PSYCHOBABBLE

PSYCHOBABBLE

The Failure of Modern Psychology—and the Biblical Alternative

Richard Ganz

CROSSWAY BOOKS • WHEATON, ILLINOIS
A DIVISION OF GOOD NEWS PUBLISHERS

Psychobabble.

Published by Crossway Books
a division of Good News Publishers
1300 Crescent Street
Wheaton, Illinois 60187.

First printing 1993

Printed in the United States of America

Library of Congress Cataloging-in-Publication Data
Ganz, Richard.
Psychobabble : the failure of modern psychology—and the biblical alternative / Richard Ganz.
p. cm.
1. Pastoral psychology—Controversial literature. 2. Christianity—Psychology. 3. Christianity—Psychology and religionl. 3. Pastoral counseling. I. Title
BV4012.G36 1993 261.5'15—dc20 93-15883
ISBN 0-89107-734-0

01 00 99 98 97 96 95 94 93
15 14 13 12 11 10 9 8 7 6 5 4 3 2 1

To my pastors
Ed Robson and Harold Harrington,
princes in the Kingdom of God.

CONTENTS

ACKNOWLEDGMENTS

I would like to thank JoAnne Bakke for proofreading and correcting the first manuscript. I would especially thank Kathy Schmidt who took that manuscript and spent considerable time reworking and restructuring it. I would also especially thank Marvin and Susan Olasky whose editorial skill brought about the present version of the book. Thank you also to William Edgar whose unpublished paper on Gary Sweeten was very helpful. I want to thank Lane Dennis who has the courage to publish a book critical of some members of the establishment. I want to express my love for my wife, Nancy, who understands that these things must be said, and encourages me to say them. Finally, I want to thank the Lord for extricating me not just from sin and death, but from a life mired in the lies and superstitions of men, and for setting me squarely in His Word.

FOREWORD
by
John F. MacArthur, Jr.

Does psychology have any valid role in Christian counseling? That question has been hotly disputed among evangelicals for several years, and the debate has heated to a fever pitch in the past few years. Richard Ganz has seen both sides of the issue, having once practiced psychotherapy in an institutional setting and now working as an advocate of Biblical counseling.

Rationally, Biblically, Ganz shows what *psychology* ("the study of the soul") ought to be and explains why modern psychological theory is so often deficient and ineffectual. He offers proof that Biblical counseling is superior to all secular models and gives a clear and convincing appeal for all believers to learn how to counsel from Scripture.

I appreciate the careful, reasonable tone with which Ganz writes. Avoiding hyperbole and emotion-laden rhetoric, he nevertheless makes his case definitively, persuasively, and in my judgment conclusively. Cutting through the jargon, he makes the issues clear enough that the average layperson can easily grasp them. From the first page through the end I was engrossed, unable to put the book aside, nodding with assent on virtually every page. Nowhere else have I seen a resource this rich or a study this helpful in sorting out and answering the Biblical questions regarding counseling and modern psychotherapy.

We who know the Lord, who have His Word, and who are indwelt by His Spirit are entrusted with too many heavenly resources to be mucking about with the utterly bankrupt wisdom that is the best this world has to offer. We err seriously if we ignore the Scriptures or the power of God (cf. Matt. 22:29). We sin grievously if we neglect divine truth in favor of the foolish wisdom of this world (cf. 1 Cor. 1:20; 3:19). The fact that such matters would be debated among Bible-believing Christians is proof of how subtle the enemy can be.

Richard Ganz is addressing what I am convinced is one of the most significant crises facing the church in our age. The role of psychology in Christian counseling will undoubtedly be one of the watershed issues of this decade. Here is a book that I pray will help divert the mainstream of evangelical believers in the right direction.

1

Confession of a Psychological Heretic

"Get it out, Immanuel!" The group looked on in astonished shock as Immanuel writhed in agony. What had begun as anxious deep breathing had progressed to violent spasms and hyperventilation. "Get it out!" I cried.

Finally he screamed, "I am God!"

I whipped out a small New Testament I had been carrying in my pocket. Just that morning I had read from the twenty-fourth chapter of Matthew's Gospel. I quoted it to him: "Then if anyone says to you, 'Behold, here is the Christ,' or 'There He is,' do not believe him. For false Christs and false prophets will arise and will show great signs and wonders, so as to mislead, if possible, even the elect. . . . For just as the lightning comes from the east, and flashes even to the west, so shall the coming of the Son of Man be" (Matt. 24:23,24,27).

Abruptly, Immanuel's writhing, spasms, and hyperventilation ceased. He calmly asked, "Where did you read that from?" I told him, tossing the Bible across the room and telling him to check it out for himself. There was not another sound or another word from Immanuel for one solid month.

Four weeks later, I was sitting in my office during lunch hour reading from the Bible and praying. Despite my earnest prayer to be used by God to bring others to Christ, so far in my eight months as a Christian, this hadn't happened. Then came the encounter that changed my life. There was a knock at my door. It was Immanuel. I invited him in and asked, "What brings you to my office?"

This man had spoken only a few words in several years. He looked at me now and clearly and calmly said, "I want to become a Christian."

It is said that people about to die experience their lives passing before them in a flash. I had that kind of experience as I looked at Immanuel. I wanted to lead people to Christ, but had never dreamed it would happen this way, in this place. I had imagined Bible study conversions or leading my Jewish family and old friends to Christ.

But that's not what happened. Instead, here was Immanuel, a patient at the state hospital where I was employed. I knew that talking about religious matters in this setting would have consequences for me. I had worked and studied for years with one goal in mind–that I would become a clinical psychologist. I had achieved that goal. Everything I had hoped or dreamed of was being realized. It was hard to imagine a better job with better conditions, opportunities, benefits, and possibilities. I had it all. Then Immanuel stood there in my doorway and made his statement.

Did I really believe in Jesus Christ? Did I really believe that salvation in Christ was the most important reality that any individual could ever possess? Did I really believe that this one man's salvation was more important than my career? I knew the answer was yes to all those questions; the proof of the sincerity of my beliefs lay in responding to his request and leading him to Christ! This was a turning point for me. It was the most important decision (apart from my commitments to Christ and my wife) that I have ever made. I said yes to this man's request, and no to my own fears.

Trembling, I asked Immanuel, "When do you want to become a Christian?"

"Right now," he responded. I sat down with Immanuel and showed him the plan of salvation, to which he heartily assented. Together we got down on our knees, and Immanuel prayed, repenting of his sin and asking Christ into his life. The years the locusts had stripped away were restored in an instant. As tears streamed down Immanuel's cheeks, the Holy Spirit gave him a new birth, and he believed God and received Christ.

The next morning the director called me into his office as soon as I arrived at work. As I sat down, he said to me, "Rich, I've just heard the craziest story in the thirty-one years I've been here."

"Let me hear it; those crazy stories are what it's all about!" I had no idea what was to follow.

"Rich," he said, "Immanuel's 'saved,' and he's telling everyone on the ward about it. He wants to get everyone, patients and staff, to become Christians." I sat listening as my worst fears unfolded before me. "What do you say, Rich?" he asked me. "Is it true that you are speaking these things on the ward, as Immanuel says?"

All I could sputter was, "It's true."

The director looked at me and explained that he didn't want to get rid of me, after having selected me over many other able psychologists just a short while earlier. He urged me to give up this "nonsense." He encouraged me to be a great Christian after work but to promise to leave my Christianity out of my psychotherapy. At the time, the rich ironies of the situation weren't readily apparent to me. The goals of my therapy with Immanuel had been to help him to speak four coherent words. Nonetheless, my director's professional curiosity was uncommonly restrained in this case; he failed to ask, "How did you do it? How did you get him to speak–and so eloquently?"

The director informed me that if I agreed to leave

Christianity out of my work, he would forget about this incident. He would be happy to transfer Immanuel to a "chronic" hospital. After a few rounds of shock treatments, all this would be forgotten!

I was profoundly confused. I thought, *The Bible teaches that I am to submit to those in authority over me. Does this mean I must accept what he asks?* I told him I would need to pray about it.

I spent the night praying and reading the book of Acts. The answer seemed unmistakable. I "must obey God rather than men" (Acts 5:29), and I "cannot stop speaking" of what I have seen and heard (Acts 4:20).

The next morning I explained to my director that I must speak at all times of Christ and His salvation and restoration, because those who most needed Christ were individuals just like Immanuel. I had not chosen to resign. I had chosen to bring Christ to the hospital. I knew that if ever there was a place that needed Jesus, this was it. The director saw it differently. As far as he was concerned, I was through–immediately. He gave me thirty days' notice.

Believe me when I say that this was not the kind of life adventure I had had in mind the day I had hitchhiked into L'Abri Fellowship in the Netherlands eight months earlier. L'Abri is a Christian community in Switzerland, with branches in the Netherlands, Great Britain, and the United States. It was founded by the late Dr. Francis A. Schaeffer IV, one of the leading Christian philosopher/apologists of the twentieth century. At

L'Abri I was confronted not only with the Biblical truth regarding man's salvation through faith in Christ, but also with Biblical counseling.

As an "expert," people at L'Abri wondered what I thought about a new book that had just come out. The book was *Competent to Counsel* by Jay Adams. I had never heard of Dr. Adams or nouthetic counseling, a counseling model that Dr. Adams developed based entirely on the teachings of the Bible. In fact, prior to coming to L'Abri, I hadn't even heard of Jesus Christ except in a disparaging way. As far as I was concerned, *Competent to Counsel* would probably turn out to be simply another psychology book. Little did I realize the profound impact it would have on my life.

I had already been in psychoanalytic psychotherapy. It was continuing (does it ever end?). My psychotherapy practice was psychoanalytic. I had spent years training to uncover the unconscious, break down repressive barriers and defenses, and analyze resistances and transferences. Life, I had come to believe, was simply "long-term analysis." I had rejected the concept of absolutes and any notions of transcendent values. I was not prepared for what I faced at L'Abri.

Competent to Counsel declared that nouthetic counseling sought as its goal, "love, joy, peace, patience, kindness, goodness, faithfulness, gentleness, and self-control," with a reference to "Gal. 5:22,23." "What was that?" I wondered! (And to which "gal" was he referring?) I was amazed that anyone even imagined such goals, let alone sought to implement or live by them. In all the years of my counseling training we had never discussed or studied such lofty ideals, nor had we ever dreamed that our patients could live by such principles. My own psychotherapy practice was devoid of such concepts.

It was a good thing that I had no idea what "Gal. 5:22,23" was. If I had known these goals were from the Bible, I would not have been interested. After all, I had believed the Bible was only for Sunday school children. As it was, in my pagan ignorance steeped in secular therapies, I found the goals and methodology of nouthetic counseling awe-inspiring.

Soon after this initial exposure to nouthetic counseling, I was confronted with the gospel of Isaiah and converted; it took me a month to realize that believing in Jesus Christ meant surrender and submission to Him, with no option to turn back.

This was the truth that my wife, Nancy, and I learned in our stay at L'Abri. Our backgrounds were as different as could be. Nancy was a genteel gentile from a small town in Ontario. I was a wild Jew from NYC. I fell in love with Nancy at first sight. She was walking alongside a canal in Venice. I was lost (in more ways than one); she pulled out her map to show me where I was going, and we realized that we were both staying at the same youth hostel. That was twenty-three years ago, and this summer we're taking our four children with us to show them where it all happened.

Nancy was studying philosophy and religion at the University of Toronto. As she got deeper into her studies, she became more and more convinced as an atheist. When our relationship grew serious, her family (and mine) began to worry. "He's a Jew. You're a Christian. How will you raise the children?"

She used to answer, "That's no problem. We're both atheists." It seemed to be the one similarity between us.

Then L'Abri happened. While God changed my life through the prophet Isaiah, he had a servant ready for Nancy as well. She began listening to tapes by Dr. and Mrs. Schaeffer. She would urge me to listen to them, but I couldn't. Finally she listened to a tape called "A Bird's Eye View of the Bible" by Edith Schaeffer, which became the book *Christianity Is Jewish*. This tape described the Biblical theme of the Lamb of God from Genesis through Revelation. Nancy had grown up in an Anglican home. She had heard "Behold the Lamb of God" many times. But it had never made sense. Now she understood the Old Testament roots and meaning of what John the Baptist was crying out. She saw her own need of coming to this Lamb, and she did, surrendering her life to Christ in the apple orchard at L'Abri on September 6, 1972, while everyone else watched a memorial service for the eleven slain Jewish athletes at the Olympic games. There was death in Munich, but life at L'Abri.

During the next eight months I taught at the university and trained psychotherapists at the medical center complex. I read the Bible continuously and grew in the knowledge of God. My desire to apply the Word of God to people and see them come to Christ also grew. Then came Immanuel, and I was fired.

But I had thirty days' notice, and during my final thirty days at the medical center, a middle-aged orthodox Jew came to my attention on the ward. He spent most of his time in a fetal position, doing nothing. I went over to him and commanded him to get up "in the name of Jesus Christ." He stood up enraged, informing me that he was a Jew. I explained that everything he longed and hoped for both as an individual and as a Jew could be found in the Messiah, Jesus. He rushed from the room, assuring me that he would prove me wrong. He went and got a Bible, and we began meeting to discuss what the Old Testament had to say about Jesus. I never again saw him in a fetal position. Rather, he was bent over his Bible, intent on proving that I was wrong about Jesus. One day I took him to lunch. To my amazement he said, "I want to become a Christian now!" His studies had brought him to Christ. Over a hamburger and french fries, I led him to the place of mercy and living waters, from which he eagerly drank.

My remaining weeks at the hospital more closely resembled revival services than psychotherapy. While these two men were growing and sharing their newfound faith, others were seeking and questioning, opening up in ways they had never dared when I was simply "staff." I heard accounts of emotionally battered and scarred people who had been locked away for years, their problems never getting discussed or resolved. They began hearing of forgiveness in Christ, and a whole new dimension of my work began to take shape.

Needless to say, the hospital and medical center personnel were relieved when my month was over. The three of us–Immanuel, the Jewish man, and I–left together, and for each of us it was a moment of liberation. I couldn't see it then, but I wasn't just saying good-bye to the hospital; it was good-bye to a whole way of life.

I was used to good-byes. I could remember the night my father died. I was twelve years old. It was the most bitterly cold night of the year and the bitterest night of my life. While it was still uncertain whether my father would live or die, I rushed in panic and hope to the one place I thought to find comfort–the synagogue. When I arrived, the doors were locked. No amount of pounding could persuade them to open. I looked into the sky and cursed God, telling Him I was through with Him. Little did I realize it, but that night I was saying good-bye not only to my father, but to my Father in Heaven. The synagogue had been a major part of my life. Every day from the time I was eight years old, I was in Hebrew school, and every Shabbat I worshiped, both Friday evening and Saturday morning. To all of this, without really understanding at all, I had just said good-bye.

I said good-bye again when I graduated from university. I had received a fellowship for doctoral studies, and my mother, with all her immense skill at arousing guilt, asked me, "Is this what I raised you for–to leave home?"

I responded simply, "Yes."

In some ways, leaving my work situation was the most difficult good-bye of all. My first weeks away from work seemed to be a good-bye to life itself. Leaving the hospital position was traumatic. I had spent my life preparing for this work, and suddenly it was gone. In the amount of time that it took to tell of Jesus, everything I'd worked for and dreamed of had disappeared with nothing left in its place, or so I thought. I hadn't yet learned of the blessings of faithfulness to Christ.

I needed to speak with someone, both to gain guidance for the future and to help me understand the turmoil I was experiencing. About this time, I was given the name of a Christian psychiatrist in New York City. I was thrilled. He was willing to see me and proved to be a gracious Christian man. I spent several hours describing my situation. I showed him my firing notice. It stated that I was fired for "using poor professional judgment, by letting my religious beliefs enter into my psychotherapeutic practice."

This Christian psychiatrist took me down the hall, showing me a lovely suite overlooking mid-town Manhattan. He asked me what I thought of the office. I pondered for a moment and couldn't help thinking that this was just what my mother had always dreamed of for me. I looked at him and told him that it was beautiful. He replied, "It's yours if you want it. Your firing letter is the best letter of recommendation I've ever received." He assured me that since he had a large private practice, there would be no difficulty starting me with a full practice as soon as I was ready.

I was encouraged beyond anything I can convey, but something nagged at me. That feeling was hard to put my finger on, but it went something like this: I knew I was a Christian; I knew I was a clinical psychologist, but I didn't know what it meant to be a "Christian psychologist." How did those two realities fit together? Could they? I asked him for a year to pray about his offer, and he agreed.

During this year, I finished teaching at the university and earnestly considered what God wanted me to do with my life. I traveled to Los Angeles and was offered a position with the Rosemead Graduate School of Psychology. Again, I was encouraged by the offer, but I knew that my psychoanalytic psychology had no Christian foundation. I wondered how I could teach at a Christian school under those circumstances. Strangely, no one seemed concerned about this conflict except me.

Providentially during this period, I met Dr. Edward Robson, a pastor in a Reformed Presbyterian Church who had a deep knowledge and love of the Bible. The months following our meeting were a veritable feast for me, as he graciously taught me the Scriptures. My demands were great. At a certain point, Pastor Robson made a suggestion. "Why don't you visit Westminster Seminary?" When I learned that Dr. Jay Adams, whose book *Competent to Counsel* I had read at L'Abri, was a professor at Westminster, I made an appointment to speak with him.

I can still remember that first meeting with Dr. Adams. Someone brought my wife and me to his office and announced, "There's a couple here to see you."

To this he bellowed, "A couple of what?"

"A couple of people," was the feeble response.

To say that Dr. Adams was consistent in his direct approach is an understatement. When I remarked to him that Westminster Seminary seemed to be a cold place, he replied, "Warm it up!"

During the course of our discussion that day, Dr. Adams asked me, "Do you want to be able to say, 'Thus says the Lord?'"

I responded, "Definitely."

He fired back, "Then you'd better know what the Lord says!"

When I asked about counseling at the Christian Counseling and Educational Foundation, his response was sharp and to the point. "I don't care how many degrees you have; no one counsels here unless they know the Word of God!" At that moment I knew I was going to Westminster. I finally understood that I needed to be the learner, not the teacher. Instead of coming to a lucrative job, I found myself coming to Westminster Seminary as a first year student. I was starting all over.

Just as it was when I came to Christ, starting all over was the only way to begin. I had to learn my lessons from the ground up. Even then I assumed I would eventually have an independent counseling practice. I was in for another surprise–I would learn not only how to use the Bible, but where to apply my gifts. I had to resolve a number of problems I had with the church. It took me five years to understand that I should use my skills in the pastoral ministry. The difficulties I had experienced in placing myself as a freshman in seminary were nothing compared to my struggle with the idea of becoming a pastor. But slowly I realized that the pastorate is the heart of truly Christian counseling, which is the ministry of God's Holy Word. I learned that I shouldn't expect or seek the approval of man.

Imagine a New York City Jew becoming a preacher of the gospel of Jesus Christ. Years later one of my relatives who would still speak to me said, "You can still make something of your life." But it was the disdain of fellow Christians that was most disconcerting. They seemed to view pastoral work with contempt.

If someone practiced law without legal training, he'd have no clients. If someone became a physician without medical training, he'd be sued for every cent he was worth, and then some. Only in the area of pastoral work, and Biblical psychology (literally "the study of the soul") in particular, is training in theology (literally "the study of God") considered, if not a detriment, at the very least, a waste of time.

Many Christians warned me against seminary, fearing that I would lose my love for God and His Word as I studied the Scriptures. Yet as I have studied the writings of influential Christian psychologists, I see an obvious problem–they are deficient in theological understanding. They don't know the Word of God or its power. They have devoted years to obtaining psychology degrees from secular institutions, training under people much like my director at the medical center. Inevitably the fruit of those years subverts even their best efforts as Christian believers. Sadly, this is true even of many who are most esteemed in Christian circles. We will take a look at some of their truncated "Christian" philosophies and see where they deviate from a truly Biblical approach to human problems.

My goal in this book is to help readers understand that the counseling concepts woven into psychoanalysis (and its secular psychotherapeutic offshoots) are inherently opposed to the Word of God. My approach will be to reveal the direct conflict between secular philosophies and Biblical principles and to strip back to its ugly roots the psychotherapy that the church has baptized and embraced. My hope is that the church will stop shuffling her hurting and broken members to the "experts" who lack the power and perspective of the Word of God, that pastors will instead seize the opportunities to teach, rebuke, correct, and train in righteousness a people fit for service to King Jesus.

Even as I write this, I am reminded that the task is

difficult. Just yesterday a desperate young woman called. A recent convert, she came to Christ with many problems. Her pastor, an evangelical, sent her to the psychiatric department of a major teaching hospital in the city. Her doctors put her on powerful psychotropic medication, and she began seeing a psychotherapist.

This young Christian asked me, "Shouldn't Christians be able to get Biblical counseling?" I hope my book awakens pastors and helps them to keep their flock from the clutches of the psychiatric establishment.

It has been said before, but we need to hear it again: Men and women of God, you are competent to counsel one another. May God enable you to accomplish this task.

2

The Psychological Views of Man

Recently my youngest daughter bashed her head into a table, leaving an ugly bleeding gash. I had to decide whether to turn left to the big children's hospital in Ottawa or right to our smaller local general hospital. The decision involved time, distance, and the anticipated length of wait in the emergency room to see a doctor. I didn't worry about which doctor we saw because I assumed that any medical doctor would be competent to put in the required stitches. The local hospital staff dealt swiftly and efficiently with Micaiah's wound, and we were home within the hour. This kind of decision, although made under stressful conditions, was relatively easy; I had a problem and I knew where to go for help. Unfortunately, for those suffering from problems in their families, with friends, at work, or with a specific personal crisis, the direction isn't as clear-cut.

"Desperate Delores" has had trouble sleeping lately. She has lost fifteen pounds and quite a few friends as well. Her husband is still around, but with all the crying jags and temper flare-ups, even he is getting a bit jagged around the edges and is threatening to take action. Delores has been to her physician and undergone the battery of prescribed tests. No neurological, physiological, biochemical, or metabolic disturbances were discovered. The problem is not organic. Fearful of a suicide attempt, her pastor has told her to seek "professional" help. Now what?

The Yellow Pages list page after page of persons who claim to practice counseling or therapy. If asked, they would all say they want to help people. They all claim to be unbiased in their approach. So how does Delores choose? Do they all practice the same "science?" Would they agree on the diagnosis of her problem? Do they accept the same definition of what is normal? Can she expect the same recommendations from all of them? Do they even agree on their definition of humanity?

The answer is startling. Clinical psychology comes to no consensus in its view of human beings–with one critical exception. It is unified in its belief that people are free from God. Aside from that exception, there are as many theories regarding human nature as there are counseling practitioners. Each one would deal with

Delores and her problem according to who and what he or she believed Delores *is*. Delores is about to begin therapy roulette. The following is a brief overview of the different schools of psychology Delores might encounter in her counseling room travels.

Sigmund Freud

Sigmund Freud was one of the founding fathers of contemporary psychiatric thought and therapy. He began as a medical researcher in neurology and almost won the Nobel prize for his scientific research into pain relief and analgesics. His experiments involved opium, to which he became addicted. Lacking the funding for his research and the interest in general surgical practice, Freud felt compelled to pursue the more profitable and intriguing world of psychiatric counseling.

At the foundation of Freud's thought was the belief that people are ruled by their *unconscious* minds. He believed that human behaviors, responses, and attitudes are governed by primitive urges combined with a vast horde of personal experiences of which they have no knowledge or conscious control. Essentially, Freud saw man as an instinct-ruled beast dominated primarily by the drives of sex and aggression.

Based on this view of man, Freud created *psychoanalysis*, a technique that involves the patient lying on a couch and *free-associating* (saying whatever comes to mind). The goal of this process is to uncover the patient's unconscious motivations. The analyst does this by interpreting the patient's so-called *defenses* and *transferences* so that he can decode and reveal to the patient the origins of his attitudes and behavior.

Freud believed that therapy could help patients know the origins of their behaviors, thereby gaining personal awareness and understanding. But in reality this type of therapy accomplishes much more. It affirms a concept that sinful human beings universally hold dear–they are not responsible for their actions. Someone else is to blame. By placing the responsibility for their behavior on their parents, environment, childhood trauma, the unconscious, or "primitive urges," patients are permitted–even encouraged–to assume a victim mentality. They are never confronted with their personal responsibility for their behavior, but must wade through years of analysis (at horrendous cost!) to discover what in their past makes them behave the way they do.

Freud's theory of human beings, like all erroneous yet warmly welcomed theories, has made some accurate identifications. People do suffer traumas, sometimes incredibly painful ordeals at very early ages. Pain and pleasure are powerful stimuli and have strong influence on our perceptions and responses to situations. People do sometimes mentally push aside and forget painful events. We are all filled with variables that make us who and what we are. However, none of these factors negate our responsibility before God for our own behavior.

We are held responsible before God for our sin and

cannot shift the blame onto some hidden event. We are also responsible for how we respond to the pain that is an inevitable part of human existence. There are always reasons why we do the things we do, but there are never excuses for sin. Christians do not deny the painful realities of life, but neither do they permit such realities to lead them into situations involving self-destructive behaviors, bitterness, sinful neglect of duties, or any other unbiblical conduct or attitude.

From a Christian perspective, a rebellious teen's destructive behavior is rooted in sin. It can be understood *in response to*, but not pardoned *on the basis of*, parental negligence. Freud, however, explained a glutton's gluttony by the fact that he was not breast-fed as a baby, or a child molester's behavior on an "unresolved Oedipus complex."

It was in the area of personal accountability to the God of the Bible that Freud parted company with his Jewish heritage. Freud hated the idea of God, and especially the God of the Jews and His Son–(as Freud saw it) the God of the gentiles. He viewed religious behavior as at best a "neurosis." The noted psychoanalyst, Erich Fromm, a follower of Freud, wrote in *Psychoanalysis and Religion* that psychoanalysis is "the study of the soul of man."[1] This is ironic because Freud was a metaphysical materialist. He did not believe that man possessed a soul.

Even though Freud hated the Judeo-Christian religion, he held a religious worldview. Gerhard Masur said, "Psychoanalysis became one of the substitute religions for the disillusioned middle class. . . . analysis is accompanied by ceremonies and rituals that resemble a religious rite. Its concepts, at best debatable, are repeated as articles of the faith."[2]

Freud created the classic psychoanalytic approach, but many others, both Freud's colleagues and those to follow, appropriated part of his theory or therapy and modified it to suit their own interpretation of man and his problems. Perhaps the most influential (and therefore harmful) disciple of Freud's was Carl Gustav Jung. Freud and Jung parted ways over Jung's involvement in the realm of the spirit.

Carl Gustav Jung

Jung went beyond Freud's theory of the unconscious by combining it with a spiritual dimension, which he called the *collective unconscious*. According to this theory, all human beings possess in their unconscious a deeply buried collective history of the race. This commonly shared knowledge is the seat of our identity as persons, represented by hundreds of *archetypes*, or symbols of universally significant persons (i.e., mother, father, etc.). According to Jung, the collective unconscious is also the dwelling place of God.

According to Jung, Jesus represented the primordial image of the *Anthropos*, the son of man and son of God. He accomplished deliverance for the enslaved people of the first century from the "divinity" of

Augustus. It was in this capacity of *redeemer* that He became part of the collective psyche of the first century. Jung saw this as consistent with the saving capacity that had been evidenced in other redeemers at other times in history. Jung didn't care if Jesus was King of Kings and Lord of Lords. All that mattered was His meaning as an archetype. Jesus became the *symbol* of sacrifice and deity, not the true Savior. According to Jungians, Jesus functions *symbolically* as an archetype for redeemer, meeting the need shared by all people for redemption.

Since Jesus exists as an archetype in the collective unconscious, we can encounter Him via active imagination. This theory of receptive visualization has its ancient roots in Tantric yoga, which deeply affected both Buddhism and Hinduism. Students are taught to visualize the image of the deity and to construct this image on their mental screens by active imagination. Agnes Sanford popularized both the visualizing techniques and this teaching of Jung's in the church. In *The Healing Gifts of the Spirit*[3] Sanford claimed that Jesus entered into the collective unconscious of the human race and is by *this means* available for healing and help. Her basis for these claims is not the Bible, but Carl Jung.

Jung's Jesus is more like a spirit guide than the Lord of history. Jung believed that the goal of therapy is not healing, but coming into contact with one's collective unconscious–a process he called *individuation*. During individuation the true self, the strongest archetype in the collective unconscious, is brought into greater consciousness. This process is considered therapeutic because it supposedly leads to wholeness or a realization of personhood. It forms the basis for the contemporary practice of receptive visualization as it is currently being practiced in the church, particularly in "healing ministries."

B. F. Skinner

B. F. Skinner was the creator of the well-known classic behavioral view of human beings. Skinner saw the mind as a black box, a series of circuits, a collection of stimulus-response connections. He rejected the idea that a person has meaning or significance. In *Beyond Freedom and Dignity* Skinner said, "Of man *qua* man we say good riddance."[4] Like Freud, he denied the existence of the soul. And he also rejected God on a personal level, although he certainly maintained a religious worldview. In his acclaimed utopian novel *Walden Two*, Skinner's namesake, Frazier, identified himself with Christ. The power he claimed for himself was divine, as was evidenced by the following chilling line: "If it's in our power to create any of the situations which a person likes or to remove any situations he doesn't like . . . we can control his behavior. Technically it's called positive reinforcement."

Positive reinforcement is not to be confused with the Biblical concept of encouragement. Rather, it is the calculated manipulation of external stimuli designed to mold human response patterns. The alteration of human behavior through these methods is called *behav-*

ior modification. Because it involves attempting to control a person's destiny by controlling his or her behavior, behavior modification is a euphemism for "man as God." It disregards the human capacity for love, patience, self-control, mercy, long-suffering, or joy. Inherent in the concept of positive reinforcement is the destruction of the personal dignity of a human being, hence the denial of personal responsibility or need to control one's thoughts, words, or deeds. The goal of behavioral therapists is to have clients manipulate their emotional and physical circumstances in such a way as to avoid pain and promote pleasure. This popular line of thinking is reflected in the humanist battle cry, "Look out for Number One!"

Carl Rogers

If Abraham Maslow is the theoretician of the human potential movement, then Carl Rogers is the practitioner. Rogers grew up in a Christian home and came to New York City to study theology at Union Theological Seminary. Not surprisingly, Rogers became increasingly disillusioned with his theological studies at Union–an institution at the forefront of liberalism in the early twentieth century. Certainly, Rogers could not have gotten any answers to hard questions concerning his spiritual life.

At the same time, and just across the street, stood Columbia University, with its cutting-edge clinical psychology program. Union Seminary had no answers. But

Columbia offered Rogers a confident faith in the incipient humanism of the day.

The young Rogers ate humanism up and never looked back to Christianity, except in dismay and disgust. However, his psychology retained a religious or spiritual character. As Rogers aged, the spiritual nature of his work became more evident, especially as he faced the death of his wife. He looked for answers, not in psychology and certainly not in Christianity, but in the occult–with its mediums, seances, and Ouija boards. He claimed to have communicated with his dead wife, who told him to have a good time in a relationship he had begun with a woman during the final stages of his wife's illness. Instead of guilt and condemnation, Rogers received his dead wife's empathy and *unconditional positive regard* (UPR) toward his adultery. His growing spiritual interest is recorded in his book *A Way of Being.*

In contrast to Freud, Rogers saw human beings as good and perfectible. He believed they needed only the guidance that was already within themselves, just waiting to be vitalized by using nondirective techniques. Rogers, like Freud, didn't believe in giving advice, only in recognizing feelings. Rogerian counselors are easily recognized by their infuriating tendency to paraphrase every statement made by their clients and then to smile in a nonjudgmental way while waiting with UPR for the next statement. They believe that as clients come to resonate with their feelings and as they experience the counselor's empathy and UPR, they will be made whole (healed). In effect, the client uses the counselor as a positive mirror to the inner self, reflecting with approval what the client sees within.

Rogers insisted there is nothing that can break into a person to help him resolve the dilemma of his suffering. There is no revelation. Thus Rogerians deny the existence of standards and absolutes and the propensity of people toward evil. In Rogerian *client-centered therapy* a homosexual can come to accept his homosexuality, but he will never receive counsel that declares that homosexuality is sin—the Biblical way out.

Werner Erhard

In the last twenty years, the field of personality theory has seen an explosion. Generally using Rogers and the human potential movement as a springboard to the study of human beings, theorists have broken new paths. One popular catalyst is New Age guru Werner Erhard, founder of est (Erhard Seminar Training), who taught that "something experienced is true; the same thing believed is a lie." In other words, there is nothing beyond that which is experienced. This means, for example, that neither guilt nor love is a reality except as it is experienced. Erhard, along with his New Age counterparts in the media, entertainment industry, and counseling clinics throughout the Western world, seduces millions with ideas such as, "You are god in your own universe. There is no God unless it is self." These theorists produce religious pronouncements that sound acceptable even to some Christians. In his est newsletter, Erhard even has clergy giving their est testimonies!

The New Age Movement that has burst upon the West is a blending of Eastern pantheistic monism, Western psychotherapy, and the occult. Many contemporary counseling practitioners are dabbling in these New Age thoughts and therapies, dragging desperate, wounded individuals and families with them unawares. One cannot look with expectant hopefulness toward secular (and even some Christian) counseling rooms today; they are as unpredictable as the toss of the dice. The New Age psychiatry is not science; it is sophisticated shamanism.

Desperate Delores needs help. But her chances of finding it by opening the Yellow Pages and playing therapy roulette are slim. Unlike Russian roulette, however, this high-stakes game comes with no warning. In fact, it comes with the patina of "science" and the approval of the American Psychological Association. In the next chapter we'll look at the science of counseling.

3

The Power of the Couch

One day a young man named Ralph came to me for help after his family suggested that he commit himself to the local psychiatric hospital. During our first counseling session, Ralph informed me of his faith in Christ. But he also made some strange statements. He said that God was telling him that a certain person had to die, that God wanted him to stop eating until a certain person was dead, and that God might want him to end the person's life himself. Ralph attributed many other impulses and desires to God. Clearly, God had not told Ralph to do these evil things.

How would non-Christian counselors have dealt with Ralph? Secular psychotherapists probably would have seen Ralph's faith as the problem. Most have been taught that Christianity is detrimental to personality development. They may not blame God pointedly for Ralph's problems, but when Ralph finished his therapy with these individuals, he would have seen man's work in his life, not God's. His interest in God may very well have ended.

Many Christian counselors make the same mistake. A Christian psychiatrist I know told me how he goes about making referrals for his patients who are hospitalized. He said, "I refer my patients to psychiatrists who won't attack their Christianity . . . unless [Christianity is] not working for the patient." Here then is a psychiatric patient in a psychiatric hospital, perhaps at the point in his life where the only reality he clings to is Jesus Christ. In walks Dr. Jones who apparently accepts completely the patient's Christian faith. That, of course, may be part of his own philosophical bias (he might accept everything). Dr. Jones looks at his new patient (clinging to his faith even in the midst of terrible problems) and says, "I'm not concerned about your Christianity . . . *as long as it is working for you.*"

What does this statement (either explicit or implicit) mean? Does he mean that Christianity is one of many reasonable alternatives? That contradicts the Bible. Does he mean that each person should judge the truth of something based upon his own private and personal experience? Does he mean that Christianity sometimes works and sometimes doesn't? However far we take this attitude, obviously this approach to Christianity is neither benign nor benevolent. Further, it is not neutral. It is saying that Christianity is allowable as long as the person "using it" conforms to worldly standards of successful living.

Few Christians would accept this thesis, and even fewer Christians would (or should) find themselves approving such counseling. So then, what does it mean when a psychotherapist tells the counselee that Christianity is fine for him, *if he is fine?* What does it mean when this professional tells him that his Christianity is fine as long as he understands that it is just one of many equally fine roads? The counselee pays the therapist; therefore, the counselee's perceptions are faulty and the therapist's are correct. Faith has been dismissed. The counselee is left shaken, but does not know why. He placed his life in the hands of this wise person who couldn't care less about Jesus Christ and the claims of the Bible.

Counseling of this sort pretends to be neutral. But it is actually the practical working out of a comprehensive world-and-life view. Could it be any other way? Beliefs about humankind, God, and values *always* enter into counseling. Many so-called neutral practitioners swear they leave all value (and value systems) out of their practice. But that does not mean they are objective. A strong presentation to counselees of a world-and-life view is still there. These therapists are merely telling the counselee that it is possible to keep all values out of a therapy intended to change a person's life. They are suggesting that valueless living is as worthwhile as a life lived according to openly stated values.

This is a powerful presentation of a worldview. Inevitably, in a counseling situation what is truly believed essential or valuable in life will be taught. Counseling cannot operate apart from both parties' view of God, humanity, and the universe. To state, "I don't speak of God in my therapy," is not neutral, but rather it is a powerful statement about God–He isn't important enough to be mentioned in counseling. All counselors state their views about these critical realities, consciously or unconsciously, explicitly or implicitly, calculatedly or in ignorance.

So-called neutral counseling is actually relativistic. It asserts that the only absolute is that all values are continually in flux. Historically, such thinking has led to the ultimate denial of all meaning, purpose, knowledge, morals, etc. Underneath pluralistic neutrality, we find that we are dealing with moral, philosophical, and intellectual nihilism, a worldview that says there is absolutely no true knowledge, meaning, values, ethics, or morals. Thus the counselor who claims to practice "value-free" counseling declares himself a nihilist and his counseling nihilistic. He is, in fact, declaring his counseling presuppositions even while claiming to have none.

Unfortunately, too many people don't understand that counseling derives from a worldview. Instead, they think of counseling as the tool that one person (the expert) applies to another person who has psychological problems. They see the practitioner apply his expertise to particular problems with the goal of bringing some relief or help. The psychotherapist, or counselor, is seen as a kind of "super-mechanic" who locates psychological shorts and disconnections, using his technical expertise to correct the malfunctionings. He is the one who, by progressive feats of wizardry, demonstrates a technical mastery of the mind.

Those who oppose this corps of cerebral supermen are met by a hostility that is hard to defend against. Once a counselee has been diagnosed, classified, and categorized, what can one really say in his behalf? If the defiant one stands up and alone defies his diagnosis, it is indicative of paranoia. After all, a sign of paranoia is to believe that one is correct and everyone else is wrong. Unfortunately, if a person agrees with a diagnosis, he is classified mentally ill (with whatever variety one happens to be labeled) and is therefore incompetent. Thus either way he is a nonperson so far as thought or will are concerned. Further, those defying the psychotherapist rarely wield power. I say rarely because there are extremely infrequent times when the science of the diagnosis and classification of supposed mental illness is shown to be what it really is–speculation at best, criminal at worst.

In 1973 Rosenhan, a professor of psychology and law at Stanford University, and a dozen friends (mostly professionals) presented themselves at local mental hospitals for admission. All repeated exactly the same opening words, "I feel empty," or, "I feel hollow." Following this admission, they acted normally. They related to others as they would ordinarily. All were admitted. The length of stay in the hospitals was between seven and fifty-two days. Requests for release on the basis that they were normal were viewed as confirmatory signs of illness. Those who spent a portion of their hospital stay writing about their time were labeled as obsessive and compulsive because of all the writing.

When released, all retained the diagnosis "schizophrenic" with the added note, "in remission." In other words, their "schizophrenias" were under some kind of temporary control, but they were all still to be viewed as schizophrenic. Had this been anything other than a research study, these individuals would have carried around for the rest of their lives the horrible appellation "schizophrenic." Unfortunately, countless others have not escaped that fate. So much for the supposed objectivity and neutrality of psychiatry in diagnosing mental illness. Of his study, Rosenhan concluded, "We continue to label patients schizophrenics, manic-depressives, and insane, as if those words had captured the essence of understanding. . . . We have known for a long time that our diagnoses are not reliable or useful, but we nevertheless continue to use them."[5]

Thomas Szasz reflects on the absurdity of this dilemma and the inevitability of psychiatric tyranny. "We are told that if a psychiatric patient is early for his appointment, he is anxious; if late, he is hostile, and if on time, compulsive. We laugh because it is supposed to be a joke. But here we are told the same thing in all seriousness."[6] As an interesting addendum, admissions to southern California mental hospitals (for a while) dropped by 33 percent because hospital staff feared they were part of a follow-up study. To be able to say with society's approval that a person who doesn't conform to a completely subjective and relativistic norm is ill and possesses a diseased psyche is an extraordinary power.

In short, counseling/psychotherapy (psychology) no longer stands as the science of behavior, but as the guardian of the soul, the maker of value, the determiner of morality, the definer of freedom. That which began as a true science of behavior has degenerated into a neo-religious cult. In the place of God is man. In the place of the priest (minister) is the psychologist. In the place of the Word is psychotherapy. In the place of confession/forgiveness is interpretation (or one of its many equivalents). Counseling/psychotherapy (psychology) emerges as the practical twentieth-century religion. Here the deception of neutrality is revealed.

A war is raging. On one side, Biblical Christianity; on the other, philosophical nihilism. Truth, meaning, and hope are placed against a moral and philosophical anarchy that can never truly meet a need or offer hope. When anarchy faces a person in despair, it can only parrot back thoughts or feelings or ask a new question. Under the pedantry and rhetoric of the psychologist's assurance, "You've got all the answers," lies another more truthful declaration, "You've got *your* problems; I've got mine!"

Remember Ralph, the troubled young man who came to me because he felt that God was telling him to kill someone? In the hands of a secular psychotherapist, Ralph would have been weaned from his fragile faith. But since I practice Biblical counseling, something else happened. I believed, despite his bizarre statements, that Ralph was genuinely converted. But Ralph had never received any discipling. After his conversion he had been virtually ignored by his church. Ralph remained plagued by many of the problems he had endured since long before his conversion.

He was angry and bitter because an old girlfriend was seeing another man. This rejection, in fact, had caused Ralph to turn to God. But Ralph had never dealt with his pain and the anger he felt toward this girl and her boyfriend. He had to learn about anger and how to handle it Biblically. He also had to learn about God and the requirements God has for us. He had to get involved in a sound Biblical church and be discipled in the Christian faith. The anger and the hurt were not completely eradicated from Ralph when I stopped seeing him, but the congregation of which he is now a member is helping him in all of the remaining areas.

The vain philosophies of Freud, Rogers, Skinner, Jung, Erhard agree that God is irrelevant. Their techniques could not help Ralph. They could only damage the one true thing in his life–his faith in Jesus Christ. Unfortunately, some Christian counselors have let their training and their desire for acceptance in this world cloud their vision. Often well-intentioned "Christian psychologists" have welcomed into their counseling rooms methodologies and perspectives that have at their root a denial of God. They begin sessions with prayer but then weave godless therapies and Freud-inspired techniques into the minds and souls of their counselees. Pastors, ill-equipped and fearful of societal reprisal, hasten their parishioners off to the "experts" at the first signs of trouble. Parishioners, ignorant and desperate, go. The counsel they will receive (or don't receive, depending on which school of thought they end up with) is based on carnal man's view of man. What does the living God of Heaven and earth think about all this?

4

Man as God Sees Him

Some time before my conversion, I remember describing my concerns about the effectiveness of psychotherapy to a colleague. Two responses of his stand out in my memory. First he said that I shouldn't trouble myself with such complex matters. What did it matter anyway? Half of the patients improved and half didn't, regardless of psychiatric intervention. His second consideration was more to the point. As we passed a road crew sweating in the midday sun, he pointed to them and said, "It's better than digging ditches." His point seemed irrefutable. (I obviously had no theology of work, unless it was simply, "Get what you can with the least amount of effort.")

I knew that what we did afforded little, if any, help; I just didn't know what else could be done. More significantly, I *couldn't* know what else to do. Without a Biblical view of man, I was unable to understand the significance and value of man, his desperate condition, and the way out.

Shortly after I arrived at L'Abri, I was introduced to Ted, who had come not long before me. I was struck by his ghastly appearance and the deep, open wounds on his skull. I found out that he had been through several U.S. mental hospitals, all to no avail. Life for Ted seemed hopeless. He had no family to care for him. His childhood had been marked by severe abuse. He was uneducated, unskilled, unloved, and had no reason to live. The head wounds were the sad reminders of a recent suicide attempt.

The L'Abri workers asked me to speak with Ted since I was a clinical psychologist. After talking to him and learning more about the misery of his squandered and wasted life, I could only affirm that his was a hopeless situation. Never before had I met someone of whom I would have said that. When the workers at L'Abri asked me what I would do or suggest, I could offer nothing. It seemed as if the entire psychological community had given up on this man.

But L'Abri did not give up. L'Abri workers offered him Christ. They did not try to change his view of himself. They did not try to help him to believe he was a great and noble figure. They only attempted to demonstrate that his life was not hopeless, because there is Another who could help him by making him into a new person.

Before I left, Ted *was* a new person. Following his conversion to Christ, I hardly recognized him. The bloodied wounds were still there, but his hair was now neatly combed, covering them. His body was clean. He was in his right mind. He had goals and a direction. Christ (and Christ alone) had accomplished this for him.

Although I had had no hope for Ted, the L'Abri workers did because they understood the Biblical view of man. The picture of humanity in the Bible is clear—we are not what we were meant to be. Every human being experiences the fight against one or more seemingly unbreakable habits, some apparently irresistible temptation, some indwelling sin. That this was not always the case is difficult to believe. There was a time, very early in the history of our race, when living for the glory of God was not a battle at all.

The Bible teaches that God created us perfect and upright in character, in moral stance, in love for God, and in a desire to serve Him. When we take a look at what we've become, we encounter one of the greatest mysteries of the ages—sin. The fact that sin could enter a perfect world and a perfect man, Adam, is an enigma beyond comprehension in this lifetime. Sin is the complete contradiction of the character of the sovereign God, who is righteous and perfect. Yet every time we sin, we validate sin's logical consequence, Hell, and deny the grace of God, the only way out of the mess into which we've fallen.

Sin is not static. Left unchecked by the Holy Spirit, people deepen in their sinful appetites and lusts. They actually come to revel in sin (Rom. 1:32). The Word of God says, "The heart is more deceitful than all else and is desperately sick; who can understand it?" (Jer. 17:9). One's thought-life is affected. "Their thoughts are thoughts of iniquity" (Isa. 59:7). In fact, every part of us has been touched by our fall into sin. The theologians call this total depravity. They don't mean that we are absolutely as bad as we can be. Total depravity means that there is no part of us that has not been corrupted and touched by sin.

Ever since sin entered the human race through Adam (Rom. 5:12, 14-19), we have been under God's curse. No one has been able to satisfy God's anger by anything he or she has done (Isa. 64:6). The sensitive soul and conscience is aware of the sentence of death (Rom. 7:24). The only compensating reality that God will accept and credit to our account is the sacrifice of Jesus Christ. He alone could provide our justification, our being declared not guilty.

The Biblical view does not deny the greatness of human beings. Rather, we would say that human greatness, created by God in His own image, is witnessed in the depth of the Fall. The French philosopher Blaise Pascal grasped this concept when he said, "Man's misery is the misery of a nobleman, the misery of a dethroned king."[7]

Man is not judged because he is man; he is judged because of his sin and rebellion. Humanists emphasize the nobility of man. But they idealize the goodness of man. What value is there in a goodness that leads only to Hell? We should reject such perversions of goodness that blaspheme God's holy name and are not truthful.

Calvin understood the tension between the nobility and the depravity of man. He quoted St. Bernard in his *Institutes*: "Man doubtless has been made subject to vanity–man has been reduced to nothing–man is nothing. How is he nothing, to whom a divine heart has been given? Let us breathe again, brethren. Although we are nothing in our hearts, perhaps something of us may lurk in the heart of God. O Father of mercies! Father of the miserable! How plantest Thou Thy heart in us? Where Thy heart is, there is Thy treasure also. But how are we Thy treasure, if we are nothing?"[8]

Calvin did not view this tension as the ultimate contradiction. It was the ultimate mercy. Man in his guilt and corruption was spared, not by self-revelation, but by the revelation of God. Man as a sinner found hope not in self-knowledge, but in the mercy and grace of Almighty God. We are not self-enclosed isolated beings. Man can only change in relationship to himself as he changes in relationship to God.

Some Christian psychologists have so intently focused on the nobility of man that they have lost the Biblical sense of humility (seeing ourselves as God sees us). They have settled on the side of the humanist. Their view of man's nature comes from secular psychology, not from the Bible. They believe that if one can just take man far enough backward or inward, the new man in

Christ will blossom. Although this view acknowledges an element of depravity in man to be dealt with, it treats man's corruption as though it exists in corrupt ideas or memories. It denies extant corruption and evil. It implies that we can't be expected to stop sinning until we have dealt with the root of our sin. It places that root not in our Adamic nature, but rather in an experience in our past that involved sin, either our own or someone else's.

The push towards the "healing of memories" is dangerous for the church because it starts from false presuppositions and leads to gross doctrinal error. Not only does this view of man prevent God's people from dealing with their sin in the only efficacious manner available (through repentance and received forgiveness through Christ), it also implies that one can live the life that was possible before the entry of sin into the race. This erroneous doctrine is not a new phenomenon for the church. In the early church the doctrine was given a name–Pelagianism–and condemned.

John Calvin refuted such heresies by pointing to the Biblical view of man. "Man," he said, "never attains a true self-knowledge until he has previously contemplated the face of God and come down after such contemplation to look into himself."[9] Calvin went on to state that the standard for perverted self-knowledge arises out of pride. When the standard for true self-evaluation (the Biblical view of man) is lacking, we are satisfied with a distorted self-picture, that of self-righteousness.

Calvin argued that man will always lack an accurate picture of himself as long as he fails to examine himself in the light of Biblical revelation. When a person does examine himself Biblically, he finds that "what formerly delighted us by its false show of righteousness, will become polluted with the greatest iniquity."[10] In other words, when a man sees his true nature, he is able to acknowledge his sin-filled nature that needs a restored relationship with God through Christ. That is the starting point for Biblical counseling.

Those searching for a Biblical approach to counseling need to understand that it is not possible to understand or deal with man's nature apart from his relationship to God. There can be no Christian plan for change apart from submission to the Scripture, which sees man in an unbreakable relationship to God–either as covenant-keeper or covenant-breaker. Basing his statement on the atoning death of Christ, Paul declares, "So from now on *we regard no one from a worldly point of view.* Though we once regarded Christ in this way, we do so no longer. Therefore, if anyone is in Christ, he is a new creation; the old has gone, the new has come! All this is from God, who reconciled us to himself through Christ and gave us the ministry of reconciliation: that God was reconciling the world to himself in Christ, not counting men's sins against them. And he has committed to us the message of reconciliation" (2 Cor. 5:16-19 NIV, emphasis mine). The only basis by which pastors and psychologists should be talking about restoration or healing is in connection with the sacrifice of Christ.

Ted, the troubled young man at L'Abri, was not changed by trying to heal his memories. Years of traditional psychological treatment had done nothing for him. Ted was a hopeless man until he came face to face with Christ. Then he became a new creation. Christ does not provide people with a placebo, but with real hope. The Bible makes this point eloquently. "Hope does not disappoint, because the love of God has been poured out within our hearts through the Holy Spirit who was given to us" (Rom. 5:5). How ridiculous to look to ourselves hopefully! Our hope is in God alone, who bestows hope on us, in spite of who we are, through the giving of the Spirit. He can take our lives, even when they are at rock bottom, and from them make something glorifying to Himself.

Leaders of the psychiatric establishment refuse to recognize that Christ changes lives. They reject the presuppositions of Biblical Christianity, but at the same time they pretend that if something works, they will accept it. I have seen Christ change people's lives, yet I have seen this reality rejected time and again by the psychological community. Immanuel's transformation into a functioning human being in my office at the hospital should have been a reason for joy. Instead, it produced defensive bitterness. Instead of being praised for having (somehow) gotten him to speak, I was castigated for "crystallizing his delusions." His delusion had been that he was the Christ. That belief was smashed. He learned that his hope was in serving the one true and living

God. Yet in the mind of my director, I had crystallized his delusion because the true religious answer replaced the former religious deception. That one was true and one false made no difference. That one helped, while everything they had tried failed, only infuriated him.

Biblical counseling is broader than the alleviation of problems and the change of personality. The Biblical reality of total depravity means that every area of a new believer's life needs to be touched by the transforming power of Christ. All our thoughts, attitudes, and presuppositions need to be filtered through our new eyes and ears and hearts. We need to be continually asking the question, "How does God view this situation according to His Word?" Paul tells believers, "Do not conform any longer to the pattern of this world, but be transformed by the renewing of your mind" (Rom. 12:2 NIV). Included in this transformation is a changed vision of who we are in God's sight.

Man has great reason for hope. Our hope lies in a reality that secular psychologists hate–we know that we are weak and need Christ's help to change. He *alone* is able to convict, forgive, renew, strengthen, comfort, protect, keep, instruct, guide, shelter, heal, and encourage us with divine faithfulness and wisdom. To offer anything less is to deny the people of God their greatest aid in times of weakness.

The Bible teaches that no part of man is unreachable by God's Word. "For the word of God is living and active and sharper than any two-edged sword, and piercing as far as the division of soul and spirit, of both joints and marrow, and able to judge the thoughts and intentions of the heart. And there is no creature hidden from His sight, but all things are open and laid bare to the eyes of Him with whom we have to do" (Heb. 4:12,13).

The Biblical counselor has confidence in the tool that God has given him for the reconstruction of individuals. He can enter into a counseling situation knowing that there is "nothing hidden which cannot be revealed" by the proper use of God's Word. Through it, God reveals how intimately acquainted He is with all our weaknesses and foibles. He even comments on our proclivity to self-deception and then declares the preventive action necessary to avoid it: "Anyone who listens to the word but does not do what it says is like a man who looks at his face in a mirror and, after looking at himself, goes away and immediately forgets what he looks like. But the man who looks intently into the perfect law that gives freedom, and continues to do this, not forgetting what he has heard, but doing it–he will be blessed in what he does" (Jas. 1:23-25 NIV).

By looking to the secular realm of psychology, God's people are forgetting what they look like. It is for this reason that Christendom must see the absolute necessity of both seeking and providing for its members *Biblical* principles of counsel at all times. As obvious as this concept should be to believers, the principles are not being sought or taught and the Church is faltering as a result.

5

The Myth of Integration

They that come to Christ, get life. . . . They get a life that is worth the having. We think much of the natural life, but this life will avail us when the other is gone."[11]

Richard Cameron, a Scottish Covenanter pastor, preached these words the week before he was martyred for his faith. He is part of the "cloud of witnesses" who proceeded beautifully in their sanctification without the benefits of modern psychology. What has brought us to the place where we Christians feel we cannot deal with our problems without the help of popular psychology? Do we realize how far from a truly Biblical perspective of man we have wandered?

Harry Blamires in the 1960s noted a shift from Biblical to secular thinking. He wrote that Christians were able to think like Christians in matters of personal morality and worship. But he lamented the inability of most Christians to think Christianly about political, social, and cultural issues. "We have prayed and worshipped Christianly," Blamires said. "Then we have gone back to talk politics with the politician, social welfare with the trade unionist, and we have emptied our brains of Christian vocabulary, Christian concepts, in advance, just to make sure that we should get fully in touch. . . . We have trained, even disciplined ourselves, to think secularly about secular things."[12]

The progressive loss of the Christian consciousness has brought us deeper into relativism and irrationalism (just note the upsurge and proliferation of occult and New Age philosophies and practices). Nowhere is the loss of a Christian consciousness more apparent than in the field of psychology. One reason is that most Christian psychologists receive an entirely secular training and are ignorant of the Scriptures. They seldom question the underlying worldview of the field in which they were trained. Instead, they take an essentially secular approach and sprinkle a few Christian insights on top. The result–secular insights that sound pious, but are dangerous and misleading.

When Christian counselors try to integrate Biblical principles with modern psychology, they run into trouble. Many end up redefining Biblical terms to bring them into harmony with psychology. For instance, Gary Sweeten redefines the theological term *sanctification* to mean "mortifying the flesh and developing our *new* (emphasis his) self or our personal self."[13] Sanctification (theological) becomes the "development of our personal selves" (psychological).

Meier and Minirth equate the *unconscious* and the *heart.* They believe that Jeremiah 17:9 is the key to Christian psychiatry. But they misunderstand what Jeremiah means when he said, "The heart is more deceitful than all else, and is desperately sick; who can understand it?" Minirth and Meier write, "The prophet Jeremiah is saying that we humans cannot fathom or comprehend how desperately sinful and deceitful our heart is–our unconscious motives, conflicts, drives, emotions, and thoughts."[14] By redefining heart, Minirth and Meier open up the door to the use of Freud's system of defense mechanisms.

Gary Sweeten also uses the unbiblical concept of the unconscious. He focuses on the unconscious of a believer as the seat of the "residue" (whatever that is) of our Adamic nature and the location of our own rebellion, guilt, and shame. Sweeten's unconscious has more in common with Freud's unconscious (with its drives and neuroses) than it does with the Biblical concept of the heart. The Bible teaches that "out of the heart flows . . . " and then numerous behaviors such as murder and fornication are enumerated (Matt. 15:19). At conversion God gives a person a new heart, a heart of flesh, and not of stone (Ezek. 11:19, 36:26; 2 Tim. 2:22). He is born again, regenerated (John 3:3). At the deepest level of his being, he is a new person (2 Cor. 5:17).

David Seamands relabels sin "difficulties" when he writes about "various kinds of sexual difficulties, from incest to prostitution."[15] Gary Collins expresses the attitude of many Christian psychologists when he writes, "Even love, hope, compassion, forgiving, caring, kindness, confrontation and a host of other concepts are shared by theologians and psychologists."[16] Collins forgets that the psychologists' definitions of these concepts are vastly different from the Biblical definitions. As so often happens with such "integration" of the Scriptures with human wisdom, the wisdom of "Nature" predominates; in time Nature will, in Francis Schaeffer's pregnant expression, "eat up grace."

By borrowing theological terms, the Christian psychologists have blurred the irreconcilable distinctions between the theories of Freud et al., and the teachings of the Bible. Many Christian psychologists believe that the therapies based on a secular mind-set are not only valuable, but indispensable. In truth, what has taken place is not integration but substitution, the substitution of secular psychology for the Word of God. Let's now take a look at a few of the areas where the substitution has occurred.

Change

What does it mean to genuinely change? Does it involve journeying back into the womb to relive your birth experience? Resolving an Oedipus complex? Discovering a functional mother archetype? Obviously Christians and Freudians would sharply disagree on the nature of behavioral change, wouldn't they? Maybe not. Sadly, the distinction in today's practice is not as clear as one would hope, and once again we see the subtle danger of "Christianizing" and incorporating secular concepts into what is essentially evangelical and well-meaning counsel.

Biblical counsel is based on the supposition that a Biblical standard exists for genuine change, but what is that Biblical standard? Even within the context of contemporary Christianity, there is confusion regarding the place, purpose, and direction of Biblical change.

In his immensely popular book *Inside Out*, Larry Crabb presents a comprehensive picture of change. He says, "Change as our Lord describes it involves more than cleaning up our visible acts. He intends us to do more than sweep the streets; He wants us to climb down into the sewers and do something about the filth beneath the concrete. He directs us to enter the dark regions of our soul to find light."[17]

Is this what it means to change? Are we really supposed to "climb down into the sewers" of our lives in order to clean "the filth" beneath the surface? This is a terribly important question because people everywhere, even those in the church, are desperately searching for ways out of the boredom, anxiety, loneliness, meaninglessness, and despair of their lives. Often the answers in the evangelical community have been cheap clichés with no Biblical substance: "Just keep praising the Lord"; "Rebuke your anxiety"; "Visualize yourself as happy"; "Just keep praying."

Crabb, to his credit, does none of the above in his attempts to take the misery seriously. But he does not provide a Biblical answer. Instead, he takes the concept of total depravity (he says, for example, "Our souls are so thoroughly stained with self-reliance . . . ") and gently brushes on top of it a Christ-colored coating of psychoanalysis.

Crabb supports his proposal for sewer-cleaning with this quote from Matthew's Gospel: "Woe to you, teachers of the law and Pharisees, you hypocrites! You clean the outside of the cup and dish, but inside they are full of greed and self-indulgence. Blind Pharisee! First clean the inside of the cup and dish, and then the outside also will be clean" (Matt. 23:25,26 NIV).

Was Jesus' condemnation of the Pharisees intended to serve as a model for deep digging within? No. When Jesus calls the Pharisees to "clean the inside of the cup," He is not concerned with the Pharisees taking a prolonged inner journey. His concern is simply that they clean up their less visible acts—greed and self-indulgence. These are inner attitudes that outwardly manifest themselves in actions. These men were not commanded to look deeply within. Rather they were told to live righteously in the realm of their actions *and* their thoughts.

Jesus did not make too fine a distinction between

thoughts and actions. He said simply that "from vile thoughts flow vile actions." They are intimately linked. Real change will not be accomplished from an inner search, except as it is necessary to identify unrecognized or unrepented thoughts or attitudes that may be impelling us to evil actions.

What will we find in a prolonged inner search? A desperately sick and deceitful heart, which *God alone* can search (Jer. 17: 9,10). Rather than calling us inward, the Bible is calling us *away* from self. The idea that a deeper analysis will bring healing is fallacious. Deeper analysis will bring deeper (ungodly) introspection and deeper self-absorption, both of which are to be deplored.

Scripture never suggests that the path to sanctification lies in therapeutically probing the "deep heart," whatever that is. The Biblical path to sanctification lies in obedience, encouraged by hope, guided by faith, motivated by love. Jesus says simply, "If you love Me, keep My commandments."

Self-Esteem—The Right of Every Christian?

Sin has always been the starting point in dealing with human problems from a Christian perspective. Yet for many contemporary Christian counselors, the concept of sin is considered dangerous and harmful. Robert Schuller writes, "I don't think anything has been done in the name of Christ and under the banner of Christianity that has proven more destructive to human personality and, hence, counterproductive to the evangelism enterprise, than the often crude, uncouth, and unchristian strategy of attempting to make people aware of their lost and sinful condition."[18] This is an amazing statement to come from one who parades across the television screen with God's Holy Scriptures tucked neatly under his arm. Indeed, *sin* has become an ugly word. The reality which necessitated the death of Christ is now "destructive" to the human personality.

Robert Schuller's "Hour of Power" is watched and supported weekly by millions, and why shouldn't it be? His message scratches right where our sinful natures itch. "Self-esteem" is a difficult catch-phrase to challenge; it sounds so good. Who wants to be against it? Schuller goes so far as to call it the "New Reformation." So much for the battles of the "old" Reformation.

But Schuller isn't the only one promoting self-esteem. Another respected leader, who has done excellent work in waking up Christians to our cultural decline, writes, "In a real sense, the health of an entire society depends on the ease with which the individual members gain personal acceptance. Thus, whenever the keys to self-esteem are seemingly out of reach for a large percentage of the people, as in twentieth-century America, then widespread mental illness, neuroticism, hatred, alcoholism, drug abuse, violence, and social disorder will certainly occur."[19] He makes that statement because in this situation he is thinking secularly, not Biblically.

Millions of Christians read authors such as David

Seamands. In his enormously successful *Healing for Damaged Emotions*, Seamands argues that low self-esteem is "Satan's deadliest weapon."[20] The ruin in Christian lives, according to this view, comes when "Satan uses this deadliest of all his emotional and psychological weapons to bring defeat and failure into your life."[21] As individuals read these words, their hope shifts, perhaps just slightly at first, from the blood of Christ and the forgiveness of sin, to the things they can learn from the psychologists.

Men like Seamands have a good rationale. They say that they preach self-esteem only because their ministries were once mired in defeat. They say they knew all about forgiveness and sanctification and yet remained defeated. Anyone who does a great deal of counseling is going to run up against much that doesn't respond to the Word. Yet I have found that the problem isn't with the sufficiency of Scripture (so that we need modern psychology), but with the failure to absorb the lessons of Church history and systematic theology. Applying psychology is much easier because the sinful nature of man is far more ready to be coddled than confronted.

Schuller says that restoration of self-esteem is the New Reformation. Seamands calls low self-esteem "Satan's deadliest weapon." People everywhere are tuned in to self-esteem. There is even a bumper sticker that proclaims boldly, "Self-esteem: the right of every child." What does the Bible say?

Proponents of this gospel of "self" argue that it is foundational for a Christian view of man. But that's not the view of the Apostle Paul, who wrote, "In the last days difficult times will come. For men will be lovers of self, lovers of money, boastful, arrogant, revilers, disobedient to parents, ungrateful, unholy, unloving, irreconcilable, malicious gossips, without self-control, brutal, haters of good, treacherous, reckless, conceited, lovers of pleasure rather than lovers of God" (2 Tim. 3:1-4). Christians today write books on self-esteem and self-love, but Paul warned the Church that the first sign of the "difficult times" of the last days will be that people are lovers of self.

To see what God thinks about self-love, look at what happened to Nebuchadnezzar, the great king of Babylon. He boasted of his feats, "Is this not Babylon the great, which I myself have built as a royal residence by the might of my power and for the glory of my majesty?" (Dan. 4:30). The words were hardly off his lips before God decreed that this proud and arrogant man, consumed with himself, would become as a beast until he acknowledged the sovereignty of Almighty God. Nebuchadnezzar had to turn from self to the service and worship of the true and living God. His self-love dissolved, by God's grace.

We need to teach people to fear God, reject sin, and live godly lives. Rather than seeking approval from others and ourselves, we need to seek God's approval, but not to gain salvation, which is provided entirely through God's approval of Christ's sacrifice on our behalf. Emphasis on self-esteem encourages truly hurting individuals to become like Pharisees. They are encouraged to delve into and build up self, rather than turn from self to God, building up the Church. They focus on themselves rather than turning from themselves and "reaching forward to what lies ahead" (Phil. 3:13).

I am not calling for an easy, superficial, or shallow approach. I believe that inward pain can be dealt with and that people can really change, but this will only happen as God's people become absorbed with Him. God wants the Church to be caught up with His glory, His righteousness, and His Kingdom. Then, and only then (when our primary focus is away from ourselves), will the aching and the longings within be dissipated. Looking to self, even with the good intentions of breaking through layers of problems, will not accomplish the liberation and joy people crave. It will only reveal the deeper levels that have yet to be traversed, a process which, like its secular twin, psychoanalysis, can easily consume an entire lifetime.

In some ways, Woody Allen, who has spent most of his adult life in psychoanalysis, said it best in his 1972 movie *Sleeper*. In this film, Allen has his body frozen for two hundred years until a cure for his disease is discovered. Upon awakening, Allen is told that he has been frozen for two hundred years. He replies (as he thinks of the intervening years), "I was in psychoanalysis. If only I had been going all this time, I'd almost be cured by now."

6

Caring to Confront

The key to Biblical change is often confrontation; yet many Christian counselors are ambivalent about its use. They depict the "nouthetic" or Biblical counselor as an unfeeling, uncaring, insensitive Bible-thumper who uses a lead-plated Bible on the skulls of impenitent sinners.

Nouthetic counseling is confrontational, but it is not insensitive and uncaring. How does nouthetic counseling work? How does it differ from a secular approach? The following example of a secular technique may be helpful.

Jane walked into my office in the medical center in obvious distress. "Dr. Ganz," she wept, "I don't know what to do." (What follows is a verbatim recording of the next few moments of that psychotherapy session.)

R.G.: Tell me about it.
JANE: I'm pregnant.
R.G.: Oh?
JANE: Yes, I just found out.
R.G.: Umhmm.
JANE: I can't stand it. I feel like I'm going crazy.
R.G.: You're feeling very upset.
JANE: I guess I have no choice but to get an abortion.
R.G.: Tell me about that.
JANE: What else can I do? I have to finish school; I have no other choice.
R.G.: [Nothing positive to say.]

I was not a Christian at that time. To know that I was in a position to offer direction, advice, truth, and had nothing for her but inane rejoinders still hurts. That kind of stupidity is licensed by the American and Canadian Psychological and Psychiatric Associations! No real Christian pastor or counselor should ever counsel as I did. But Christians (of all stripes) endorse the thinking and mind-set that make such drivel acceptable. Since then I've had numerous opportunities to counsel women in crisis pregnancies. Let's look at another example so that we can see what Biblical counseling offers to the person in this genuine crisis.

SALLY: Dr. Ganz, Fred and I never meant for anything like this to happen, but I'm pregnant.
R.G.: Have you discussed what you are going to do about it?

SALLY: Of course, this hasn't been easy, but we know we're not ready for a family, so the only thing we can think of doing is to have an abortion.

R.G.: Both of you consider yourselves Christians, don't you?

SALLY: Yes, of course, but we don't see what that has to do with it.

R.G.: Wouldn't it be important to know what God has to say about this?

SALLY: Of course, but certainly God knows how we feel and can understand that we have no choice.

R.G.: It is absolutely correct that God knows you see this as impossible. But God also knows that it isn't impossible. What's important is what God says about this. Does God approve of abortion, even in such difficult straits as you seem to think you are in? God says, "You shall not murder." Sally, that is a child in your womb . . . a growing child. If you have this child aborted, that is murder, and that's what you will be responsible for, for the rest of your life.

SALLY: But we don't have a job or the right place to live. There's so many things.

R.G.: We'll work together with your congregation. I'm sure they'll want to help you find work and a good place to live.

SALLY: Oh, I could never tell them. They would judge me and treat me like a prostitute.

R.G.: Sally, you and Fred have to show them that you know what you did was wrong and that you've asked God's forgiveness. God's people

> know that they are no more perfect than you are, even if they haven't committed the same sin. Furthermore, your struggles are not just yours. God says in His Word that "no temptation has overtaken you but such as is common to man; and God is faithful, who will not allow you to be tempted beyond what you are able, but with the temptation will provide the way of escape also, that you may be able to endure it" (1 Cor. 10:13). That's right, Sally. Nothing has happened to you except what is common to man. You are not alone.

Fred and Sally kept their child. In the process they came to a deeper walk with God and with God's people. What is even more important for our purposes, however, is the contrast. Here as a counselor, I had a standard by which to operate. Here as a counselor, I offered words of rebuke, words of encouragement, and a plan to help them deal with the difficult situation in which they found themselves.

What about the first situation? Whether she would deliver or would kill her baby was virtually irrelevant to the counseling situation. Even though I had received individual training from some of the world's finest psychotherapists, there was absolutely nothing I could offer. That statement is not totally accurate. I did offer reinforcement of the view she already held, that as master of her fate and captain of her soul she could discover "truth" within herself. *There is no neutrality; we worship the Creator or we worship ourselves and other creatures.*

When we confront the way Jesus did, we "admonish the unruly, encourage the fainthearted, help the weak, [and are] patient with all men" (1 Thess. 5:14). Even our patience has an end in the exercise of discipline, for we are to discipline the unrepentant and have nothing to do with a divisive person after a second warning (Tit. 3:10). Clearly this approach following Biblical guidelines cuts deep. But it does not mean we lack care, concern, warmth, understanding, or patience.

Opponents of nouthetic counseling have many objections: It's "far too threatening to use early in the helping relationship"; it can "make the final healing even more difficult to achieve"; "it is the fertilizer of fear"; it is "deficient in love."[22] They argue that the nouthetic idea of confrontation is unbiblical. But nouthetic counseling is only unbiblical if sin does not exist.

According to Jay Adams, author of *Competent to Counsel*, nouthetic confrontation suggests "there is something wrong with the person who is to be confronted nouthetically. The idea of something wrong, some sin, some obstruction, some problem, some difficulty, some need that has to be acknowledged and dealt with, is central . . . nouthetic confrontation arises out of a condition in the counselee that God wants changed. The fundamental purpose of nouthetic confrontation, then, *is to effect personality and behavior change* (emphasis his)."[23]

Adams did not say that the goal of nouthetic counseling was simply to change behavior. The concern of nouthetic counseling is to see personality and behavior change. It is all encompassing. This change often comes about through confrontation, but confrontation of sin does not have to be ignorant, ill-timed, adverse, or fear-provoking. Confrontation can be gentle. The model is Christ. "A battered reed He will not break off, and a smoldering wick He will not put out" (Matt. 12:20).

Let's look at some examples of Christ counseling nouthetically. When confrontation was demanded, Jesus used it forcefully and with immediacy. He used a different approach with the Pharisees than the one He employed with the woman at the well. Both times, however, he used strong and pointed confrontation.

With the Pharisees, His confrontational approach often involved condemnation. They deserved it, and they got it from Him. He didn't say to Himself, "Am I being empathic enough?" Jesus' approach with the woman at the well would also have to be considered abrupt and harsh. Listen to it: "You have had five husbands, and the one whom you now have is not your husband" (John 4:18). If anything can be perceived as an attack, this is it!

Let me make three observations. First, the teaching of Jesus is dramatically confrontational. Secondly, some counselors assume that people would not want to be confronted in this dramatic fashion. But should that prevent us from confronting? Should the counselors of the church pamper sin? Third, I am appreciative when people confront me. Although we might prefer to feel good rather than be faced with the deep sin in our lives, there is more to life than feeling good, especially when we are in sin.

Gary Sweeten, an opponent of nouthetic counseling, wrote, "It is grace that leads to change (repentance)." But the woman at the well changed (repented) because she was confronted with the holiness of God and His just demands. The people of God, in fact, need more confrontation than ever we dreamed.

Sweeten suggests that even deep, sinful habit patterns shouldn't be immediately confronted. For instance, he wrote:

> The homosexual lifestyle is a result of bondage, rebellion, guilt, and shame, usually beginning in the womb, with strong reinforcement in early childhood. Such traumas and the resulting roots of bitterness must be healed if the release from the homosexual neurosis is to be found. Simply 'cutting off the fruit' by stopping the sexual behavior is not enough. In fact, such a remedy will lead to strengthened roots and more destructive fruits. If such pruning is used too early in the helping relationship (i.e., a call for repentance from obvious fruits of the flesh), stronger fruits will result even if the outward fruits do disappear from the seeker's life.[24]

Does he mean to say that fruit worse than homosexual sin will develop if the command to repent comes too early? Paul says that God commands all people everywhere to repent (Acts 17:30). That means us. That means now. That means even if we have never heard another word and never will. Leviticus 20:13 speaks of the homosexual practice as an abomination demanding death. Is there fruit more destructive than this?

Sweeten calls homosexuality a "neurosis." The Bible nowhere views homosexuality as a neurosis. It is sin. A nouthetic counselor will never let a man continue in his sin. He will warn that the way of the transgressor is hard (Prov. 13:15 KJV). He will, after the behavior ends, continue to work on all of the problems that surround this behavior. (Homosexuality is of course a life-dominating problem.) However, counseling ends if the person refuses to repent and change his ways. Jesus departed from those people who refused to obey Him. He didn't hang around developing a warm, gushy relationship. Instead, He warned that the wrath of God was upon them. Hard words. Necessary words though, because sin kills. Sweeten thinks these things are caused by pre-birth and early childhood trauma. Does he forget that Jesus, with an immediacy that startles even the nouthetic counselor, demands immediate repentance? "Go and sin no more." That's it. Final. That's the way it has to be.

Some Christian counselors and pastors are uncomfortable with confrontation because they are uncomfortable with the concept of sin. They want to soften it. Instead of sin, we are taught that "conflicts exist because people have never been taught to communicate adequately." The remedy is said to be "conflict management."[25] Regardless of the conflicts or faulty communication, the basic problem with "hurting" Christians is their sin, not their hurting! The shift from sin (lawbreaking) to "hurting" (the consequences of sin) is subtle and dangerous. In this scheme Christians focus not on their sin, but on their pain. Thus they are tempted to work on problems and seek change, not because they have done wrong, but because it feels so bad. Sooner or later the individual drifts so far away from law as a standard that the things causing pain bear no resemblance to transgressions against the law of God. Then you have defined a "hurting," not a lawless society.

The Bible teaches the necessity of change. It also teaches the possibility of change. The Bible urges believers to replace their sinful behavior with righteousness. "Let him who steals steal no longer; but rather let him labor, performing with his own hands what is good, in order that he may have something to share with him who has need" (Eph. 4:28). Rationalization and blame-shifting have no place in the life of a believer. Sin can't be blamed on someone else. We take responsibility for it, repent of it, and bring forth fruit in keeping with repentance (Luke 3:8-14). The Bible, when it deals with sin, doesn't call us to be healed, but to repent.

The new psychological elite and their mass of discontented churchgoers find this call to repentance totally unacceptable. All that was sufficient for godliness and joy for two thousand years is suddenly deficient. We have a problem—we have little gratitude for the great salvation we have received in Christ and the all-sufficiency of His Word.

I trust that by now my reader is, if not convinced of the folly of secular psychology, at the very least prepared to entertain some thoughts on the Biblical alternative to problem-solving and counseling. Specifically, we will direct our attention to the healing power in the church.

7

The Healing Power in the Church

For five years I had the privilege of working with Dr. Jay Adams at the Christian Counseling and Educational Foundation (CCEF). Dr. Adams's goal was to train pastors to take congregational care out of the hands of the professional psychological community and put it back into the hands of the church. First, he had to convince church leaders they could do it. His book *Competent to Counsel* launched a revolution in Christian circles. While not everyone agreed with Dr. Adams, at least the church began to rethink the passive, submissive role it had assumed in these vital areas.

In my counseling ministry at the CCEF, I typically saw a counselee for one hour a week and only in a counseling setting. I did not see him at church or at home or work. Often these people attended unbiblical churches that effectively minimized, if not outright negated, the help they received. Although I worked diligently to extricate people from liberal churches, the pressures of time and unfamiliarity with their affiliations made this aspect very difficult.

I began to see that the way I could best help people would be to counsel from within a church. I knew that the regular expository preaching of God's Word is the most therapeutic confrontation the people of God receive. But the thought of pastoral ministry terrified me, and I fought it! I would have preferred to do anything else, but God had other plans. It was only a matter of time before He had me serving in a pastoral capacity.

In 1980 I accepted a call to plant a church in Ottawa, Ontario, the capital city of Canada. During the course of that work my view of the pastorate began to change. Previously, I had seen it as the position from which healing and restoration was to come. But I began to understand that as Jesus Christ blesses His Church, the body (not a solitary pastor) is the source of blessing to countless hurting individuals.

This understanding came when the Holy Spirit impressed upon me some verses from Ephesians: "He gave some as apostles, and some as prophets, and some as evangelists, and some as pastors and teachers, for the equipping of the saints for the work of service, to the building up of the body of Christ" (Eph: 4:11,12). In short, these verses teach that the job of the pastor is not to *do* the work of the ministry, but to equip *the flock* to do this work. Christ assigns His ministry to the Church, not to one person in a church, no matter how gifted that individual may be. This understanding is not something new or radical. The work of the ministry is, and always has been, the work of the Church. Pastors are guides or trainers to help people identify and implement their gifts for the Lord.

When we fully understand this principle, however, the entire life and direction of a church changes. Members are not simply individuals drawn into the church to receive something, but are a body drawn together to strengthen one another and the church. Through this process lives are restored, and the Kingdom of God is advanced.

Everyone who comes to Christ and into the Church has real needs, concerns, fears, hurts, scars, and sins which must be faced. Counseling is part of this process. It involves dealing with the batterings of a former life and bringing the healing balm of the new life in Christ. But counseling is not the whole picture. The work of healing and restoration requires a more inclusive view of the local church.

Building up an entire congregation is a challenge, especially for someone like me who has always thrived on my own resourcefulness. The difficulty is not in backing off to let others work, but in setting up procedures necessary to adequately disciple, not just a few individuals, but a whole congregation. I have to build a team, not a group of super heroes. We see in Ephesians that the way to accomplish this goal is through church officers. As the leaders are equipped, they are able to equip others; lives are restored and the kingdom advanced. This is one of the cardinal principles of nouthetic counseling. "Nouthetic activity is the work in which all of God's people may participate."[26]

Most pastors view their work as the *doing* of the ministry. Yet Paul says in Ephesians that the primary work of the pastor (within the context of consistent Biblical preaching) is for the equipping of the saints, that *they* may do the work of ministry. Generally, Christians expect the pastor to do pastoral things *to* them. The pastor, for his part, agrees. He then wonders why he cannot get help, especially for the things he is unable to do. The reason–often he has failed to communicate to his congregation that they have, not only the ability, but also the responsibility to minister to one another.

Matthew Henry, the great Puritan preacher and commentator, wrote, "[The pastor] is to bring into an orderly spiritual state and frame, those who had been as it were dislocated and disjointed by sin, and then to strengthen, confirm, and advance them therein so each in his proper place and function contributes to the good of the whole."[27] In other words, the church is the place where broken people are put back together again, to the good of the church.

Let me illustrate. One time my wife took our youngest child to the physician's office for a simple immunization shot. We had spent much time reading about immunization. When she arrived, she asked the doctor several questions. He responded tersely, "I'll do the doctoring around here."

My wife did not return to that doctor. You see, she believed she had a responsibility at least to know what was going on in the care of our children. Christians have even more responsibility for the living of their Christian lives. No one, not even the best pastor, is responsible for your behavior and work. Unfortunately, many pastors act like that pediatrician. They convey the attitude: "I'll do the ministry around here." Instead they need to prepare, expect, and encourage the saints to be responsible for the work of ministry.

Many people view the church as they would view the secular service industry. You pay your money and get your service. They do not realize that for the church to function well, each member must function to the limits of his/her capabilities. The church can not accomplish the ministry entrusted to it if only pastors do the work. We must rid ourselves of our inherent and radical individualism.

In addition to pastoring a church, I own a sheep farm. Watching the behavior of sheep has taught me some lessons that apply to people as well. Sheep are rather defenseless. When they are attacked by wolves, there is only one way they can protect themselves. They draw together into a gigantic white mound during an attack. The wolf won't attack this white mound, but will go after other prey–often the sheep on its own outside the flock. For my sheep to be safe they must stay together as one and work together as one. Similarly, in the church safety and strength come when the congregation works together as one body. Such unity does not come naturally to any of us. Perhaps that is why Paul repeats his concern for oneness seven times in the fourth chapter of Ephesians. The saints can't be equipped for works of service if they are bickering among themselves.

The pastor equips the church, as Paul says in Ephesians 4:12, "for the work of service." This is further defined as the "building up of the body of Christ." The phrase "building up" comes from a term that means "house" or "household." From its earliest usage it had a heavenly sense to it. The apostle says that the one who came *from* Heaven (Christ) wants the church equipped so that it can make it *to* Heaven (verse 12). In 2 Corinthians 10:8, Paul speaks of his apostolic authority which he received for "building you up." The same word is used in both Ephesians and 2 Corinthians. Paul wants the church to be the heavenly house of God. He wants the church established so that it makes it to Heaven. It must be willing to receive from the apostle, or it will never possess the obedient nature necessary to fulfill its heavenly mandate.

The church in Corinth battled authoritative apostolic teaching. We see this in several places in 2 Corinthians. Notice 2 Corinthians 13:10: "For this reason I am writing these things while absent, in order that when present I may not use severity, in accordance with the authority which the Lord gave me, for building up and not for tearing down." Today we continue to fight against authority. When we resist, we miss being established, strengthened, and built up. Congregations that submit to God's instruction will "be of one mind" and will "live in peace" (2 Cor. 13:11). What wonderful blessedness results from being "built up."

Everyone who is called into union with Christ is also called to minister to the body so that strongholds of sin are torn down and the body of Christ is strengthened. The Church may be strong even when there are weak members in it, but the principal Biblical teaching is to "strengthen the hands that are weak" (Heb. 12:12). In the next chapter we will see what is meant by strengthening these hands.

8

Equipping the Body

The world is filled with broken, sinning, and hurting people. Counseling centers of all kinds, Christian and non-Christian, are overloaded. As a young Christian, I was still working at a medical center complex when I was invited to a Katherine Kuhlman healing service. What was most incredible to me was not what happened (or didn't) to those people. The incredible reality was the enormous number of people clamoring for healing. There must have been 20,000 people in attendance. One must conclude that masses of people are desperate, even within the church. People are running blindly here and there for healing and restoration. Few of them realize that the church itself, under the Holy Spirit's direction, is active in the process of restoration.

The Spirit of Christ working in the church restores the "brokenhearted." The church ministers to people who have been torn apart by sin. Sometimes the sin is of their own doing. They have lied, cheated, abused their wives or children, cheated on their wives or husbands, or destroyed their bodies with alcohol and drugs. The consequences have ravaged them. Often when they come to their senses and repent, the situation for them is dramatically less fortunate than that of the prodigal son.

Sometimes people are victims of someone else's sin. A strong, tough man once described the years of sexual abuse he had received at an orphanage run by a religious order. He detailed how he had been abused from the very first day he arrived. He described how good people who had wanted to adopt him had been told lies to keep them from taking him so that he could remain a sexual plaything for the leaders of this religious order. He had only recently uncovered those lies.

The man's voice broke as he recounted the years of suffering. Clichés won't work with such wounded people. Only the Word of God applied to the hurt and pain of his life through the Holy Spirit by the body of believers ministering compassionately could heal him. It is not enough for a counselor to speak about a person's wrecked past and offer hope; the whole congregation must accept the one who is scarred, marred, and torn.

The salvation God offers is not just from sin, death, and Hell. Restoration is available now by God's grace to all of God's people who admit their hurt, pain, and suffering. People do not need to talk incessantly about a "dysfunctional past," although many do. I have ministered to such people. They use their past as an excuse to avoid both solving their problems and ministering to others. The truly dysfunctional (although I reject this term) do not dwell on their "dysfunctionality," but rather quietly carry their bruises and brokenness. They are damaged goods. Often the real problem is not the damage, but their belief that they are irreparably damaged. In fact, without Jesus Christ they *are* beyond repair. Often these people go on to a life of crime, or they inflict on others the sin and criminal behavior done to them. But with Christ restoration is possible.

In the previous chapter we looked at the concepts of equipping and building up. Let's now look at the concept of equipping the body[28] in more depth. In Greek the word for equipping is *katartidzo.* In classical Greek it was used to describe the refitting of a ship or the setting of a bone. It can also be translated as "perfecting" or "completing what is lacking." It is used thirteen times in the New Testament and in different ways depending on the context. It is also used in Ephesians 4, the passage that is the basis for understanding not only the work of the pastor/teacher, but also the work of the church.

In Matthew 4:21 James and John are in a boat with their father, and they are mending *(katartidzo)* their net. In order to make a living, a fisherman must keep his net repaired. If he does not, he can lose his entire catch. This passage gives us a picture of a church as a body of people–a grand net. Pastor Ken Smith points out that broken relationships are like a hole in the net: "What if [the hole] becomes a large tear?"

Most churches are filled with tears and holes. The people of God must constantly be on the lookout for them. They must be ready at all times to do the work of mending. They must show interest and sympathy in the hurts and sufferings of those around them and be willing to do all that is possible to mend those tears. Only in this way can the body be built up. This is easily said, but more difficult to do because we live in an age when people coming into the church are largely consumed with self. Self-absorption is a habit that is hard, but not impossible, to break.

All people hurt at some time. Few are prepared to look beyond their own troubles to help someone else. They have developed the habit of thinking, *Make me feel better; then I'll help you (if I have time)*. They do not realize that their problem will often seem smaller if they step out and enter with encouragement (not commiserating gossip) into the world of someone else's problems. I do not want to suggest that all problems go away when a person gets involved with others. But it is true that people are helped when they know they are not carrying their burdens all on their own, that others are interested in them and are prepared to help.

Martha had been hospitalized five times for various psychiatric disorders. She is doing beautifully in our church. It is the counseling and ministry of *others* in the church that have accomplished this. She said recently, "This is the first time in my life that I am not lonely." I don't think we can ever overestimate the force for good of Biblical involvement in other people's lives.

The term *katartidzo* is also used by Luke. In Luke 6:39 Jesus told a parable about a blind man who was unable to lead another blind man because both of them would fall into the pit. He said a pupil is not above his teacher, but that everyone, after he is fully trained (*katartidzo*), will be like his teacher. He then goes on to ask, "And why do you look at the speck that is in your brother's eye, but do not notice the log that is in your own eye? Or how can you say to your brother, 'Brother, let me take out the speck that is in your eye,' when you yourself do not see the log that is in your own eye? You hypocrite, first take the log out of your own eye, and then you will see clearly to take out the speck that is in your brother's eye" (Luke 6:41,42). Jesus is asking, "How can you minister to the blind if you are blind?" *Katartidzo* is used here in the context of dealing with ourselves first so that we can minister to others.

Pastors often have blindness that leaves them unable to help others. They need to deal with their personal problems in order to be of any help to others. For pastors to pretend nothing ever troubles them is foolishness. It is even worse when pastors attempt to lead the flock without dealing with their own problems first. Christians, especially pastors, need trusted friends with whom they can share the details of problems and receive honest and straightforward Biblical counsel in response. Otherwise, they are walking in blindness, and one of the great problems with blindness is that it persists; if not dealt with, it persists through the generations.

Parents can also train their children in blindness. Unrenounced patterns of hate, bitterness, and resentment are passed from one generation to the next. When we refuse to deal quickly with our sins, our churches and our families are torn apart. Many churches are shepherded by pastors and elders who are blind. Many families have children who are clones of their parents–possessing their parents' worst problems. What a shame! If we were willing to look at ourselves and deal with our blind spots Biblically, many of these problems would be smashed and swept away.

Katartidzo was also used by Paul in 1 Corinthians 1:10. The Corinthian church, largely composed of

Gentiles, had many problems in connection with its growth. Paul exhorted the brethren, "By the name of our Lord Jesus Christ, that you all agree, and there be no divisions among you, but you be made complete in the same mind and in the same judgment." Here *katartidzo* means "that you all agree" or be "perfectly united" (KJV). Paul told the Corinthians to come together in Christ. They were to stop choosing sides, as far as apostolic leadership was concerned. Paul gave this advice to those who sided with himself as well as to the other factions.

In the Corinthian situation factionalism had reached new heights. Church members were quarreling over who had the greatest gifts. One part of the body said it didn't need the other parts. Paul reminded them that the gifts are given in order that the whole body might work together, that Christ's people and work on earth would not be divided. Finally in chapter 13 Paul gave the ultimate antidote to the foolishness and pride characterizing the church—love.

One commentary pointed out that the word for "umpire" is almost identical to *katartidzo*. The idea is "to bring together," as an umpire mediates between two opposing factions. We have a much greater umpire, Paul said, in the Holy Spirit. He makes no bad calls. Paul argued that Christians need to do whatever is necessary to bring about perfect unity, without tossing out truth.

That means that Christians must strive to work out differences that hinder their unity. People must not seek supportive "grumble groups" for their particular grievances in the church. Even when there are legitimate differences of opinion, the people of God will continue to strive with one mind for perfect unity in the faith.

Finally, we see *katartidzo* in Galatians 6:1. "Brethren, even if a man is caught in any trespass, you who are spiritual, restore (*katartidzo*) such a one in a spirit of gentleness; each one looking to yourself, lest you too be tempted." The word is used commonly in relation to church discipline. It conveys the sense of recovering a brother or sister who has been caught up in a trespass. That person is to be restored gently. Even if he is not ready to give up his sin, he needs help, the kind of help which will restore him to the place he ought to be. So Paul tells the church to restore him, not waiting until the person comes forward (which is the usual scenario in counseling). It involves going to the person hurt (by sin) even before he may be fully aware he needs help.

Today if there is a sin of omission in Christ's church, it is that the church (especially its leaders) sits back and does little regarding sin. I am not suggesting that we rush around looking for sin. At the same time, when someone is caught in it, the church must be mobilized to bring about restoration. Otherwise, people become firmly entrapped in sin from which they might have been rescued had the church responded quickly with gentle confrontation.

If we understand the meanings of the word *katartidzo*–to mend, to train, to promote unity, to restore–and apply them, I believe we will see the church equipped and strengthened immeasurably. As we keep our eyes and hearts open for those who are broken, their restoration and the "knitting of their bones" will bring considerable health and energy to the church. The church needs to be encouraged in this task, knowing that Christ will restore His hurting flock. Understood in these ways, *katartidzo* is an essential concept for an effective counseling ministry.

9

Building Up the Body

A man and a woman recently left our congregation because they "didn't get fellowship." I talked to them about their complaint. They thought the body of Christ existed to serve them. No amount of encouragement succeeded in motivating them to reach out to others. Others were there for them, but this family was never there for others. The family believed its problems were so great that they had no time or energy left to think about others. Nevertheless, the family thought that others should always (if they were loving) be ready to give to them.

God created us needing fellowship. He said, "It is not good for the man to be alone" (Gen. 2:18). Following this pronouncement, God proceeded to make a wife for Adam. Not all Christians marry, but all need, should have, and should seek fellowship. As we open ourselves to the real needs of others around us, we can receive great blessing. In a community that operates in this way, everyone will be looking out for everyone else. This is the antithesis of "looking out for Number One." We care for others because we have been touched by God, shown mercy, and seen our guilt and sins washed away; now we want others to receive that same benefit. Out of gratitude to God we reach out to our Kingdom family and beyond. This motivation can only exist for those who have been converted from death to life in Christ.

At conversion, our lives are taken over by a new and glorious Person–the Holy Spirit. Even a superficial overview of the fruit of the Spirit reveals what a powerful force we actually have become. The Bible says, "The fruit of the Spirit is love, joy, peace, patience, kindness, goodness, faithfulness, gentleness, self-control" (Gal. 5:22,23). These functional realities in the hands of dedicated Kingdom workers are incredibly powerful tools for comfort, encouragement, and change.

Learning to comfort one another is one of the positive aspects of equipping that takes place in the body. It is "putting on the new life in Christ." Paul said, "Blessed be the God and Father of our Lord Jesus Christ, the Father of mercies and God of all comfort; who comforts us in all our affliction so *that we may be able to comfort those who are in any affliction* with the comfort with which we ourselves are comforted by God. For just as the sufferings of Christ are ours in abundance, so also our comfort is abundant through Christ" (2 Cor. 1:3-5, emphasis mine). We are to follow Paul's example. The fruits of the spirit–love, joy, peace, patience, kindness, goodness, faithfulness, gentleness, and self-control–are not for personal enjoyment, but for the building up of the body of Christ.

Each person can extract from his own struggle that which can edify and uplift his brothers and sisters in Christ. To act contrary to what is sinfully natural takes education, an act of the will, and the help of God. It is natural to behave like the family that left our church. In their difficulties, that family demanded that the body of Christ serve them. The result was their separation from the body of Christ. It is unnatural and takes deliberate effort to look to the interests of others before our own interests. This does not mean that we are to defer indefinitely dealing with our own problems. Rather, we must not be so intently focused on our own situation that we fail to see those around us who may be facing situations far more serious than our own.

Self-deception plays a significant role in our failure to fulfill this command. I have never heard anyone say, "Yes, I saw they needed help, but I didn't feel like it"; but we are all guilty of intentionally *not* seeing those in need, as if this somehow negates our responsibility. We must resist the temptation to "duck down the alley." We need to meet, not avoid, people and their needs. At times we must put our own needs on the back burner.

This is not done slavishly, by compulsion, but heartily, out of gratitude.

We must also avoid playing the game of "hide and seek" with our Christian family. Often people who truly need assistance, intervention, or just an encouraging word stroke their self-pity by thinking, *Well, if they can't see I'm hurting, they mustn't care, so why should I tell them?* Implicit in Paul's command is that we are to both take *and* receive the comfort that is ours in abundance in Christ.

The structure of the church provides an often-ignored opportunity. This opportunity comes because a church meets as a group. We are called to place ourselves in physical proximity with one another. (This is just one of the reasons that "the church of the air" (TV) is a deficient notion; the "members" never know each other, or connect in any way at all!) The primary purpose of "coming together" is to worship God, but this group structure serves many other purposes as well—providing encouragement, support, accountability, and a physical confirmation of belonging to God's Kingdom. The world recognizes the value of this concept and utilizes it with great success.

Those in the midst of change need to affirm publicly their thankfulness for victory over sin. They also need to be part of a group that will keep them accountable. This is not primarily the responsibility of a Biblical counselor but of the church. The counselor must direct his counselee to seek out a good, solid, Biblical church, not only for the *whole* counsel of God provided through steadfast exegetical preaching, but also for accountability and acceptance in the struggles of life. We need to be helped or "lifted up" when we stumble, not left to flounder on our own. We shouldn't always think that we have to send our people to one of the "anonymous" groups. We have everything they have and more. We can keep people accountable and do so on the basis of the Word of God. The church must learn that its ministry is not only preaching and worship services, but also the mutual encouragement and edification of one another. The Scriptures are replete with such commands. In fact, a quick tally shows more commands for a "one-another ministry" than for the pastoral side of the church's ministry.

Recently I had the privilege of helping a young man recognize the necessity of personal commitment to Jesus Christ as his Lord and Savior. While we were talking afterward, he said that he wanted to tell me something. He told me that I intimidated him. This wasn't the first time I had been told that, so it didn't surprise me. But I was surprised that this young man, with whom I had been so careful not to do anything that would push him away from Christ, would say it.

I asked him why he felt intimidated. He said he felt overwhelmed by someone who got up early in the morning, had a full day of work and other activities, and continued working until late in the night. Reflecting on his comment, I realized that I often spoke about my rigorous schedule. Was my speaking about it encouraging others to a more disciplined and productive life, or was it instead pushing them in the other direction? Was there a way I could encourage better time usage without provoking the human tendency toward comparison and despair?

This man had the courage to confront me. I could have defended my schedule; in fact, I could have urged it on him. Instead I accepted what he had to say and thought about it. I realized that unless what I say can be a real encouragement to others in this area, I should be silent. Most important, this young brother in Christ took a risk in telling me something that I needed to change–perhaps a pride in certain accomplishments that may have been causing others to stumble. Often we don't realize that interactions such as this are God's tools, used to mold us into the Christlike people He wants us to be.

We don't often take criticism well because by nature we are self-protective. By nature we guard ourselves from insult and injury. By nature the person we want to promote is the lord Self, not the Lord Jesus Christ. Our sinful natures notwithstanding, Christians must learn to receive confrontation regarding harmful or sinful traits and habits. We can do this only when we understand that we don't have to protect ourselves. In fact, if we truly desire to become like Christ, we must not protect ourselves. That would be like a surgical patient "protecting" himself from his competent and caring physician by refusing to expose his wound, saying, "But he'll touch what is hurting me!"

Some people say, "I'm perfectly willing to be confronted by God through the Scriptures, but not by *him/her*, thank you very much!" Well, yes, seeing one's errors while reading or hearing the Word is less publicly embarrassing, and God in His mercy does use this channel often in the lives of believers, but He also sometimes chooses to use fellow sufferers and sinners to do His good purpose as well.

The best people to help are those who know us best. Do we avail ourselves of that help? Do we indicate that we want to grow and change? Or do we give off signals that say, "I've arrived; that's all, folks!" Imagine what it would be like if everyone who knew (by observation or relationship) and cared for you told you something about yourself of which you were not aware. There would be numerous areas for growth and change. Do it! Ask the question and then listen to the answers. Certainly there will be some pain in the self-discovery, but nothing close to the pain of being a stunted Christian. The pay-off is tremendous–a life more closely conformed to Christ. The best person to help others become like Christ is that person who himself is becoming more and more like Christ. Do you want to be used in many people's lives for growth, restoration, and strengthening? Begin with yourself.

People are touched when others open up to the Spirit of God and in turn open up to the church. As a body, they stop hiding and instead seek to include others in the freedom they now have in Christ. Sometimes Christians hesitate because they have been harmed before. It seems safer to stay out of the line of fire, but this is a faulty strategy. The line of fire is also the lifeline. The obstacles, self-protection, apathy, discouragement, and strife are difficult to overcome–but not impossible.

A Biblical church is a living body, willing to listen to the hurts of others, even as it acknowledges hurts of its own. Not all hurt and pain can be eradicated in the Lord's Day preaching. Church members need to be sensitive to the needs of others, seek ways to comfort the hurting, acknowledge their own sins, and be willing to confront and be confronted. When that happens, a church is built up.

Wherever church members are part of a Biblical counseling ministry, they are seeing their churches revitalized as individuals live out Biblical truths. And thus the words of John are fulfilled: "In this is love, not that we loved God, but that He loved us and sent His Son to be the propitiation for our sins. Beloved, if God so loved us, we also ought to love one another" (1 John 4:10,11).

10

Becoming New Creatures

God's people are meant to bless, strengthen, encourage, and Biblically counsel one another. Church leaders should spearhead these activities. All too often, however, they do not do it. Pastors who will otherwise be committed to the principle of the "sufficiency of Scripture" will compromise at the point of counseling. They will relinquish their God-given and God-ordained authority at the doorway of the high priests of psychology.

I was forcefully reminded of this in the case of Betty, who came to my attention when a pastor called me for advice. Betty was not in his congregation, but she had been a friend for years. He knew her to be a committed Christian.

Betty's husband had recently been laid off from

work. She still had a good job, her children were grown, her husband wasn't worried, and the house was paid off, but Betty nevertheless brooded about possible dangers. She became obsessed with fear that she and her husband would be impoverished.

Betty's sister recommended that she be taken to the local psychiatric hospital for help. After a quick evaluation, the doctors admitted Betty to the hospital. She was placed on medication but was still depressed. At this point my pastor friend called to ask my advice. I told him to get her out of there and begin dealing Biblically with her fears and the inaction that her depression caused. The pastor said that the family was unwilling to take her out of the hospital even though weekend home visits were Betty's best times.

Two weeks later the pastor called again. He was alarmed because he had just discovered that Betty was about to begin a series of electroconvulsive shock treatments (ECT).

ECT was discovered in the 1930s by the Italian psychiatrist Ugo Cerletti. As he walked past a slaughter house, he noticed that the cattle had electrodes attached to their heads. He found out that a relatively small shock rendered them unconscious; thus it was possible to slaughter them in a more humane fashion. He began applying the shock in his psychiatric practice at the local hospital. In the last half century, shock therapy became one of the most widely practiced therapies in the world. Although there have been numerous outcries against it, it remains a staple in the arsenal of the modern psychiatrist.

I told the pastor, "Bob, contact her pastor and warn him of the dangers of ECT–that it begins a treadmill of regular rounds of ECT in increasingly serious depressions. Remind him that ECT will not deal with Betty's fears and her lack of trust that God will take care of them during this difficult time." He told me that Betty's pastor was at the hospital during his last visit. He overheard him telling Betty and her family that ECT was a wonderful treatment.

About two weeks later Bob called me to say that he had just returned from a visit with Betty. She appeared in better spirits than he had seen her in a long time. I could sense his underlying confusion. He was wondering if ECT really was a wonder cure after all. I told him to ask Betty about her experience with ECT. He came back and told me (as I knew he would) that she had absolutely no memory of ECT or *of any of the events immediately preceding it.*

Sure, Betty seemed better. Her recent memory and all that had triggered her depression had been removed, as if magically. Yes, Betty could expect a brief respite from fear and depression. But ECT was no cure. ECT had not dealt with the root of her distress. There was absolutely no reason to assume that continuing problems in Betty's life wouldn't prod her to return for ever-decreasing periods of "peace" through an ever-increasing number of ECT treatments.

Betty is a Christian woman with a Christian family and a Christian pastor, all of whom allowed a barbaric form of "treatment," with negligible (if any) long-term benefits and potentially serious long-term effects, to be used instead of the Word of God.

Biblical counselors are committed to God and His Word, not just in our prayer closets and on the Sabbath, but in our work. We want to "bring every thought captive to Christ," and in so doing, witness the power of God, not the power of man. This is just what God offers. "If any man is in Christ, he is a new creature; the old things passed away; behold, new things have come" (2 Cor. 5:17).

Young Christians know that the Bible says they are changed. But they often understand this change to be primarily an *affective* reality. That is, they assume that because they *are* changed, they must *feel* changed. They believe they will *feel* more loving, gentle, self-controlled. (This too does take place in the course of our sanctification; our feelings, like all else, are redeemed by God to be used for His glory.) When their feelings don't change immediately, it can lead to massive disappointment in poorly instructed new Christians.

These new believers often react with anger and disappointment: "I don't want to be a Christian anymore. I don't *feel* any different"; "I still have homosexual feelings"; "What good does it do being a Christian? I thought that God would take those feelings away or at least take the temptations away."

Every Biblical counselor has heard similar accounts dozens or perhaps even hundreds of times. Yet God never says He'll take away bad feelings or temptations. He says instead that "with the temptation, [He] will provide the way of escape also, that you may be able to endure it" (1 Cor. 10:13). The glory of God is not that you are never again tempted, but that in the midst of your trials, instead of giving in to sin, you flee to Him and do what's right. To the glory of God you learn to say no to sin and yes to God and to His standard of righteousness.

Failure to understand this point leads to cruel bondage. We open ourselves to the suggestion that our Christian faith isn't working and whip ourselves into the psychotherapist's office at the first available appointment. But this is *not* what God tells us in this passage. His power is real, but corruptions still continue to plague the child of God until the end. This is the reason for the constant admonitions in the Scriptures to "put off the old and put on the new." It is confirmation that certain areas of our lives, though truly set free from the law of sin and death, stubbornly resist relinquishing their hold on sordid but familiar postures and attitudes. Hence the commandment, "Do not conform any longer to the pattern of this world, but *be transformed by the renewing of your mind.* Then you will be able to test and approve what God's will is–his good, pleasing and perfect will" (Rom. 12:2 NIV, emphasis mine).

Being a new creature means to be part of a new

order. We do not have the old thoughts immediately eradicated. Don't be discouraged when facing a difficulty. Don't be disheartened at temptations. What did you expect? Don't answer. I know what you expected . . . at least what you hoped. You hoped as a holy person to be out of the battle. You hoped your lusts and wrong desires would never again trouble you. Not so! We are holy in spite of the continuation of sin and sinful impulses. We are holy *in the battle!* And the battle wages in us! We are a battleground, every bit as much as the national (political, civil) scene, every bit as much as the family is a battleground. Yet by God's grace we can stand our ground in the power of the Holy Spirit, by His strength–and we can see personal victory.

So then rather than despairing at the difficulties, remember that what you are really experiencing is the tension of living between two worlds. Every believer is appropriating the powers of the age to come *in this age.* To expect no difficulty is to deny sin and its power. The mighty change is within, as God's Spirit takes progressive control of a believer's life and equips him or her to face the tension between the two worlds and win. Every believer must realize that only the miracle of grace accounts for his or her change from a natural to a spiritual person (1 Cor. 2:14,15). Every believer must realize that to be regenerated is to be emancipated from Satan's kingdom and to be placed into the Kingdom of Christ. It is to be transformed from a "child of disobedience" (Eph. 2:2) into a "child of obedience" (1 Pet.

1:14). It is to take an unbeliever, including his mind and heart which are at enmity against God, and make him into a loyal subject of the King.

Indeed a war is being fought. In any war the major issue must never be how the troops feel in the battle, but rather, are the troops battling regardless of how they feel? Sure, the King wants happy troops. He has done everything to facilitate this. But the King demands our active participation in His cause even when we don't feel like it. This is where many people have trouble. They believe the change in coming to Christ should make them *feel* different. While changed feelings follow obedience, coming to Christ doesn't necessarily make a person feel better at first. In fact the changes one undergoes and the possible friction in relationships with people who don't understand what is happening often contribute to feeling worse.

However, there is one principle that facilitates peace during the early and more trying times in the Christian life–the Christian grows in his or her understanding of the truth gradually. Advance in the Christian life comes a little bit at a time. One of the great problems of young Christians is their proclivity to act as though they know all the truth. Many people, highly excited and almost intoxicated with their new-found faith, act as though they can learn nothing from anyone. Some of them, while learning very little, parade about in arrogance and presumption. True Christian knowledge inevitably leads to humility because the knowledge of God is humbling. Thus the hope of the believer is to be progressively deepened in faith and progressively conformed to Christ. Those who shepherd the flock of God ought to instruct their people in perseverance, not only for salvation, but also in order to taste more deeply of the good things of God.

11

When Christianity Doesn't Work

I had been a Christian no more than a month when Harry came to see me. He told me a lurid story of countless homosexual escapades he'd had while traveling with the circus as an acrobat. He described his conversion to me, and I was able to rejoice in his deliverance from sin—or so I thought.

What actually emerged was not a story of deliverance but a narrative of complaint. He complained that Christianity did not work for *him*. I asked what he meant. He told me that although he had not practiced homosexuality since becoming a Christian several months before, neither had his interest or desire in homosexuality abated. He told me that he could not go on as a Christian if these feelings were not removed.

Harry expected that Christ would remove his

desire for homosexual contact. When that didn't happen, Harry decided he was an example of a case where Christianity didn't work.

I was a young Christian at that time, and there was a certain cogency to Harry's argument. I too thought that being born again meant the obliteration or instant zapping away of all lusts and angers–that one shouldn't have to be struggling against sin. Fortunately, I moved beyond this point. I came to see that the glory of our faith is not that we have no desire to sin, but that we do not have to act on that desire. I also came to learn that it was God who gave us the power to say no to sin. It was God who made us "both to will and to work for His good pleasure" (Phil. 2:13).

I lost contact with Harry at that point. But I haven't lost contact with the fact that countless Christians walk around all their lives believing what Harry believed and are thus defeated before they begin. They never seem to understand that when it seems as though Christianity doesn't work, they have misread the problem.

Is there a time when Christianity doesn't work? Yes. Christianity does not work when there is a false expectation regarding what the Christian life is all about. It doesn't work when there is little or improper teaching of Biblical precepts and standards. It does not work when there is a lack of commitment to the disciplines involved in perseverance and growth. It does not work in isolation from other believers. Most important, it does not work apart from the saving grace of God through Christ.

But Christianity does work for sinners.

The first step necessary for anyone's ultimate good is to enter into a personal relationship with Jesus Christ as Lord and Savior, submitting to His Lordship and then living according to His plan. This is the definition of righteous living. A person who *incidentally* lives a good life aside from a conscious submission to God will be blessed by the common grace associated with the avoidance of evil, but he or she will not be living a righteous life. Righteousness is attributed to believers through the sacrifice of Christ. The one who rejects Christ will face the penalty for failure to receive Christ's righteousness, no matter how apparently good the person is. "The wages of sin is death" (Rom. 6:23). Cleaning up the externals of a life without cleaning the inside (possible only through the blood of Jesus) brought the serious charge of "Woe to you" on the Pharisees. For this reason, the presentation of the gospel is an important part of nouthetic counseling.

The end result of a superficial quick fix is that a relatively clean (e.g., sober as opposed to drunk) sinner still stands before God in judgment. Therein lies both the foundational need for nouthetic counseling and the grave danger in shipping people wounded by sin off to the secular professionals. Without a changed heart, any "put-off" sinful behavior is merely put on hold. The counselee remains bound by "the law of sin and death," not yet released by the "law of the Spirit of life" (Rom. 8:2). Biblical counseling expresses the demand, not only to put off the sinful habits of life under the old regime, but to put on the righteous habits of new life in Christ.

If a person refrains from sinful habits but puts nothing in their place, he eventually will be back where he began. On the other hand, if he ceases his iniquitous behavior and replaces it with new depraved activities, he can wind up worse than before. The only antidote for sin is a righteous life lived according to the Word of God. This is not a one-step operation. We are responsible to do right, day by day and moment by moment. This can be either an overwhelming responsibility or a wonderful opportunity. Seizing the opportunity involves making sure not to succumb to the numerous and inevitable temptations of the moment. It means being ready in prayer. It means being ready to act in accord with the teachings of the Bible even when it is difficult and may hurt. How can it hurt? It hurts enough that most people never engage themselves in doing what the Bible teaches.

Relinquishing sin can be like giving up a cherished part of ourselves. The Bible is uncompromising and unbending in its moral boundaries. Because of this, it is an entirely trustworthy, sure, and solid standard for behavior. It is unyielding in its intolerance of sin. It will never say, for example, "You're committing adultery, but hey, you really love her, and you have such a nice relationship. Your wife is such a nag. I guess in this situation it's okay." No, never! Instead it demands righteous living that is pure and spotless. The Bible demands not just any action, but righteous action. This is easier said than done. How many times have we seen people who, despite what seem to be the best of intentions, fail repeatedly? Counselors, friends, and all concerned wonder why.

People fall short of genuine change either because they don't want to change or because they don't know what is required of them. The patterns from the past become deeply ingrained in their lives. They learn habits that are incredibly destructive, yet counselors often neglect to teach them how to break with those patterns and do what is right. Often counselors do not know themselves. They have not understood the awesome implication of these words, "You were taught, with regard to your former way of life, to put off your old self, which is being corrupted by its deceitful desires; to be made new in the attitude of your minds; and to put on the new self, created to be like God in true righteousness and holiness" (Eph. 4:22-24 NIV).

The Bible is replete with counsel on how to put off sin and put on righteousness. Biblically, a thief is no longer a thief when he stops stealing *and* starts working with his hands to provide for the poor (Eph. 4:28). We are not to get drunk on wine, *but are* to be filled with the Holy Spirit (Eph. 5:18). Paul commands us to "not be anxious about anything, *but* in everything, by prayer and petition, with thanksgiving, present your requests to

God" (Phil. 4:6 NIV, emphasis mine). He states elsewhere that " . . . each of you must put off falsehood *and* speak truthfully to his neighbor . . . " (Eph. 4:25 NIV, emphasis mine). The successful dismantling of sinful habits is a two-step process–breaking old patterns and forming new ones. While all of this takes place in the reality of the Spirit, the seat of both of these operations is in our thinking.

We assimilate negative attitudes about ourselves that we allow to determine much of what we do or do not do. I am not talking about self-esteem or self-image; I am talking simply about learning. If a person has been told all his life that he is stupid, he may very well believe that he is dumb even though he may be intelligent. If he has grown up being told he is an awkward klutz, should it come as any surprise when he fails repeatedly in tasks and skills demanding coordination and dexterity? He may even want to do these things, but finds himself stuck behind the message that says he cannot. So he doesn't try, therefore failing before he begins. If he does try and then fails, he sees that as confirmation of his inabilities.

What people tell us about ourselves influences (although it does not determine) what we believe about ourselves and what we can do. Parents especially should be aware that their comments to their children will mold much of these young lives. For example, when a child comes home from school with mediocre exam results, reacting properly is important. "What an idiot!"

or "Any moron could have done better than that" is not a proper response. I mention this because the best situation is to get it right from the beginning.

Treating a child like a criminal contributes to future criminality. But the adult criminal is still without excuse for his behavior. He cannot blame his parents, his siblings, his environment, his teachers. That notwithstanding, good and godly parenting will foster godly children. The Bible is clear and summarizes this for us when it says, "Train up a child in the way he should go, even when he is old he will not depart from it" (Prov. 22:6).

In other words, we learn to be (*be*have) good, and we learn to be (*be*have) bad. We learn to view ourselves as those who can accomplish much, or we learn to view ourselves as hopelessly incapable. Since learning is so important, we should not be surprised at how important teaching is. The first and most important teachers for a child are the parents. They must be careful to teach according to Biblical guidelines. If all that ever comes from their mouths is criticism, often their children will give up. Perhaps parents criticize because the child attempts something new–something he doesn't know how to do. He may create a mess, which is no big deal, but if he is harshly criticized, he may fear to try again. When the child becomes an adult and finally gains knowledge and skill, he may respond as though he is still the incapable child who made a displeasing mess. It has become his habit to do so.

Bad habits are most deadly in the realm of values and morals. It is tragic when individuals act like criminals because that's what they have been taught they are. These individuals are responsible for their actions, but others retain responsibility for their influence. We must make sure that the fruit of the Spirit is operative in our lives. This demands patience, gentleness, and a lovingkindness to discipline and nurture children who do not live up to our (often unrealistic) expectations.

The "new" Ten Commandments for some parents seem to be: "Don't touch," "Don't grab," "Don't speak," "Don't enjoy," etc. Yet when the children grow up morose and habitually negligent of God's commandments, parents wonder why. Children have been taught another set of commandments. Then when it is to our advantage, we expect them to shift gears and become happy, content Christian young people. They aren't interested in such hypocrisy and often respond with harmful, destructive, and sinful habits. These habits are the "former way of life" that Paul insists must be put off and replaced with the "new self, created to be like God in true righteousness and holiness."

Sin not only is entered *into* habitually; sin *is* habitual. No sins, left to themselves, just go away. Sin is either atoned for by the blood of Christ and then put off day by day in the Christian, or else it is left to spread like cancer. This is not to say that all negative habits are sinful. A person may drink a lot of coffee, which is a negative habit, but it is not necessarily sin. Habits like this can easily lead to sin. If a person drinks too much coffee, he can harm himself with nervous disorders, ulcers, and lack of sleep. Excessive coffee-drinking for him has become a self-destructive sin.

Most sinful habit patterns are something an individual believes he cannot get along without. There is security in following a pattern even if that pattern is sinful and destructive. Counselors often forget that it takes courage to tear oneself from these long-term, life-dominating patterns. People need to realize that the Word of God speaks truth, demands righteousness, and offers hope. There *is* an alternative to sin. There *is* a way out. God's commandments must be obeyed; He provides the strength to obey them, even when it hurts. This is where growth takes place.

Paul gives great encouragement to the struggler, "Not that I have already obtained all this, or have already been made perfect, but I press on to take hold of that for which Christ Jesus took hold of me. Brothers, I do not consider myself yet to have taken hold of it. But one thing I do: *Forgetting what is behind and straining toward what is ahead*, I press on toward the goal to win the prize for which God has called me heavenward in Christ Jesus" (Phil. 3:12-14 NIV, emphasis mine).

The willingness to obey is the starting point. Let me put it more simply. We have a will to do either what is right or what is wrong. The fruit of the Spirit includes self-control. The dramatic changes needed in our lives are under our control. I don't mean by this that we are sovereign; I simply mean that no allowance is made for default on our responsibility. The choice is ours—whether to live or to groan. The choice is ours as children of God whether to sit and snivel over past hurts or outrages and squander our lives, or to seize the opportunity to live joyously and hopefully. Nothing, not even the greatest sin, need stand in the way of the new life.

12

Pre-counseling Standings

Countless counseling sessions have taught me that two basic kinds of people come for counsel–those who want help and those who don't. Some come wanting to change at any cost. The others come with a pre-set limit on what they are willing to "pay." These folks usually show up wanting to change their boss, pastor, neighbor, child, or spouse. They feel that by coming for counsel, they have "done their bit." They definitely *do not* come to hear how *they* need to change.

My colleagues used to wonder why I almost always preferred the most desperate counseling problems. The reason was simple. Counseling is far more difficult with people who don't have much distress or aren't highly motivated. In the toughest cases, where the problems seem insurmountable, those who come desperate for help are more willing to accept what I have to say. They have a far greater chance for restoration. This is not to say that desperation is a prerequisite of counseling. Yet it is true that those who are more desperate are more amenable to help. (Desperation is often a golden opportunity to share the gospel, and giving someone the good news that Christ can help him should not be seen as "taking advantage of an individual." The gospel is "good news," and it is meant specifically for those beaten down by their sins or who see themselves as abject failures.)

Generally, most people who come for counsel are not desperate but merely uncomfortable. With a person like that, I first determine whether he really wants to see me. My work is to counsel; thus I don't need to work with individuals who aren't interested in receiving counsel. This of course doesn't mean that I won't help those individuals. I will, but I make it clear that I am helping at *their* request. I know that many people are skeptical about counseling at the beginning, often for good reasons. They have been disappointed before so they hold back.

They stand aloof and wait to see how they will be handled. They may not reveal the real problem, but will present a superficial test case first. For this reason, I am careful before terminating a case. I often take a wait-and-see approach, remembering that when a person comes for help, he is brought into contact with the gospel.

Should conversion take place, he gets a new heart and is therefore open to a whole new set of attitudes about himself and his problems.

There is a third pre-counseling attitude that one encounters as well. Some people beg for help but will never take it. They want help but not change. They *like* being desperate, drawing others into their whirlpools of misery. The beauty of nouthetic counseling is that as the counselor demands Biblical change of this counselee, the mask drops, and they both understand very early on what they can expect as a result of their time together—nothing. Until the counselee is willing to make changes and actually accomplish something, it is foolish to waste time with this person.

Even if a person wants to change, there are two prerequisites (one for the counselor and one for the counselee) for effective counseling. The counselor must believe that God is sovereign over the lives of both counselor and counselee. Without that fundamental undergirding, the counselor cannot demand the necessary Biblical life-changing behaviors. For his part, the counselee must either come with or be brought to a position of submission, not to the counselor but to the Word of God.

Submission means that those needing help must honestly admit their situation. They must admit that their problem is *their* problem, not the problem of a parent or a spouse. The anger or rage is not just something that others provoke, but is something they responsibly acknowledge and are prepared to renounce. In other words, they become accountable. They place themselves before God and confess that they alone are responsible for holding the attitudes that are damaging their lives.

Blame-shifting (refusing to be accountable) can be traced back to Adam and Eve. Immediately after eating the forbidden fruit, the first couple hid from their best Friend, God, because they were afraid (Gen. 3:10). Until this point they had communed with God and each other in total openness. There was no hiding, no shame, no embarrassment, no disgrace. Sin changed all that in an instant (an instant that we cannot comprehend because we have never experienced life without sin, as did Adam and Eve). "I was afraid because I was naked."

When God confronted Adam, he denied his guilt. Instead, he blamed both God and the woman for his sin. "It is the *woman* that *you* gave me." Eve also blame-shifted. "The *serpent* deceived me, and I ate." Despite their efforts to extricate themselves from their sin, God found them guilty, and they suffered the consequences.

Submission also means counselees seek the power to accomplish change through the Holy Spirit, not relying on their own strength. They must see that all they are, all they have been, and all they ever will be are part of God's wondrous plan. He uses even the former sins to glorify His name. Submission to the hand of God in both the acknowledgment of sin and its relinquishment is critical.

Submission means that we dismantle and demolish attitudes and thoughts that lead to destructive living. We must stop making allowances for all the so-called small sins that ultimately cripple us. Persisting in even small sins can have devastating results.

Recently, I headed out to visit someone in the hospital. The snow that had fallen in the night on the partially thawed ground was heavy and wet. My driveway was blocked by a snowdrift. I decided to try to speed out over the field, which was relatively free of snow. Within fifty feet, the van stopped–not exactly stuck, but not moving freely either. It was doing a two-inches-forward-then-slide-and-dip cha-cha. *Never mind,* I thought, *I have just hit a soft spot. A little more playing around, and I'll be on my way.* And that, folks, is exactly what happened, except that instead of being on my way forward, the van and I were on our way down.

Tiring of the light-hearted (light-footed) approach, I got down to business and tried to gun my way out. I tried forward, I tried backward. I would gain a few inches, but at the same time I was sinking deeper and deeper into the soft muck. The word *mire* was taking on new dimensions. Mud was flying on every side. Soon I had created four mini-sinkholes around each of the tires, and our front-wheel-drive van looked, as my daughter said, "like the *Titanic* going down." I stood there in horror, gazing at this sight, wondering how I could have gotten into this mess. The thought came to me—*Inch by inch, little by little, I am getting myself in so deeply that eventually there will be no way out.*

It was a time-consuming, messy, expensive, and embarrassing situation, but it did give me an illustration for this book. I am convinced that this is the way life-dominating, sinful habit patterns develop for most of us—inch by inch, little by little. Eventually, we find ourselves in a dreadful situation. The question of the day becomes, how do we get out?

My mud situation offers some insight. At a certain point, I saw that all my efforts were accomplishing nothing. I saw that to get free, I would need outside help. I couldn't get a tractor onto the field because, even with its exceptional traction and size, it too would have sunk deep into the mud. I knew that there had to be a way out, but as yet I did not know what it was. It was not going to be an issue of applying knowledge I already had, e.g., tractors pull out stuck cars. I needed new knowledge.

Biblical freedom operates in much the same way. God promises that "no trial will overtake you" (1 Cor. 10:13). Yet at the same time, He doesn't specifically tell us the way out. He leaves it to us to look carefully at our situation, to pray, and to be open to an honest means of escape.

I put together the factors involved in my situation. I needed a piece of machinery that could get out onto the field, light enough not to sink in, with enough traction not to get stuck, yet still have the strength to pull a van out of heavy-duty muck. I realized that I needed a small four-wheel-drive vehicle for this job. I found a neighbor with just such a vehicle. After several hours of carving new ruts through the field and grinding mud into every pore of my being (and I'm sure my neighbor's as well), I was free. The next day I surveyed the damage. The van went through car purgatory, but oh, that field! The ruts were knee-deep in places. The restoration was going to require substantial labor.

So it is with sin. Sin has consequences. Thieves, drug-users, drunks, adulterers, gossips, gluttons, and murderers all leave behind a trail of destruction that must be cleaned up. Bodies take time and care to heal; trust takes time and diligence to restore; financial loss takes time and labor to rebuild; offenses require time and commitment to be forgotten.

When Mike and Ruth came to me for counseling, I sized up them and their situation right away. My judgment turned out to be wrong. They told me that they had come for help because there had been adultery. They failed to mention (or note on their information inventory) that Mike was a successful pastor, and Ruth was everything a pastor's wife was supposed to be.

I learned that Mike was always working, and his young family was left alone all the time. I had assumed that Mike was the adulterer. It turned out that Ruth was. This young, attractive (openly evangelical) woman was committing adultery with every man who came near their home, including delivery boys and even a bill collector!

As the story unfolded, I saw a man who had come to despise his wife for her unbelievable infidelity. I saw a woman who had done all she could to punish an inattentive husband, a man who cared more about other people's problems than his own wife's needs.

I thought that a church board had sent them for help before the inevitable (as I saw it) divorce. I was surprised to learn that Ruth did not want a divorce. I was startled to learn that Mike did not either. If you think this is some kind of Cinderella story in which everyone lives happily ever after, you are right. But the agony of getting there should not be overlooked.

It would have been easy to send them on their way, promising to be faithful and to spend more time with each other. I knew, however, that for even a possibility of success for this marriage, Mike and Ruth had to be extricated from many sins. They also needed to ask and receive forgiveness. We had to develop life principles that would keep them from sinking into those sins once again. It had to be a repentance "which brought forth fruit" (Luke 3:8-14).

Both of them were quick to acknowledge their sins and ask forgiveness. Mike was not sure how he could forget an almost total betrayal. Ruth (interestingly) had fears that she might commit adultery again. After all, this was a habit she had mastered. Mike was out of the ministry, so he was more able to devote regular blocks of time to Ruth and their children. He was no longer on call twenty-four hours a day. Ruth knew that she could count on Mike to be there. She stopped looking to other men's arms for the support and affection she needed from Mike. Mike learned to check in with his wife during any time of absence, and Ruth came to see that Mike's work didn't mean she was being abandoned. Mike also learned to pick up warning signals; Ruth learned how to tell Mike her fears and temptations before matters erupted.

They left counseling to take a job in a new city, but the real test came when, after several years, Mike had an opportunity to reenter pastoral work. He accepted that call and about a year later when they came back to town, they made an appointment to see me. They showed me a newspaper clipping reporting that Mike had been voted husband and father of the year–over eight hundred other men. It certainly didn't erase the sins of the past, nor did it completely eradicate the pain and misunderstandings of the past, but Ruth and Mike were well on their way to being the family God had always meant them to be.

There is no question about it. Getting out of sin can be extremely complicated and messy. Liberation is impossible without cooperation. The one in need must desire *and* work toward his extrication. Even after he stops his sinful behavior, the job isn't over. People have to learn how to deal with the temptations to return to sin or with the pride of new accomplishments. They must put off the old habits *and put on the new*. This is why nouthetic counselors insist on God's sovereign rights and the need for a submissive heart toward Him. First, God *is* sovereign and requires this submission of His people. Second, the reality is that without His aid and aside from His decrees, authentic and permanent change is impossible. But the alternative to deep and lasting change is deep and lasting sin. This is the alternative that confronted Mike and Ruth. It is the alternative facing each person alive today.

13

The Time and the Place of Godly Living

Jesus said, "Do not worry about tomorrow," yet most Christians obviously pay no attention to Him. They spend more energy on yesterday or tomorrow than on the present. The concept of "the present" *is* an illusive thing; yet of all people, the Christian should live in the present reality. We have been forgiven for the past and are guaranteed the future. The present is the reality in which we live. We can neither redo yesterday nor prelive tomorrow. The present is in effect all we get, yet many fail to embrace it with enthusiasm. Sadly, they squander the present in useless regretting of the past. They waste it on worry about the future.

Of course, a life oriented in the present without

God at its core will degenerate into a hedonistic, idolatrous enthronement of the present. As Christians, our enjoyment of the present has to do with the fullness of possibility for rich and meaningful service for God. We can cast off the defeats of a lifetime. We can go beyond a million hurdles presented by the future. Today is alive with possibility for both the enjoyment and service of God.

It is possible for the Christian to live in the present without falling into hedonism if he remembers the answer to the first question of the *Westminster Shorter Catechism,* "What is the chief end of man?" The answer is, "Man's chief end is to glorify God and enjoy Him forever." That is the ultimate goal of the Christian. Embracing this goal eliminates as our ultimate aim the achievement of health, wealth, or happiness and indicates a readiness to sacrifice all for the Lord. As a matter of fact, the joy of the Lord comes when we break free from dependence upon health, wealth, or happiness. When a person is right with God, it brings a real contentment that nothing can take away. He knows his Redeemer lives, and he rests in the new life given by Him. Thus he spends his life serving God and others, not in playing political games to gain certain advantages for himself. He is not thinking of a big payoff; he is thinking of the Lord.

Embracing this goal is crucial to the Christian life. Most of those who feel themselves enmeshed in unbreakable habits have no orientation to anything beyond the present moment and the need for relief from whatever is pressing upon them. These individuals desperately need a spiritual or future orientation, which the Bible gives them.

But there is a tension for the Christian. Our citizenship is in Heaven, and yet we are called to live out our lives in a particular place at a particular time in history. The Christian must walk in the Spirit while living in a body of flesh in the present. Everything will fight against success in keeping a spiritual orientation. Something always needs to be corrected from the past. Something always remains to be done for the future. There is always something to crowd out the now. Yet there is a better way.

Why spend your life fighting against an oppressive past and a terrifying future? Why not instead use both to help you glorify God right now? We can look at the past and learn. We possess the insight born of a lifetime of struggles and joys, failures and victories, that can help us live in the present and plan with discernment and confidence for the future. We are not existentialists who journey through a meaningless situation from a senseless past on the way to an indifferent future. Instead, we acknowledge that life is a challenge, ripe with profound possibilities. We acknowledge the importance of the battles, realizing that the outcome has genuine significance in the course of time and history. We acknowledge that life is a gracious gift from God and that the future is in His hands. Viewing life from this perspective stimulates a godly determination to serve Him every day we are alive.

Determination is vital in a successful bid for a productive and joy-filled life. God has granted us the ability to determine much of the course of our lives (from a human perspective). The ability to live today for God requires determination. Jesus makes this clear: "If any man wills to come after me . . . " The word translated from Greek "to will" actually means more than determination. It is the firmest resolve, decision, or choice. It is rigorous religious striving, which in this case will take a new direction in order to follow Christ. The disciple of Christ denies self, takes up his cross daily, and follows Jesus (Luke 9:23).

In a parallel passage in Matthew, Jesus says that this determination should be so strong that every earthly attachment, including that to parents, is to be placed under it. This is the force of will. Jesus says, "He who loves father or mother more than Me is not worthy of Me; and he who loves son or daughter more than Me is not worthy of Me" (Matt. 10:37,38). We possess the power to live each day fully because we possess the power, given by God, to choose and determine what will receive our attention, affection, and concern. Through the operation of our wills God advances His Kingdom by bringing us, His people, into conformity with Christ.

14

Moving Toward a Free Will

What do we mean when we talk of the will? Simply put, the will is the power to choose. This power involves much that can change our lives. We can choose one thing and refuse another, approve or disown, enjoy or dislike, embrace or repudiate, reject or accept, command or forbid, deny or affirm, persist or give up, and so on. From the human perspective, we are what we choose, because what we choose, we do. Some choose for the good and to their blessing. Some choose for evil and to their cursing.

The natural man chooses in a way consistent with his desires. A Christian, however, often wills (or chooses) something on a fleshly level (so to speak) that he wouldn't truly desire on a spiritual level, because often the old carnal desires conflict with the new spiritual desires. But the Christian is called to conform his desires to those of Christ. A non-Christian doesn't understand this kind of choice, but it is an integral part of the increasingly sanctified walk of a believer.

Christ made the same kind of choices. In Gethsemane, He prayed, "Not my will, but Thine be done." He separated desire from will, for He said in effect that He did not desire the cross, but rather a way of escape. As a human, Christ was repelled by the anticipation of the wrath of a holy and angry God; yet He submitted His own will to the will of God. "Not My will, but Thine be done" were the words of One who determined to place His desires in subordination to the will of Another.

We Christians have to learn that our own desires can be modified. Desire functions as a subset of will. Our controlling reality is the will in subordination to God. We must choose the right way in spite of our desires. Praise God, we can and are changed to the extent that God works in us both to "will and to do of his good pleasure" (Phil. 2:13 KJV). These concepts–willing and doing–are not separate, but are one idea joined together for emphasis. What a person wills he does; what a person does he wills.

Of course, this principle operates only within the boundaries established within the Scriptures and creation. I can will with incredible determination to fly, but without an artificial apparatus, I cannot fly. A kind of magical thinking is promoted in some Christian circles–

that they can "name it and claim it." According to this school of thought, if I set my will to get something with enough determination ($5000, the publishing of this book, or whatever), it will happen. This mistaken notion is simply an excuse for superstition.

Willing is involved in making decisions, either to behave righteously or to sin. The Bible teaches, "But each one is tempted when he is carried away and enticed by his own lust. Then when lust has conceived, it gives birth to sin; and when sin is accomplished, it brings forth death" (Jas. 1:14,15). The deed was birthed in a desire. We could say that this desire develops a determination. Connected with the determination is a degree of both deliberation and motivation. Jesus points out how our deeds are reflections of what goes on in our hearts (Matt. 15:18).

To recognize desires and motivations that are contrary to Christian living is important. Lust (desire) gives birth to adultery (deed). Greed (desire) gives birth to theft (deed). Rage (desire) gives birth to murder (deed). The thought-behavior (attitude) precedes the action. Adultery does not suddenly occur, overtaking one by surprise. Desires have been aroused. Motivations are strong. Regardless of what the adulterer says, he or she wanted (willed) the adultery more than purity. The desire for innocence/righteousness may even have been present throughout, but it wasn't strong enough to cause him or her to desist. It was one of several conflicting desires, leaving the person in a state of ambivalence.

Rhonda's story illustrates the point. She said she wanted to stop drinking. I had no reason to doubt her except that her husband said she was drunk "all the time." Rhonda liked the idea of sobriety, but she loved drunkenness more. Let me put it another way. Rhonda hated the guilt of drunkenness. It was an obvious sin, but she wanted to drink more than she wanted sobriety. I know this because, conflict and all, Rhonda was drunk more often than sober. You ask, "If this is so, why did Rhonda ever come to you for counseling?" Rhonda didn't come for counseling. She was *brought*, still claiming that she had no problem–even though while drunk she'd driven her truck into a ditch, almost killing herself and her daughter.

You ask, "How could she deny that?" This will be hard to believe, but since she and her baby were unhurt, she saw no problem. Denial works mightily in such people. Rhonda was drunk, and she really only wanted to stop the guilt, not the drinking–until a cigarette dropped during a drunken stupor touched off a small fire, again almost killing her and her child.

At that point Rhonda was forced to see the problem. She almost lost her child in the courts because of her negligence. Finally, she wanted her baby more than alcohol. For several months, she stopped drinking. As soon as the legal pressures eased a bit, however, she convinced herself that she could drink "responsibly." She wanted no more counseling, and it was not long afterward that she lost her child to her husband who had left her.

Conflicting motivations exist in almost every decision we make. We want to do the right thing, but we don't want to spend the time, money, or effort. We are tempted to do the lawless thing, but it will cost us fellowship, unity, and innocence. This conflict of motivations is often manifested in inaction or indecision.

Inaction is also willing–willing not to act when the decision is too demanding. In some scenarios this may not be the worst decision. At the least it buys time to think and reevaluate alternatives. The problem comes when inaction becomes a habit or a coping mechanism. Copping out appears to avoid stress, but it also avoids the rewards and gratifications of a life actively and rightly lived. In reality, it only postpones stress or substitutes one kind of stress for another. It may, for instance, avoid the stress of social engagement, but it cannot avoid the stress of self-knowledge accompanied by the inevitable self-judgment and self-condemnation.

So then the process of willing is certainly more complex than just "making a decision," although every decision is an act of will. We assess whether a situation is potentially pretty and pleasant or ugly and bothersome. We determine whether our action will bring good or bad consequences. These consequences may be difficult to assess. They may be so far in the future that the decision-maker feels safe ignoring them all together. Thus a drunk confronted by a bottle of liquor is more prone to drink because the thought of its immediate pleasure is stronger than the thought of guilt afterwards. People by nature want things now. They do not like to defer their enjoyments to the future. Without other variables, we will always choose the immediate pleasure. The Christian faith, however, is a real variable that sets this pattern on its head.

Deferment of gratification is inherent in Christianity. We have a Kingdom waiting to be revealed. Ours is a heavenly citizenship; the Lord Himself promised, "I go to prepare a place for you [His Father's house]. And if I go and prepare a place for you, I will come again, and receive you to Myself; that where I am, there you may be also" (John 14:2,3). In view of the "eternal glory that far outweighs" all his "light and momentary troubles" (beatings, imprisonment, chains, desertion by friends, sleep deprivation, hunger, thirst, nakedness, etc.), Paul states that "we look not at the things which are seen, but at the things which are not seen; for the things which are seen are temporal, but the things which are not seen are eternal" (2 Cor. 4:18).

Historically, Christians have been the ones in society who have deferred gratification. They have invested their lives rather than squander them ("kill time"). They have used the present to gain future rewards. Christian faith and obedience produced an active and decisive willing that was in every way contrary to the natural affection or inclinations, yet not contrary to the way the reasonable mind wills. The future pleasures of Heaven and the Kingdom were seen by Christ's followers as sure and certain. Thus opting out of immediate gratification was a postponement, not a pain or a loss.

In addition to our ability to "fix our eyes" on the unseen and receive succor there, our determination to abstain from immediate gratification is affected by other factors. The degree or strength of temptation is a powerful determining variable. A person is more apt to will for the good when he is removed from the evil. A person is more apt to be faithful in the arms of his wife than when out of town in the company of his gorgeous coworker. A person is more likely to choose sobriety while in his home than while sitting with friends in the local pub, watching them guzzle beer. To minimize temptation is irrefutably wise, good, and reasonable. To do so is not an indication of character weakness, but of moral strength; we all have weaknesses, areas where we are in danger of stumbling. To have learned from past failings and cut off the progress towards sin at the "assessment" level indicates maturity and a God-honoring choice for righteousness. To maximize the good ("whatever is true and good and lovely") also is wise because there is a sense in which man can only choose what he deems at that moment to be the most worthwhile.

Great energy should be aimed at redirecting or rightly directing the will. What is obedience? Is it not the compliance and consent of the will to commands, followed by the execution of those commands? If education in the Law of God is lacking, what moral basis does the will have for choosing the good? Knowledge of the Law of God, or lack of it, will influence every stage of behavioral decision. God's people need to know, not only what is expected of them, but also the tools established in Scripture to fulfill those expectations.

15

The Power of God in the Changing of Lives

"Twice I have heard this: That power belongs to God" (Psalm 62:11). Even though evangelicals are enamored with it, secular psychology contradicts the simply stated truth that God is the God of power. We talk as though we believe this verse, but we refuse to look to the Bible for real counsel. The Bible, given by the mouth and by the love of God, is designed to bring His healing power to bear on the shattered people who flee to Him. Instead of using God's Word, we send people to "the professionals." If we believe that the power of God has been exerted in our salvation, why would we neglect its use in sanctification? That is what counseling is all about. Does not God want His people to have abundant life? The answer is obvious.

As we observe ourselves from a Biblical perspective, we must affirm our initial enmity against God. We "were by nature children of wrath, even as the rest" (Eph. 2:3). We hated God and were His enemies. "But God, being rich in mercy, because of His great love with which He loved us, even when we were dead in our transgressions, made us alive together with Christ" (Eph. 2:4,5). "You see, at just the right time, when we were still powerless, Christ died for the ungodly . . . While we were still sinners, Christ died for us" (Rom. 5:6,8 NIV). The incredible potential for real change began while we were helpless, powerless in our sins. We could do nothing; the Bible teaches that everything *was* done for us. We *were* changed. We were changed from objects of wrath to children of God (Rom. 8:17)! Instead of enmity toward God in our hearts, God's love fills our hearts. "God has poured out his love into our hearts by the Holy Spirit, whom he has given us" (Rom. 5:5 NIV).

What has God done in regenerating us, causing us to be born again? By His power He has changed us. We are no longer the same. He says, "If any man is in Christ, he is a new creature; the old things passed away; behold, new things have come" (2 Cor. 5:17). Many individuals will testify that the change that God wrought in them produced a holiness that completely changed their lives.

I have seen this in counseling. One situation in particular stands out. The man was immersed in a life of deceit and theft. He was converted and instantly he was a new person, not just in relationship to God, but also with regard to former habits and desires. In the six years since, this man has continued to grow in holiness and has never (to my knowledge) even experienced temptation to return to the former sinful ways.

Of course, he is not the norm. While God in His power and mercy makes us new by giving us a new nature, rarely is there a turnaround such as this. Instead, counseling is necessary for new Christians because they need to understand the warfare raging within them. People want to do right, yet they find themselves assaulted by evil motives, desires, thoughts, and actions. Often they feel like anything but recipients of divine power. They do not experience a completely changed life. In fact, it is a grievous error to lead people to believe that in this life their battles can be over. The demonstration of the power of God is not in bringing us to a place where there is no battle, but in causing us to see that the power of God will be present in whatever battle we find ourselves. Then we can endure trials and temptations (1 Cor. 10:13), and we can change!

God says, "My grace is sufficient for you" (2 Cor. 12:9). His grace is not only sufficient, but available; yet believers will often run in every other way but to that place of grace. But not only is His grace to be sought; once received, it is to be used (Luke 8:18). Then a believer, living a grace-filled life, will expect even more. "He gives us more grace" so that we can fight all the battles in which He places us (Jas. 4:6 NIV). A dear old saint I know has this to say every time I tell her about a battle in which I am engaged, "The devil is mighty; but the Lord is Almighty." Put simply, "Greater is He who is in you than he who is in the world" (1 John 4:4). What does this mean? The Christian is called in the midst of fierce battle "to be strong in the Lord, and in the strength of His might" (Eph. 6:10). Our strength is in His might, not our own.

Our Lord promises rest (Matt. 11:28,29), but this promise is appropriated in the midst of the world, the flesh, and the devil. This rest will never be perfect serenity of heart and mind until we are with the Lord. Although we face many crises during our lifetimes, the true believer can testify that God has both been with him and seen him through these seeming disasters. Jesus tells us numerous "sheep" stories in the Bible because He wants us to learn from these little woolly creatures. As a shepherd of a flock of about one hundred sheep, I have faced numerous crises with them and learned many lessons that aid my work as a pastor.

Not long ago, my youngest child came running to me announcing that she had found a young lamb with its head caught under a fence. The logical question is, what was its head doing under a fence? You know what they say about grass and fences! This little lamb got stuck in its quest for greener grass. In a field filled with lambs running around, it was easily overlooked. Without help, this lamb would have died. Fortunately for it, a little shepherd girl carefully scanned the perimeters of the field, noticed it, and saved its life. That night I would have counted my sheep and, unless they were running too fast and jumping too high, I would have noticed a missing lamb. I would have done what my daughter had already done–searched for the missing lamb–until I found it.

We find ourselves in many disastrous situations. We get caught, trapped, or ensnared in one thing after another, but the Lord delivers us from them all (Ps. 34:17). He is truly our Good Shepherd.

Nonetheless, our lives are filled with troubles. Jesus says, "In this world you will have trouble" (John 16:33 NIV). Does this mean that we have embraced less than a perfect Savior? Does this mean that salvation is not perfect because of our imperfect experience? No, but many Christians enter into the Christian life hoping that sin will be eradicated from their experience, and they are not taught otherwise. They are understandably disappointed and often distressed when this does not happen. They could be saved that disappointment if they had a solid Biblical understanding of how God intends for us to be changed.

"But thanks be to God that though you were slaves of sin, you became obedient from the heart" (Rom. 6:17). What has happened? God is saying, "Now that you have been made free from guilt and the dominion of sin, you are free (have the capacity) to serve God." What is perhaps most illuminating for our purposes in this passage is that God says that the transformation is carried out when you obey Biblical doctrine that demands hearty acceptance (Rom. 6:17). This is called in Titus "the truth which is after godliness" (Tit. 1:1 KJV). The picture is of a form or pattern placed upon our hearts to mold them like molten liquid in order to retain the exact impression required. Our hearts, in other words, are being molded in order to conform us exactly to the image of Jesus Christ!

We are to fight willingly against the sin that threatens to destroy our character, relationships, and witness because Christ is with us–strengthening, empowering, and shaping us, not only to act like Him, but to be like Him. The psychologists may teach us many techniques through which they promise peace and prosperity, but there are no shortcuts to change. God chisels away at us piece by piece until the completed person is, in glory, a replica of the Christ who redeemed us.

Woe to us if we replace conviction of sin with self-esteem, self-love, or even self-knowledge. Woe to those who counsel such action! Those who swallow the medicine of the secular psychologists, tonics disguised with a Christ-flavored coating or remedies straight from the textbook, are condemned to wander through their lives with the nagging despair that accompanies the barrenness of such foolishness. Instead, turn to Christ. Acknowledge your brokenness, not as a gimmick, but as a reality based on your struggles with sin, so that God might begin the work of mending your brokenness according to His will, expressed through His Word.

Then the Church of our Lord Jesus Christ will be able to rejoice in its identity, for its members will know that they are washed, cleansed, renewed, restored, and mended in every way. The Church will exult, for believers will see beyond the twentieth-century perception of themselves as a motley band of walking wounded who should be grateful for the attention and assistance of godless soul-menders. People of God, denounce that vision! The Church of the King of Kings and Lord of Lords is His glorious bride. He will not have His precious possession limping into the wedding feast with mud clinging to the wedding clothes, but instead will present us pure and radiant. Therefore, throughout eternity, beginning now, let the glorious body of Christ exult, for we are

MORE THAN SURVIVORS.

Appendix

Learning to Communicate

All the best intentions of Christians to comfort and encourage one another will come to nothing if church members can't communicate. I disliked it when one of my mentors said to me, "Communication is the name of the game." It sounded so cheap, so carnal. I'm embarrassed to admit that he was right. In my counseling practice, and that of the men and women I have trained, problems in communication account for the vast majority of cases we see. That is not meant to suggest that everyone coming for counseling says that the problem is communication. Not at all. Some could never imagine that. Yet the problem becomes evident rather early on; it is not so much what was done, as what was or wasn't said, that causes most problems.

Jay Adams said, "Communication is the basic skill needed to establish and maintain sound relationships. A sound husband and wife relationship is impossible apart from good communication."[29] Amos put it tersely, "Can two walk together, except they be agreed?" (Amos 3:3 KJV). Communication is crucial to counseling. First, the counselor must elicit information. Even prior to the actual beginning of the sessions, forms are filled out that ask basic questions: What is the problem as you see it? What brings you here? What have you done about it? What do you hope I can do?

But the counselor soon learns that what counselees write may not be what actually most deeply troubles them. As a matter of fact, numerous individuals who seek counseling will not put their main concerns on the forms. At the beginning of counseling, I never push much deeper than the "presenting problem," that is, the problem they write on the form. I take that problem seriously. I work with them on it. I help them to solve it. Often after I have dealt with the presenting problem, a counselee will say, "I'm glad that's dealt with. Now I know you can be trusted with the really serious problems."

Sometimes, sad to say, people never get beyond the presenting problem. Perhaps they are embarrassed by the real problem. Sometimes they are enmeshed in lies.

Nowhere did I see these barriers more clearly than in the case of Ron. He and Stephanie came for counseling because their marriage was crumbling, and he (not she) wanted it saved. The crisis had come the previous week when Ron stayed late at work one more time. I asked him to tell me what was so important about work that again he didn't make it home until late. He described an important business meeting he had had to attend.

As he described this meeting, I watched confusion spread across Stephanie's face. I asked her what was wrong. She said that a week earlier he had told her a completely different story. She reminded him of what he had said. He suggested that she was mistaken, but she stuck to her guns.

In fact, when Ron refused to change his second story, Stephanie got up to leave, saying she refused to live with a liar. As the door was shutting, Ron called her back. He swore he was about to tell "the whole truth and nothing but the truth." I think he did that. He explained that there had never been a business meeting, ever. Instead, Ron spent his nights as an active participant in gay bars. Incredibly, Stephanie never knew.

Tears streamed down his face as Ron confessed his sin. Stephanie sat there stone-faced, getting (as it seemed) more rigid by the moment. Finally she left the room again–this time for good. While there was no fear of Ron's having passed on AIDS to his wife since this happened before that plague, she left him because of his adulterous, homosexual relationships.

Ron was broken. As he sat and wept, I couldn't be

sure whether he was crying about his sin, about getting caught, or about the breakup of his marriage. I knew that if he and I were going to work together, we would have to work on his life, not on his marriage. Ron agreed.

What emerged was that Ron's life was a total sham. Not only was his relationship to his wife a lie, but his whole life–every significant aspect and relationship–was dominated by perverse sexual desire and actions and by deceit. Ron had lied about that Friday night because he could no longer keep straight the massive number of lies he had told to his wife, his children, his employer, his colleagues, his homosexual partners, and his parents. Life for Ron was a mountain of lies that had finally collapsed.

He had a choice. Like Harry (mentioned earlier) his desire for homosexual relationships was strong, but he didn't get a chance to tell me that "Christianity didn't work for him." In the intervening years, I had learned clearly that victory was not in being immune to former temptations; victory was in standing firm in the midst of temptations. We are not kept from the "valley of the shadow of death." We are kept safe in the "valley of the shadow of death."

Ron saw how this sin, which he thought had been hidden, had blown up in his face and destroyed his life. He did not want to stop homosexual sin, but he did want to make one last try to get right with God. He knew that this would not guarantee his wife's return (she didn't come back). At the same time, he knew he could no longer live the lie. Interestingly, the lives of many homosexuals are characterized by deception. Ron was not unique in this sense. What made him unusual was his willingness to do what was right, in spite of what he desired.

No one will ever be successful in the battles against sin unless he or she is willing to do what's right above any and all desires. Ron persisted in a changed lifestyle. He found it became easier to live a straight life after his paths had been straightened. After he repented of the lies, he began developing a pattern of honesty. As an honest man, he did what was right–daily putting off sin and putting on righteousness.

The battle isn't over for Ron, but each day's righteousness makes tomorrow's just a little bit easier. Our paths parted with Ron's life shattered, but in the brokenness he was being made whole by God. He was experiencing success because he didn't allow the conflicting emotions, desires, and drives to let him choose against God. He saw that in these battles, he was no different than anyone else.

The counselor often finds it difficult to probe people who are obviously concealing something. Yet this must be done gently if there is to be Biblical change in people's lives. Ron had to be pushed to present the real problem, because he did not have an unhappy wife, but a miserable wife who knew (on some level) that something was terribly wrong in the marriage.

The Lord is gentle. "A battered reed He will not break off, and a smoldering wick He will not put out" (Matt. 12:20). But there is an interesting twist here. It is the smoldering wick and the broken reed that Jesus doesn't crush. It is not all people. Those who come crushed, hurting, and broken are to be gently helped and encouraged in the ways of confession, repentance, reconciliation, and restoration. But those who come cocky and bold, arrogant and proud, are not treated as broken reeds. They are to learn, perhaps very soon, that the way of the transgressor is hard (Prov. 13:15).

Communication skills are used in counseling and in every part of life. Paul told the Corinthians that his mouth was open to them. He kept nothing back (2 Cor. 6:11,12). When people are closed-mouthed, hiding things, keeping things back, or misrepresenting truth, serious problems result. Biblical counseling must help people learn how to communicate in their present crisis and make a lifelong commitment to godly communication thereafter.

If I suggested that the basic communication problem is what people don't say, and I stopped there, I would be misleading you. Even more potent is what they do say. James hinted at this problem:

> So also the tongue is a small part of the body, and yet it boasts of great things. Behold, how great a forest is set aflame by such a small fire! And the tongue is a fire, the very world of iniquity; the

> tongue is set among our members as that which defiles the entire body, and sets on fire the course of our life, and is set on fire by hell. For every species of beasts and birds, of reptiles and creatures of the sea, is tamed, and has been tamed by the human race. But no one can tame the tongue; it is a restless evil and full of deadly poison. (Jas. 3:5-8)

Few things are more difficult than picking up the fragments of lives smashed by words that can never be retrieved. I remember telling one counselee that every word that proceeded out of his mouth was to be (only) a gracious word that brought edification to the hearer (Eph. 4:29). He looked at me and said that would ruin his spontaneity. For a moment I was taken aback. Yes, what about his spontaneity? Then it hit. What is spontaneity anyway compared to the damage thoughtless words inflict on another human being?

This spontaneity stuff is part of a culture determined to do whatever pleases it, whatever makes it feel good, even if that rips and tears someone else apart. Christians have accepted the Esalen mentality[30] that says, "Let it all out." It is the honesty-for-honesty's-sake cult. There is no sense of speaking the truth in love, but simply of getting it all out. That man with whom I spoke had no idea of the philosophy behind what he was saying, but his attitude has to be opposed. Yes, many people have spent their lives spontaneously tearing others up, but they are going to have to learn new patterns of communication that are gracious and edifying. If they are Christians, then they will have to submit themselves to God's demands for loving and for godly speech.

They will have to renounce the "deadly poison" of the tongue.

If we are to honor Jesus Christ and bless one another, we must remove from our lives various kinds of ungodly speech. These include:

Blowing Up at Others

Proverbs likens speech to the "thrusts of a sword" (Prov. 12:18). Many will say that it is better to blow up than clam up. Both are ungodly communication practices and should be renounced. Recent studies indicate that blowing up may be just as harmful physically as clamming up. But even if blowing up were more physically healthy than clamming up, these would both still be wrong because they are unkind and unloving. When there is a problem, you must attack it, and not another person, even if you perceive that person to be responsible for your problem.

Continual Sarcasm

If some people are not using sarcasm, they do not communicate. Everything is a put-down. Think of how it would feel to hear statements such as these addressed to you all the time, "Oh, you're a nerd," or "You weren't always obese," or "You really think you're holy, don't you?" What would these remarks do to a Christian struggling with sin?

Merciless Teasing

Sometimes teasing is confused with playfulness, but not by the recipient. It is one thing to be playful; it is another to never let up on teasing. Ask the young children of a parent who never stops teasing if they like it. Sure, it sounds funny, but not to the child with braces to always be introduced as "metal-mouth." And not to the employee to be introduced by his employer as, "Homer our accountant. Too bad he never learned how to add." There is a place for playfulness, but when you are asked to stop, that should be it. If you say that you are never asked to stop, that it doesn't bother anyone, perhaps they have just given up asking you.

Joking About a Spouse to Others

Few things undermine a marriage more than to have one partner make jokes about the other to outsiders. Recently I spoke at a conference on the family. My wife was in the audience. I was talking about this principle and communicating how important it is. I still don't know why I did it, but I made a joke about her. She was embarrassed and flabbergasted. I felt rotten. That kind of thing occurs with couples all the time, but I had prided myself on being above it. Perhaps that is why I fell, with my wife and a large audience present.

Telling Others About Intimate Problems

Married persons should not speak to their parents or

others about intimate problems with a spouse, especially if the spouse doesn't know. It isn't good even if the spouse does know about it. Problems should be worked on together. If couples cannot resolve them, they should seek out the pastor or someone trained in nouthetic counseling. If the married person speaks to parents or others, he or she will dissipate the energy needed to tackle the problem. He or she will become accustomed to talking about problems rather than doing something about them.

Criticizing One's Spouse to the Children

So much has already been said about this one that I won't belabor it. Suffice it to say that the long-term harm alone warrants stopping this practice. If one has a problem with the spouse, he or she should deal with the spouse, not the children! Children should not become the battleground of a couple's contention. If a parent does tell the child, yes, the child will probably grow up to hate the other parent, but he will also probably grow up hating the criticizing parent. Even more important, not having seen Jesus Christ in his home, he may grow up not knowing Christ as well.

Gossip

Gossip murders a person's character or reputation. For example, "Is she sleeping with him? I thought she was a Christian." Even if "she" is sleeping with "him," there is a way to handle this Biblically. That way is not by gossip or slander. Many people wouldn't know what to say if they didn't talk about others. Make sure you don't gossip. And make sure you don't listen to gossip either.

A Biblical counselor must be careful to spot any of these areas of improper and ungodly communication. He or she must be able to point out how these operate in the lives of counselees and help them to introduce new patterns of godly communication to take the place of these sinful patterns.

NOTES

1. Erich Fromm, *Psychoanalysis and Religion* (New Haven, CT: Yale University Press, 1950), p. 7.
2. Gerhard Masur, *Prophets of Yesteryear* (New York: Macmillan, 1961), p. 311.
3. Agnes Sanford, *The Healing Gifts of the Spirit* (San Francisco: Harper and Row, 1966), pp. 116, 136, 160.
4. B. F. Skinner, *Beyond Freedom and Dignity* (New York: Alfred K. Knopf, 1971), p. 175.
5. D. L. Rosenhan, "On Being Sane in Insane Places," *Science*, January 19, 1973, pp. 250-258.
6. Thomas Szasz, *The Manufacture of Madness* (San Francisco: Harper and Row, 1970), p. 8.
7. Blaise Pascal, *Pensées*, (Paris: Dalmas Publishing, 1952).
8. St. Bernard, quoted in John Calvin, *Institutes of the Christian Religion*, III, II (Louisville, KY: Westminster Press, 1973), p. 25.
9. *Ibid.*, I, I, p. 2.
10. *Ibid.*
11. Richard Cameron, quoted in John Stone, *Sermons Delivered in Times of Persecution in Scotland* (Edinburgh: Hunter and Co., 1880), p. 384.
12. Harry Blamires, *The Christian Mind* (London: SPCK, 1963), pp. 4, 16, 38-39, 41, 45, 190-191.
13. Gary Sweeten, *The Theology of a Caring, Equipping Community* (Cincinnati, OH: Christian Information Center, 1989), p. 36.
14. Paul Meier and Frank Minirth, *Happiness Is a Choice* (Grand Rapids: Baker Book House, 1979), p. 97.

15. David Seamands, *Healing for Damaged Emotions* (Wheaton, IL: Victor Books, 1988), p. 19.
16. Gary Collins, *Can You Trust Psychology?* (Downers Grove, IL: Inter Varsity Press, 1988), p. 129.
17. Larry Crabb, *Inside Out* (Colorado Springs, CO: Navpress, 1988), p. 33.
18. Robert Schuller, *Self-Esteem, the New Reformation* (Waco, TX: Word Books, 1982), pp. 14-15.
19. James Dobson, *Hide or Seek* (Old Tappan, NJ: Revell, 1974), pp. 12-13.
20. Seamands, *Healing for Damaged Emotions*, note 5, p. 48.
21. *Ibid*, p. 49.
22. Gary Sweeten, *Apples of Gold II* (Cincinnati, OH: Christian Information Committee, 1983), pp. 4-5.
23. Jay E. Adams, *Competent to Counsel* (Philadelphia: Presbyterian and Reformed, 1970), p. 45.
24. *Ibid*, p. 15.
25. Sweeten, *Apples of Gold II,* chapter 5, p. 7.
26. Adams, *Competent to Counsel*, p. 42.
27. Matthew Henry, *Commentary on Ephesians,* vol. 6 (Old Tappan, NJ: Fleming Revell, n.d.), pp. 704, 974.
28. Dr. Ken Smith, a pastor in the Reformed Presbyterian Church, has worked with this concept for several years. I am indebted to him for this chapter.
29. Jay E. Adams, *Christian Living in the Home* (Philadelphia: Presbyterian and Reformed, 1972), chapter 3.
30. The Esalen Institute was the center of the human potential movement in the sixties and seventies in Big Sur, CA.

INDEX

Sweeter GETS *the* JOURNEY

— The Life of John Stoltzfus —

A Man of Faith, Hope and Courage

by JEANNE WILBER

Sweeter Gets the Journey

— The Life of John Stoltzfus —

A Man of Faith, Hope and Courage

Design and Layout *by* **box43 LLC**

Unless otherwise noted, Scripture quotations are taken from the KING JAMES VERSION of the Holy Bible.

Other Scripture quotations are taken from the NEW AMERICAN STANDARD BIBLE®, Copyright © 1960, 1962, 1963, 1968, 1971, 1972, 1973, 1975, 1977, 1995 by The Lockman Foundation. Used by permission.

box43 books – *formerly* RCW Publishing Company
box43 LLC | RR 3 Box 43 | Old Post Lane
Columbia Cross Roads, Pennsylvania 16914

Printed in the United States of America by
Reed Hänn — Williamsport, Pennsylvania

ISBN 1-889825-10-7

THIS BOOK IS PRESENTED BY JOHN'S SIBLINGS:
Naomi, Kathy, Sam, Mahlon and Louise

IN MEMORY OF Daudy Beiler and Grandma Stoltzfus. Daudy stood by Mom and Dad from the very first night. He always gave wise counsel and we were strengthened by him. He was patient with John and guided him with gentle persuasion. Grandma loved all of us but she had a special relationship with John. She filled his emotional needs from the day he came home from the hospital and never tired of holding him, rocking him, singing to him and praying for him.

IN HONOR OF Aaron and Susie Stoltzfus, our Dad and Mom. You have set a high goal for each of us by your example of faith and strength. Never once did we feel deprived or neglected because of the time and extra care you had to give to John. You kept us happy and involved in all of the activities of family, farm life and church. We are thankful to have been taught good work ethics. The daily nourishment from the Word led us to have our own personal relationships with the Lord. We are also grateful you tied such a strong knot when you taught us about family ties – ours cannot be broken!

IN DEDICATION TO our brother, John – this is your story! You are the one who has enriched our lives beyond measure (even when there were situations that caused embarrassment – we considered you a blessing). You have kept our hearts alive with love for you. You have taught us much and we are always proud to call you our Boy – our brother!

ABOUT THE COVER

The cover photo was taken of a route near the author's home some time ago. It represents a journey. A view looking on ahead, towards what is to come. We never know what or whom we will meet over the next knoll or around the next bend. We never know if calamity will strike or if peace will prevail. However, we can know that every day with Jesus is sweeter still...

> Psalm 16:11 – **Thou wilt shew me the path of life: in Thy presence is fulness of joy; at Thy right hand there are pleasures forevermore.**

The use of purple on the cover was intentional as well. For many years purple has been John's favorite color. Since this book is about John and dedicated to his life, we thought it only appropriate to use a color that John would enjoy.

CONTENTS

CHAPTER I

A Fragile Beginning

Susie lay on the hospital bed. The nurse had spread and tucked the crisp sterile covers over her with care – deftly folding the sheet down in order to place her patient's small arms extended beside her on top of the sheet. Susie was too exhausted to move but, because it was her nature to be grateful, she thanked her as the nurse quietly stepped out of the room to continue her nightly rounds. Did that nurse give Susie extra care out of sympathy for her most unusual situation or was she trying to control the surge of empathy that was flooding her very being?

In the semi-darkness Susie was unaware of the hushed murmur of nighttime noises that came from the nurses station, the far off pulsing of a monitor, the muffled sound of an ambulance siren, a cough, a moan and the even rhythm of someone snoring. Her body was sore from giving birth, her mind was swimming with Dr. Munteanu's words, "Don't get your hopes up – there is not a chance in this world that he will make it – your baby will not be able to live through the night." Fear, disbelief and grief weighed so heavily on her heart that silent tears kept falling from her closed eyes. The burden was more than her twenty-two-year-old life wanted to accept. It was then that she sensed Someone in the room with her and she felt *that* Someone take her hand and hold it. She felt comforted. After moments of quiet assurance she opened her eyes but no one was in the room with her. A gentle peace fell over her.

> "The satisfying peace from God exceeds our comprehension. God knows everything and makes no mistakes. Commit your *unknown* future to *Him* and someday you will understand. Put your focus on God and His greatness – rather than the obstacle you are facing. Long-suffering and patience are helpful factors." [1]

> James 1:4 – **But let patience have her perfect work, that ye may be perfect and entire, wanting nothing.**

Pleasant thoughts of her husband, Aaron, and their sweet, 20-month-old daughter, Naomi, came to her as she began to drift into a needed slumber . . .

Aaron and Susie met at a wedding when they were young teenagers. Because they were Amish and their families lived twenty long miles apart they did not see each other again until they were a few years older, when they belonged to the same youth group. It was then that they became friends.

Aaron was eighteen when he and his older married brother, John, who lived on the adjoining farm, were helping their father fell a tree. There was a tragic accident and his father, John F. Stoltzfus, was killed by the falling tree. Aaron became a man very quickly as he took on the responsibility of the large farm. His mother, Mary B., still had two younger boys and two younger girls at home (Aaron was one of fourteen children). Aaron was a hard worker and was grieved over the loss of his Dad but as time went by thoughts of Susie helped to lighten his load – especially after they began to court. His horse became familiar with the twenty-mile journey between the Stoltzfus farm and the Samuel U. Beiler farm in Gap, PA. Susie's heart leaped a bit when she saw his horse and buggy coming up the drive.

Beiler farm where Susie grew up.

Aaron Stoltzfus and Susie Beiler were married on November 19, 1957. He was twenty-two and she was twenty. They moved to his home in Morgantown, PA and lived in the larger part of his family home. It was a large stone farmhouse with a grand history. The farm was part of a 340-acre tract that was granted by William Penn's sons to John Bowen in 1743. John Bowen sold 150 acres to his son, Evans, in 1752 and then Evans sold it to the Jenkins family who owned the iron ore works at Pool Forge. They built a lot of stone mansions in the area including the one that would become the John F. Stoltzfus homestead. The farm and eighty acres of fertile Lancaster County farmland were purchased by John U. and Rachel Stoltzfus in 1859. Later a 35-acre farm was added to the homestead. John U. (Aaron's great grandfather) built the west end for their retirement home in 1892. That section of the house was frame and was called the Daudy House (Grandfather's house).

The Old Homestead and the back enterance to the Old Homestead.

The homestead continued to pass from father to son. In 1935 the original barn was struck by lightning and a new large barn was built. John F. and Mary B. Stoltzfus bought the farm in 1942. Six generations have lived there. The Stoltzfus home, from the outside, gave the appearance of a single family dwelling but inside there was a separation – a big farm house for the growing family and a little house for the grandparents. The larger section, which was closest to the farm, had a big kitchen with a dining area, two bedrooms and a very large living room on the first floor. Upstairs there were three bedrooms, a bathroom, hall and a huge closet. There was a door on the opposite wall of the downstairs living room that opened into Mary B.'s smaller section (the Daudy House). She had a kitchen and laundry room, large bedroom, small sitting room, bathroom and a closed-in porch, plus three upstairs bedrooms. She also shared the large living room with Aaron and Susie. Aaron's younger brother, David, lived in the farm house with Aaron and Susie and helped with the chores.

Outside was an interesting building made of block. It was their wash-house with a wringer washer and a place to heat water. The stove was a brick shelf-like ledge with two round holes large enough for two huge kettles – one iron and one copper. On the brick wall beneath the holes were openings to put the wood in the fire pit. The wash-house was very versatile – not just a place to do laundry, as the name suggests. They also did the butchering there, made pear or apple butter, soap and did the canning. They processed the food by placing the filled jars in boiling water in the iron kettle. On hot summer days with so many vegetables to be canned, the hot coals of the fire and the steam from the boiling water in the kettles gave another use to the apron – thankfully it was always handy to lift and mop a sweaty brow.

Further out in the back yard was the vasah shonk (water cupboard) where fresh spring water perpetually flowed. It was cool and refreshing inside – a good place to go when the heat in the wash house became too torrid. The pool of water inside the vasah shonk was cold enough to keep glass gallon jars of milk and jugs of tea cool. There was a water wheel that turned and supplied power for the pump that provided water for the house.

Life was *"güt"* (good)! Susie and Aaron loved each other and his mother (Mary B.) was an absolute blessing! They worked hard but the Amish do much of their work together and that puts pleasure in what could have been a grueling day's work if one man did it alone. They raised barns, prepared the fields for planting, harvested and did any emergency work that came along, while the women prepared food and provided wonderful picnics and harvest dinners for all the families to enjoy. The men laughed and talked, the women served and chatted and the children hurriedly ate so they could get back to their play. After the men had refueled their bodies, they took a few minutes to relax. The older girls and boys generally stood in separate groups but occasionally a young man would notice that the young woman he fancied would be looking in his direction. If he caught her eye she would lower hers and try to fight off the flush that came to her cheeks. Young married men were happy to sit with their brides for this period of respite. One or two older men found a tree to stretch out under or sit and lean against, to take a little snooze before they continued their joint labor for the afternoon. When it was time for each family to leave they climbed in their buggies shouting loud farewells and the host family stood together waving and saying "Denki" (thank you)! Soon the single line of horses and buggies separated as they turned off the farm lane and each family made their way home. A stillness came over the precious cargo – the tired bodies, the contented hearts were lulled by the metered clopping of the horses' hooves on the pavement. The quiet journey gave these gentle souls rest enough to return home and do their evening chores.

When peace like a river attendeth my way . . .
It is well, it is well with my soul." [2]

Susie's parents, her four brothers and eight sisters were very supportive and a vital part of their lives. A year after they were married their first daughter, Naomi, arrived and brought untold joy to the united Stoltzfus and Beiler families. The following year Susie became pregnant again but this pregnancy was not the same as when she carried Naomi. For the first five months Susie was sick and "threw up" every morning but the doctor assured her that it was a normal pregnancy. As any good Amish mother would do, she kept up with her chores and enjoyed caring for Naomi.

Two weeks before their new baby was born, Aaron asked Susie a strange question. He said, "Have you ever thought what it would be like to have a handicapped child?" The question took Susie by surprise – she thought about it a lot and couldn't get his query out of her mind. The due date passed and now she was two weeks overdue. The Dr. had her admitted to Ephrata Community Hospital on Saturday morning for x-rays. Dr. Munteanu told Aaron and Susie there was a problem and their baby was deformed.

They kept Susie in the hospital. On Sunday they induced labor. Evening came and by then the baby was under stress. Aaron had gone home to do chores and the Dr. had him called and told him not to come alone. Susie's parents came with him. Before they arrived Dr. Rifford had to perform a Caesarean section. They gave Susie a spinal anesthesia and she was conscious when their baby boy was born. Susie cried when she saw him and the nurses cried with her.

CHAPTER 2

Take Him Home and Love Him

Gradually Susie became dimly aware of the stepped-up activity around her as the hospital began to come alive again. The dull pain was there in her abdomen and then the heart sickness came and she was fully awake. It was Monday morning (Dr. Munteanu was still there – checking Susie and the baby – he had not left the hospital since he had gone there Saturday morning.) The events of Sunday evening June 26, 1960 came rushing back. At eight o'clock PM she had given birth to their 8lb. 10oz. baby boy. She remembered … and she cried again.

The baby's appearance was shocking. He had a black rupture on his left side as big as a fist. He had no rectum, the neck muscles were shorter on one side than on the other causing his head to rest on his shoulder, there was a large hard lump on his head – he had no soft spot, he had no hip on one side and the knee and foot were compressed into that area. These were the problems seen at first observation – they would find other deformities.

Something had to be done immediately about the rectum. The surgeon, Dr. Rifford, gave them two options – colostomy or make an opening. Aaron asked Dad Beiler for his advice and his wise words were, "Have them do all they can to make him as normal as possible."

Within hours after his birth the baby went into surgery where they made a rectum. He had convulsions during the operation and in spite of all the predictions – he survived! God loved his little soul. God had His hand on him. God had a plan for his life! ***(Thank You, Lord!)***

That night a friend, Madge Benton, brought a book to Susie. It was *Angel Unaware* by Dale Evans. She had written this inscription on the inside cover page:

> *Susie:*
> *From Madge*
> *Hope this book will prove a blessing to you.*
>
> *Proverbs 3: 5-6 –* ***Trust in the LORD with all thine heart; and lean not unto thine own understanding. In all thy ways acknowledge Him, and He shall direct thy paths.***

The day after the baby was born, a woman was crying in the room across the hall. The crying went on for hours. Becoming concerned, Susie asked the nurse what was wrong and the nurse said, "She had a girl and wanted a boy." Susie couldn't help but think how thankful she would be to have a healthy baby – it wouldn't matter if it was a girl or a boy.

Aaron and Susie named their son John F. Stoltzfus – after Aaron's father. They could not hold him or even touch him because he was kept in an incubator, but they spent much time near him.

The Amish community was very concerned and came out full strong. As many as could fit, came into Susie's room – nurses had difficulty getting to her bedside – and the hallway was filled with Amish who were waiting their turn. Aaron and Susie were grateful for their sincere support and the hospital staff felt such compassion for Susie and Aaron that they overlooked some of the hospital rules. Much as Susie appreciated everyone's concern – after they left in the evening and the hospital became quiet again she felt weak and tired and confused. She longed to have time alone with Aaron – they needed to talk about it – they needed to comfort each other. She thanked God for Aaron.

Today handicapped children are looked at differently than they were in the early 1960's. Having a handicapped child was looked on as having a curse. Susie had to deal with her feelings. What was she going to do with this child??

Romans 10:11 – **For the scripture saith, Whosoever believeth on Him shall not be ashamed.**

Susie was in the hospital for six days and John remained there until he was five weeks old. Susie went every day to be near him. Before John was ready to leave the hospital, Dr. Munteanu talked to Aaron and Susie about having him put in an institution – he told them their baby would never talk – but Aaron and Susie said they would take him home. It seemed to them that Dr. Munteanu was glad they made that decision because his last words to them when they left the hospital with John were, "Take him home and love him."

And that is what they did but it took great courage to overcome the fear that overwhelmed Susie. The hardest part was that the doctors still gave no hope. She would need to rely on God's help.

> Isaiah 41:10 – **Fear thou not; for I am with thee: be not dismayed; for I am thy God: I will strengthen thee; yea, I will help thee; yea, I will uphold thee with the right hand of My righteousness.**

John never cried out loud – his only sound was a whimper and his sad little whimper tugged at their hearts. He never smiled until he was about a year old. His hernia had to be dressed every day and they had to do exercises to lengthen the left neck muscles. They also noticed that John's eyes began to look cloudy when he was six months old and they wondered if he was blind.

Susie, Aaron and Grandma Stoltzfus took shifts and held John for more than a year – he was only out of their arms during hospital visits. He was rocked, talked to, sung to and prayed for every minute day and night. He was loved! He was a fortunate boy to be born into such a caring and loving family. He was sent by God and his little life was turning hearts to God.

John was put in a cast when he was six months old to try to get his hip to go back into place. He wore the cast for five weeks but it didn't work. It was an awkward time – he had to be carried on a pillow and his diaper could not be pinned properly. They had to continue carrying him on a pillow until he was two and one-half. It was very hard to hold him and carry him around.

John had digestive problems. He was always throwing up and had diarrhea most of the time. They tried all of the very best formulas – including soy – but nothing seemed to be exactly right for him. When he was old enough to have baby cereal and other pureed foods he choked a lot. They learned that he had thrust tongue. The normal function of the tongue is to move the food forward to the front of the mouth to be chewed by the teeth and then the food is ready to be swallowed, but John's tongue thrust it backward and down the throat. Consequently, John was a year old before he regained his birth weight.

Life was a little easier when John was able to be put in a crib to nap during the day and sleep at night. There was a nursery next to Aaron and Susie's bedroom but they needed John closer to them so the crib was in their bedroom near Susie.

During the year that John was being held night and day,

Aaron and Susie had to stay home from church. Occasionally if church met in a relative's home where they felt comfortable to take John, they would go. During the time they stayed home, they began to read the Bible and study it in a way they had never done before. They had an understanding of the new birth but realized they had a limited knowledge of the meaning of **grace.** John's birth made them desirous of a more personal relationship with Jesus.

> Romans 10:9 – **That if thou shalt confess with thy mouth the Lord Jesus, and shalt <u>believe</u> in thine heart that God hath raised Him from the dead, thou shalt be saved.**

> Romans 10:13 – **For whosoever shall call upon the name of the Lord shall be saved.**

> Ephesians 2:8-10 – **For by grace are ye saved through faith; and that not of yourselves: it is the gift of God: not of works, lest any man should boast. For we are His workmanship, created in Christ Jesus unto good works, which God hath before ordained that we should walk in them.**

> 2 Corinthians 7:4 – **Great is my boldness of speech toward you, great is my glorying of you: I am filled with comfort, I am exceeding joyful in all our tribulation.**

They were happy when they were able to go to church again as a family on Sunday mornings. A typical Amish Sunday is to get up, do chores, eat breakfast and then get cleaned up for church which always met in different homes. The women of that home provided dinner for everyone after the church service. Sunday afternoons were generally spent visiting widows, children or someone that was housebound and then it was home again to milk the cows, do the other chores and spend a quiet evening with their own family.

Aaron and Susie were members of the Old Order Amish – the conservative branch of a Protestant religion developed from the Mennonites during the period from 1693 to 1695. The group was named for Jacob Ammon, a Swiss Mennonite leader. The Amish came to America with the Mennonites, in large numbers after 1740.

It is believed that all people having the Stoltzfus name in the United States are descendants of Nicholas Stoltzfus, who came from Zwibrucken, Germany on the ship "Charming Polly." They landed in Philadelphia on October 18, 1766 with 181 passengers on board. He settled with his family near Sinking Springs in Berks County. The house that he lived in has been preserved and restored by his descendants. Nicholas had a son born in 1749 named Christian. He was a bishop in the Amish church in Berks County. In about 1800 Christian moved to Lancaster County. Aaron is a direct descendant. His ancestors had strong faith; they really knew the Bible and preached mostly from the Old Testament.

When John was little, van loads of company would arrive to see him (the van and drivers were hired from a taxi company).

It was never a surprise when they came because visiting is very common among the Amish. Many times they came late, after John had been put in his crib for the night and he was sleeping soundly, but they wanted to see him so Susie would get him up. Susie did not resent having to wake him. Instead she felt grateful for their love, prayers and continued support. She still refers to the van loads of company as a blessing! Only occasionally did she detect an element of curiosity and feel the sting of hurtful comments. But negative words were a blessing, too, because they caused her to love her Johnny all the more. God filled her with a greater desire to protect him and gave her new strength to care for him.

John was not quite sixteen months old when Susie had their third baby – a beautiful little girl and they named her Kathy. She was born by Caesarian on October 18, 1961 and Susie had the same surgeon that had delivered John. Dr. Rifford remembered and asked Susie how long the boy had lived. He could not have imagined the fortitude of that little wonder boy or the love, encouragement and strength John was deriving from his caring family. The doctors called it a miracle but did they really understand and give the credit to God for John's life – as his parents and grandparents were doing?

John's digestive problems continued. Susie began to wonder if he would ever stop having diarrhea and throwing up. His doctors prescribed adult doses of a stomach medicine that brought relief but because he could not chew, the choking continued. He could only eat Junior baby food, mashed potatoes and soft foods until he was twelve years old. The medication stunted his growth but

Aaron and Susie looked on that as another favor from God because it made him easier to lift, hold and carry. God was watching over John because he never put toys or food in his mouth. All babies and small children seem to have an inborn drive to find objects and stuff them in their mouths, but God did not give John that desire – if He had, the results could have been disastrous.

John was two years old when the constant stomach irritation began to improve. With that relief he could respond to those he loved with smiles and even laughter. The whole family took delight in these changes and began to enjoy him in a new and more relaxing way. His development was slow but when he expressed happiness – a great load was lifted and taking care of him became more pleasant.

John learned to carry a tune before he could talk. He hummed to his heart's content and to the great pleasure of Aaron, Susie, Grandma Stoltzfus and Daudy and Grandma Beiler. His humming was not just a tonal meandering from low notes to high notes – he sang hymns and the family could fill in the words because the melody was so clear. Again they were told that he would never talk – he would only be able to imitate sounds. At that time John hummed "*Christ Receiveth Sinful Men*". Aaron said, "He'll be a soul winner some day!" But Susie still did not think he would live.

"Christ Receiveth Sinful Men"

Sinners Jesus will receive
Sound this word of grace to all
Who the heav'nly pathway leave
All who linger, all who fall.

Refrain:
Sing it o'er and o'er again
Christ receiveth sinful men
Make the message clear and plain
Christ receiveth sinful men.

Come, and He will give you rest
Trust Him for His word is plain.
He will take the sinfullest
Christ receiveth sinful men.

Now my heart condemns me not
Pure before the law I stand
He who cleansed me from all spot
Satisfied its last demand.

Christ receiveth sinful men
Even me with all my sin
Purged from ev'ry spot and stain
Heav'n with Him I enter in. [3]

His Grandma Stoltzfus was instrumental in teaching John to sing – she spent hours and hours rocking him and singing to him. Tears came to her eyes when he first started humming the tunes that she had sung as lullabies to him when he was a baby. She truly loved him and would never regret the time she had devoted to him. She had filled his emotional needs and was always ready to give him even more love.

Another boy arrived in the Stoltzfus family on November 16, 1962. They named him Sam and he was a joy to his parents! Now they had two girls and two boys and they felt blessed indeed! God is so good!

CHAPTER 3

He's Going to Make It!

At one of John's regular office visits with Dr. Munteanu, the kind Dr. said, "This boy has a will to live, he's going to make it!" Other doctors concurred and they began the long process of planning and performing corrective surgery. But the doctors shook their heads when they studied x-rays that were taken when John was three years old. Everything, inside and out, was damaged on the left side except his arm, hand and ear. He had only one kidney but it was double and the liver was on the wrong side. There was much to be done and this would not be a simple task!

John was four years old when they began to work on his eyes. He had three operations to repair the muscles and nerves that had never developed in back of his right eye. They removed cataracts that they thought might have resulted from the bright lights in the incubator. John was totally blind in his left eye so it was imperative that they do all they could to correct the many problems he had in his right eye.

The easiest way for Johnny to get around was to roll. He never could crawl but he devised a method of travel that was uniquely his. He curled in a ball and used his one leg to push and propel himself ever faster. He rolled so fast you would think he was going to take off and fly. He rolled so much that he wore the hair off the sides and back of his head – giving him the most unusual "hairdo" in Lancaster County. His favorite place to go was through the large living room to his Grandma's door. When he arrived he would thump on her door with his foot and she would open it with a jovial, "Come in, John!" How they enjoyed their time together!

In 1964, John was admitted to General Hospital in Lancaster where Dr. Kent amputated the webbed clubfoot from his left hip socket in preparation for a prosthesis. Dr. Zelkie made the prosthesis and carefully fit it to John. Daudy Beiler made parallel bars that were just his size and then Daudy spent many hours patiently teaching John to balance and walk between the bars. He started wearing a helmet at that time and then continued wearing it for ten years. After John bravely accomplished walking with the bars, he started using a little walker, then three legged crutches and finally regular crutches. Learning to walk was a long, difficult process – consequently John most generally used his wheelchair that he maneuvered with great expertise. He was such a good-

"Look Mommy – no hands!"

natured boy. God had blessed him with a happy heart.

The city of Lancaster had an Easter Seal School that John was able to start attending when he was four years old. The programs were based entirely on physical therapy. Countless hours would be spent on learning coordination and how to better manage his deformities. Much time was also spent on his speech and making the various phonetic sounds. Gradually John began to repeat the sounds and form the words. At first, he repeated the things people said to him. Then he made the transition from humming a melody to using words in a song. It wasn't until he was six years old that he said words and short phrases on his own.

Mrs. Gill was his teacher. Aaron and Susie grew close to Mrs. Gill and the other staff members. Soon Mrs. Gill, the staff and some of the other students were making regular visits to the Stoltzfus farm and of course, Johnny (as well as Naomi, Kathy and Sam) loved that! They took many pictures – these were the first ones ever taken of John because the Amish didn't take pictures.

Easter Seal School hayride and picnic at the Stoltzfus Farm.

His first bus driver was Lavern Petersheim and she took very good care of him. John could not sit alone so Easter Seal provided a seat to strap him in. Lavern taught John many new songs and poems. He became so familiar with the route the bus took that he would tell the bus driver exactly where they were. One landmark was a large maple tree with branches that arched over the road and provided shade in that area. Lavern called it "Nature's Bridge" and after John learned to form his words, he always made the announcement when they arrived there. He became so familiar with the trip that he knew every bump and every turn. It didn't seem to bother him that he could not see – he was too busy singing songs, reciting poems and mentally observing every movement his Volkswagon school bus was making.

Following is a letter from John's first school bus driver:

John lived on the eastern end of Lancaster County and Chet Sweigart was in charge of Bus drivers. My sister Bette was driving a station wagon for him and taking a load of special children to a school in Lancaster. He asked her if she knew anyone in the Morgantown area who would drive a VW and start from Morgantown and pick up a load to be taken into school. He came for me and drove me around to my stops: 1st–John, 2nd–Luke Sauder, 3rd–Connie Wenger, 4th–Eddie Mertz, and 5th–Janie Echerling (I think that was her name). She was the little queen for the special children one year. I thought I could do it. It was 89 miles a day, more or less, both ways.

I lead singing at Conestoga Bible School so had lots of songs in my head and singing helped to keep the children from picking at each other.John was the only one that helped me sing. Luke was very quiet. He could walk but didn't talk. Connie jabbered a lot but her words all ran together and you couldn't understand her. A very pretty child. We didn't have seat belts so she usually stood. I would hear John say, "Move over Connie." Janie could talk but was very slow and hard to hear. She couldn't walk. A dainty little thing. Eddie also had to be carried and didn't talk but gave me great big smiles. He sat in front with me.

Coming across the Mt. or hill from Johns to Morgantown, there was a tree across the road high up so I always said we're going under nature's bridge. John began to ask "Where's nature's bridge?" So I would tell him. One morning to my surprise he called out, "Nature's Bridge, Mrs. Petersheim." After that I always let him say it.

One morning I drove a different way in back of Churchtown -and John said, "I can't find the road, Mrs. Petersheim." I said, "I'm taking a shortcut this morning." I went that way for several weeks then changed again.

John said, "I can't find the shortcut, Mrs. Petersheim." I thought, What! This boy is supposed to be blind, how does he know? I guess he went by the Bumps and bends in the road. They were felt easier in a little VW.

We had a traffic light on 222 so when we stopped, I would count 1, 2, 3, 4, 5, 6, 7, 8, 9, 10 red light, 1, 2, 3 green light, then we'd go. One time I was counting and John said, "green light." How did he know? I'm sure he couldn't see it from where he sat. I guess he felt me release the brake and start pressing the gas so he quickly said Green light. He had me puzzled many times. Lots of times he would say, "Sing, Mrs. Petersheim." I guess it kept the others happy and content and they left him alone so we sang. John moved to Chester County then but finished out the year at Lancaster school. I wasn't needed any more.

I was so thankful for the safety God gave us over all those miles. At times I felt it was the guardian angels of the children that alerted me to the traffic around us.

Thank you, Jesus!
Lavern Petersheim [6]

Aaron and Susie made a frightening trip to General Hospital with John when he was five years old – he had begun to vomit again. The doctor discovered a bowel blockage and would have to remove four inches of intestine. Before John went into surgery Dr. Munteanu again told Aaron and Susie that it would take a miracle for him to survive – but there was no other choice. Another concern was that whenever he had anesthesia his chest would fill up and he would become ill – this time was the worst. While he was in the hospital he developed pneumonia and was a very sick boy!

With great faith Aaron and Susie turned to God again
and with even greater love
He answered their prayers.

During that same year, 1965, Dr. Kent operated on John again at General Hospital. This time the doctor put a six inch pin in John's hip to keep the ball in the socket. After a few days a pimple-like bump appeared on the skin of John's hip and then the point of the pin broke through. The pin had to be removed. Even though the operation was not successful John's hospital stay was beneficial in more important ways. His love for singing could not be squelched by his physical discomfort. He had learned all the words of *Whispering Hope* and gleefully sang it for the nurses. *(Read the full text of Whispering Hope in the Endnotes on page 192.)* He won the admiration of the nurses and as Susie puts it, "He wiggled his way into their hearts!" One nurse was so moved by his rendition of the song that she accepted Christ. She said, "This child has changed my life – because of what he can be – I can be a follower of Jesus, too." All of the doctors and therapists had said that John would never talk and if he did he would be a "repeater," but look what he was doing with words. How he loved to bring glory to God. Did God empower him with the ability to use words for moments like this?

Thank You, Lord, for John's precious life!

CHAPTER 4

A Place of Their Own

It always seemed that God gave Aaron and Susie refreshing (though sometimes labor intensive) breaks from their times of deep concern over John. His bowel blockage and hip surgery made 1965 an eventful year but another happening made it memorable for the Aaron Stoltzfus family. They moved from the family farm in Morgantown, Lancaster County to Honey Brook in Chester County. Aaron's younger brother and his new bride were ready to take over the farm. They would live in the farmhouse and Grandma Stoltzfus remained in the Daudy House. Aaron and Susie hired a driver and truck to move their furnishings and belongings to the new farm they had purchased in Honey Brook. The children were excited and Aaron and Susie found contentment when they were finally settled in a place that was their very own. Cattle trucks moved their registered dairy. The cows adapted easily to their new barn and lush pastures.

Because John was progressing at Easter Seal School, those

in charge allowed him to keep coming even though the Stoltzfus family had moved out of the county. His dedicated driver drove twenty-five miles, one way, and Easter Seal paid everything. It was very helpful to have him go there for the many and various types of therapy; but his parents were especially grateful for all they did to teach John to feed himself by using a spoon and fork. He had to go to Children's Hospital in Elizabethtown to develop the ability to chew. His inability to chew caused many worrisome experiences. John was six years old when one evening during supper, he choked on a piece of finely chopped meat. Aaron worked feverishly to remove the meat, trying every method he knew but John continued to choke and could not even gasp for air. Aaron feared that John was not going to make it; Susie was praying, Naomi, Kathy and Sam were wide-eyed with fright. John was turning blue and limp when finally Aaron was able to remove the meat from his throat. To this day John only eats what is set before him at his place on the table. He never gets food for himself or goes to the refrigerator. He does not like candy or foods with unusual texture. Evidently his diet has been good for him because he had his first cavity last year when he was forty-three years old.

In 1966 John had surgery on his knee. The cap was on the side of his leg and had to be moved to its proper place on top of the knee. He was put in traction for a week at Elizabethtown Hospital. He went home with a cast on his good leg which he wore for a few weeks and then he had to wear a brace for nine more years to strengthen his knee.

While he was trying to adjust to the knee problem, John

began seeing dots in his good right eye. He became very frustrated and afraid when the spots would appear – this went on for weeks before the doctors decided to take him to Wills Eye Hospital in Philadelphia. His retina was detached and that was reason enough for a little six-year-old boy to be fearful. No wonder John had cried out "Swatza heat" (black heat) so often during those weeks when his pain became intense – "Swatza heat" was his way of describing the sensation he got when the retina was detaching. Surgery helped but within a year the spots appeared again. The doctor at Wills Eye Hospital wanted Dr. Shay to see him. Dr. Shay was renowned for his skill and knowledge. He had his own hospital and traveled throughout the United States to teach other surgeons. Aaron and Susie became friends with Dr. Shay and he assisted with John's surgery. It was a very tedious operation due to an accumulation of scar tissue from previous surgery. Aaron and Susie waited in the hospital from nine o'clock AM to five o'clock PM without a word from either doctors or nurses. It was January 1967 and they think it was the longest day of their lives. They were alone in a city hospital – they did not know a soul – they did not know that it would take all day and they had no cash to make a phone call or buy something to eat. It was a dark, dark day but God was so good. After two weeks of bandages they knew that John was not totally blind. The Doctor had told them it would be a slim chance that they could attach the retina again. It was a very risky operation but it was successful! After John was fitted with glasses that had a telescopic lens on the right side, he had tunnel vision (comparable to looking through the hole in a spool of thread) with no peripheral vision. It is still like that today. John is actually legally blind but he is so thankful for what he has.

On June 26, 1967, John had his seventh birthday and two weeks later, on July 10, another son arrived, and what a blessing he was. They named him Mahlon, and John was delighted to have a new baby brother. Now there were five children for Susie and Aaron to love. This was surely a time of celebration and thanksgiving! John was the happiest one of all and he looked so smart in his first, very thick eyeglasses.

Evaluators from Reading Special School came to observe John and they were amazed when he identified the pages in his books. John's family had spent a great deal of time reading to him from the time he was little and he had memorized thirty books. The evaluators were baffled because he did not recognize letters but the colors in the pictures told him what page he was on. They would turn the pages from front to back and he would "read" the story, using the right words for every page. Then they tried to fool him and turned the pages from back to front. John "read" the book backwards.

The first year they lived in Honey Brook, Aaron and Susie had a tutor, Mr. Sugar, for John – but John did not like it. He had gotten used to the social part of going to school and he missed it very much. The tutor, however, was able to teach him phonics and John began to read but it took great concentration because of his limited scope of vision. He also learned Braille during that year. John was a very happy boy when he was able to go to Reading Special School in Shillington, PA the following year.

The next letter is from Rachel Stoltzfus, the bus driver that took John to Reading Special School.

August 6, 2004

Our family was first introduced to Little Johnny (as we called him then) when we received a phone call from his mother inquiring if we could transport Johnny to and from school to Reading, PA. After a few more calls it was explained that a vehicle would be supplied by the Morgantown School thru Harvey Eshleman who also had the school buses, all they needed was a driver behind the wheel. We decided I could do that and started soon after.

It was in 1968, we had a 13-year-old son, Howard, a 9-year-old son Darrel and Wanda was 4 years old. We lived in town, the boys could walk to school and Wanda didn't go yet.

We left quite early for the ride to Reading. I would take Wanda right out of bed in her pajamas, her blankie and her thumb. She would often take another nap on the way. Wanda liked Johnny a lot and I was impressed by him and his handicaps – the way he dealt with them.

She sometimes would take her prize possessions along to show Johnny even tho' she knew he couldn't see too much. She had a book, Curious George, she would try to read it to him, one day he asked what color the cover was.

We dealt with Nature's Bridge every morning and afternoon. This was a tree grown over the road to the other side and created a bridge. Johnny would always know when we approached it.

He talked a lot about his family. His sisters, Naomi and Kathy, and especially Baby Mahlon. He would tell us they often made home made ice cream and how they turned it by hand. His Mother baked a lot and our family enjoyed lots of her goodies.

We soon had another passenger for school (Jeff Jones). He was a 10 year old with many disabilities. He wore two leg braces. He was quite active and misbehaved many times. We had to take the handles off the door on his side. He would open the window then the door and would soon be on the floor. He would sit in the front seat with me. Johnny would be in the back seat begging Jeff to behave. Wanda looked on and would find her thumb and blankie and lay down in the back of the station wagon.

Johnny had leg braces, too, also an artificial leg. Coming home one afternoon his leg fell off. He called to me and said, "Rachel, my leg fell off." It was quite a shock. We stopped and I tried to put it back on. We started for home again and soon Johnny said his leg is pinching him so I stopped again and this time I laid it beside him and left for home.

In 1969 in February our family moved to Chester Co. on a farm. It was quite a distance from where Johnny lived. It didn't seem practical to continue doing the school run So I finished out the school year and then someone else took the job. For quite awhile we didn't see the Stoltzfus family very much.

In 1976 we moved to Dundee NY and a little while later (1981) Johnny's family did, too. We now live about 8 miles from each other.

I don't see John too much but some members of his family every Saturday at the Windmill.

I greatly appreciate John's Christian Testimony his music talent and singing for the Lord. I find it a privilege and a challenge to have known John and his family all these years. Also to be a small part of his life.

Thank you John for your friendship. You have been a Christian Witness to our family and many others.

Rachel Stoltzfus [8]

Aaron and Susie had a wonderful Christian neighbor and his name was Magnus Tournquist. He took a special interest in John and introduced him to musical instruments. He also taught him to play each one. Magnus gave him a xylophone, then an autoharp, a guitar, an accordion and even a record player! John loved to listen to music on his record player and he became so familiar with it that if he wanted to hear a certain song again, he was able to pick the needle arm up and put it back down in the exact spot where the song began so he could hear it play again. It took great dexterity to perform that feat without scratching the record.

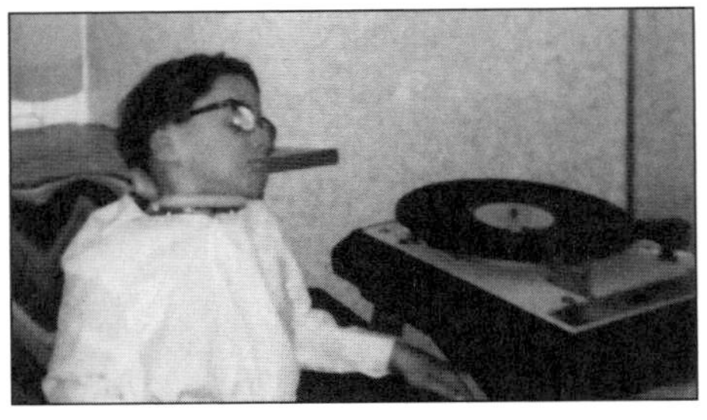

Enjoying his record player.

When John was seven years old he had an organ. As soon as he arrived home from Reading Special School he would go directly to his organ and play, to his heart's content, from the Christian Hymnal. He still knows all of those hymns and what page they are on. One Christmas vacation he played through the entire hymnal (657 pages). He has always had a dogged determination and his family laughingly says, "Perseverance! – it's the story of his life!"

Aaron and Susie's faith had grown steadily since John's birth. They were so aware of God's constant care and His abiding presence in their lives. Even though they had both made commitments to Him when they were children they now felt the need for a more personal relationship with Jesus. They kept wanting more of God. They loved their Amish foundation, family and friends but when they moved to Honey Brook they visited the Pequea (sounds

like Peckway) Mennonite Church where they heard a message from the Bible that started to quench a thirst that had been building in their hearts. They had such a hunger to study and learn more about Jesus that they soon became involved in Small Group and Bible Study. Aaron Glick, a Godly man, led the Bible studies and they learned much from him. It did not take long to fit in and feel at home at Pequea and become an active part of the Christian fellowship there. The friends they made at Pequea will always be their friends.

Romans 8:38, 39 – **For I am persuaded, that neither death, nor life, nor angels, nor principalities, nor powers, nor things present, nor things to come, nor height, nor depth, nor any other creature, shall be able to separate us from the love of God, which is in Christ Jesus our Lord.**

Romans 12:9 – **Let love be without dissimulation. Abhor that which is evil; cleave to that which is good.**

"Without faith it is impossible to please God. We must believe that God <u>is</u> – and He is a rewarder of those who diligently seek Him. <u>Without faith it is impossible to</u>

please God. Without faith our religion is in vain – faith keeps our eye on the goal.

Jesus is forbearing with us. We are far from perfect, but don't give up! God is willing to help us with our onslaughts or trials if we allow Him to have control of our lives.

Today the choice is yours. Today we are sowing seeds. The choices we make in life will determine our destiny." [9]

CHAPTER 5

Willing Worker

Some of John's happiest times were those days when he had a job to do and could be helpful. He loved being involved with the family and working on the farm. Quite often Aaron would carry him to the tomato patch, put him on the ground near a plant and give him a bucket. How he enjoyed picking tomatoes! He could not see well enough to see the tomatoes hanging on the plant, even at that short distance, but he found his own system. He could reach and feel the tomatoes. If they were big enough he would pick one and hold it close to his right eye. If it was green – he threw it, if it was red – it went in the bucket.

John wanted so much to help do the chores with Naomi, Kathy and Sam that Aaron, being the good Dad that he was, thought of a way he could help. John carried milk from the big milk bucket to the bulk tank in a little plastic bucket. He could only manage an inch or two of milk but he was helping. The disadvantage was that the bucket bumped against his crutch, causing the milk to spill, which made his wooden leg smelly – he quit!

John started leaving his prosthesis in the house (probably to keep it smelling good). Susie watched from the kitchen window as he went off to the barn by himself in his little stroller. It was an uphill climb and took a lot of determination for John to make the journey from house to barn. He had to push with all his might using his one leg to not only push the stroller forward but also to keep it from rolling backward. The struggle was well worth it because his Dad had given him another chore. The milker pump was turned on with a switch. When the milking was done Aaron let him turn it off by pulling a string that Aaron had attached to it.

John thought the best part of chores was having the cows bed down for the night. Milking was done, the barn was cleaned and each cow had fresh bedding underneath her. Talk about contented cows! One by one each cow made a groaning sound as she lowered her heavy body down to the clean straw. When the descent was completed, she gave a satisfied grunt. Lying there on her fresh bed of straw she methodically began to chew her cud. John knew when one was ready to lie down by the sounds she made, and he would quickly maneuver his stroller to be behind her when she heaved her final sigh upon reaching the floor. He laughed. Then he would hear another cow start her descent to the floor and he had to hurry to get behind her. How he laughed! And how he loved those girls – he knew every cow by name. This ritual took place every night and he did not want to leave the barn until they were all in bed

but the minute the last cow was down

he scooted out of the barn.

In the spring of 1968 Aaron was preparing a field for planting and had to get the stones picked up. He hitched the stone wagon to the tractor and his eager helpers: Naomi, Kathy and Sam, were with him and ready to go. At the last minute seven-year-old Johnny came out of the house in his wheelchair and wanted to go with them. Aaron lifted John in his wheelchair up onto the front of the wagon – it was an easy lift because John only weighed 25 pounds. John had ridden this way many times before, but he had previously been in his stroller which had a protective bar in front of him. Aaron did not give that a thought as he securely strapped John's wheelchair to the wagon.

Off they went to pick stones. Hard work always seems easier when you are having a good time with each other and this was a happy crew of workers. Aaron felt blessed to have his four children with him on a perfect spring day, working the land that he loved. God is good! Before they knew it the wagon was full of stones and they were going down the field lane to dump it when John slipped out of his wheelchair, flipped off the wagon and landed on the lane under the wagon wheels. It was a dual wheeled heavy-duty wagon and was loaded with tons of stones and rocks. The wheels ran over John's chest.

Laughter changed to screams as the children saw what was happening. Aaron jumped off the tractor and rushed to John. He was not breathing. As Naomi ran for help, Aaron carried John toward the house, praying for him to breathe. That quarter-mile from the field to the house seemed ever so long that day. After several minutes (Aaron believes it was five to seven minutes) John started breathing again. Aaron laid him in the field and Kathy, Sam and Aaron surrounded him, kneeling in the high grass while Aaron prayed. He worked over John and then carried him the rest of the way to the house with his two little children running beside him. Susie had called the Dr. and he made arrangements for them to meet an ambulance in town. John regained consciousness in Susie's arms in the car. His breathing was labored but he looked over at Aaron and said, "Goodbye, Dad, I'm going to heaven now."

The ambulance took John to Ephrata Community Hospital. Aaron prayed most of the two nights and one day while John was on oxygen. On the second day John recuperated so quickly that he went from intensive care to home. What a great relief to Aaron and Susie. They thanked the Lord for hearing and answering their prayers. John still had a longing to go to heaven and for two weeks after he got home he was very sore and weak. It was a serious accident and they were thankful for his brace with its strong metal bars that protected his rib cage. There were wheel marks on his chest above the brace. Surely God would have loved having John in heaven with Him, but He still had work for John to do here.

There was another near accident that could have taken John's life. His younger brother, Sam, loved tractors. Aaron had parked their large Farmall tractor just inside the shed attached to the barn near the milk house. The drive went slightly downhill from the shed. Sam was only four or five years old, but he thought he knew everything there was to know about tractors. He climbed and crawled up onto the tractor and released the brake. As the tractor started to rumble forward, Sam thought it was great fun but then he saw John in his stroller part-way down the hill, near the driveway. Sam yelled, "Go back, John, I'm coming!" The tractor hit the front of the stroller and missed John's face by a fraction of an inch. The stroller was crushed but John was all right. Aaron was on the run and jumped up on the tractor with Sam. He stopped it before it could do any more damage. John had many narrow escapes but God's guardian angels were always alert and watching over him.

> Psalm 91:11 – **For He shall give His angels charge over thee, to keep thee in all thy ways.**

Elizabethtown Crippled Children's Hospital became John's home away from home for most of 1969. Because John had always had curvature of the spine and had worn a brace, it was time now to be fitted for an even stronger one – a Milwaukee brace. It would tilt his head back and support his back. A bar on the brace would go across his upper chest and support both sides of his ribs. It would limit his mobility but he was not old enough to have his back fused.

Preparation for the brace was long and tedious. It was expected to take three months, but John's bones did not cooperate so he spent every week-day and night there for nine months. The curvature was so bad that his hipbone went two inches up over his rib cage and there should have been a space the width of his hand between his ribs and his hip. They needed to fit the brace below the ribs so they had to use an articulator to separate the rib cage from the hip bone. The articulator was a machine to stretch the left side of his body (a very painful procedure) and John had to be on the machine for one hour every afternoon.

For five days each week John lived in a ward at the hospital with other children. There was a houseparent with them all of the time. It was very difficult for him to stay and very heartbreaking for his family to leave him there. Aaron picked him up at four o'clock every Friday afternoon. What a joyous time that was! And how John enjoyed spending Friday nights sleeping in his own bed with his brothers in the room, participating in Saturday's activity on the farm and going to church with his family on Sunday.

The trips were long – fifty miles, one way – from home to the hospital. The Sunday evening rides were very special because the whole family went and they spent most of the time singing. Mahlon was two years old and he usually found his way to Susie's feet below the dash with a pillow. (This was before seat belts and seemed quite normal at the time – but now looking back, it was actually rather dangerous.) The family joy left John when they arrived at the hospital. When they took him in, John did not want to stay and he clung to his Mom, pulling her covering strings and cape off – this was the <u>most</u> heartbreaking time for Susie!

After a few weeks went by, John adjusted to being in the hospital. His mornings were full of activity that he came to enjoy. The hospital had classrooms where the long-term patients could be taught. John's classroom had a nice group of children whom he could interact with while they were learning. The teacher was very helpful in teaching John better reading skills. His love for reading

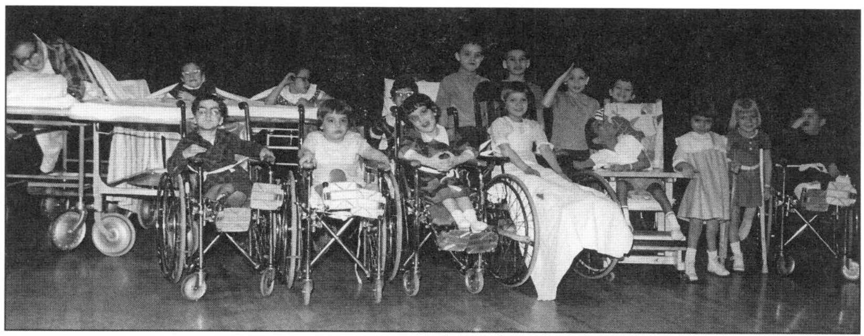

John and classmates in a program at Elizabethtown Crippled Children Hospital.

started then. Susie went to visit him one day and found him lying on his back in his crib with a book nearly covering his face because he had to hold it so close to his eye to read. He was very excited and wanted to read the book to her. Every word was correct except the word sweater. He pronounced it "sweeter" and to this day they call sweaters "sweeters." By afternoon he was tired and his therapist, Mrs. Tome, was amazed that, in spite of the painful stretching, he was so relaxed that he fell asleep during the procedure. This was surely another favor from God. John had such a positive reaction to the wonderful sleep that God gave him – nothing like the negative reaction he always had to anesthesia.

Nine year old John with his new Milwaukee brace.

It was a very happy day when the arduous nine months were over. John left Elizabethtown Crippled Children's Hospital wearing his new Milwaukee brace! – He would be wearing it for the next six years.

Back home again life was just the way John wanted it to be. He loved being with his family – basking in the love of his parents, playing with his brothers and sisters and going back to Reading Special School. His doting sister, Naomi, loved having him with her – she carried him on her hip much of the time. If she had outside work to do she would carry him out, put him in a safe place and get her chore done. Naomi liked to play Sunday School near the wood pile. They had slab wood and the flat pieces of wood were just right to use for imaginary people. She lined them up and placed them in a good arrangement for conducive learning and then she taught the lesson.

John was her favorite student

and Naomi was his favorite teacher.

John had missed listening to the train that regularly passed by their farm. He had always become mesmerized by its first far away sound and as the mighty locomotive drew closer, he loved to hear the rhythmic clatter of the huge wheels as they rolled over the iron rails causing the train cars to lurch and squeal as they lumbered down the track. The mournful wail of the whistle thrilled him as it faded in the distance.

One day Naomi was alarmed when she found him leaning out of the second story window of their farmhouse. He had climbed up on the sill and had gotten himself into a very precarious position to be nearer the sounds of the train. He probably thought, "The closer I can get to it – the better I will hear it." (Perhaps if his eyesight was better and he could have seen how far he was from the ground, he would have experienced a little fear and might not have been so brave.) Naomi was a caring big sister and helped him back to the safety of the bedroom floor, explaining the danger he was in and showing him how well he could hear – just by standing by the open window. Susie never knew about it.

The three boys shared the same bedroom and since John had a penchant for helping, Sam and Mahlon devised a system for John to turn off the light at night. The light switch went from side to side (instead of up and down) so they were able to attach a long string to the switch which was on the same wall as John's bed and they tied the other end to his bed. After night-time prayers and everyone was settled in bed Sam would tell John to "Outen the light" and then they all said "Good Night" to each other. It was such a good feeling to be needed!

CHAPTER 6

The Age of Awakening

John was small for his age but he was growing in heart and mind. He had a great love for the people in his life. School was always exciting for him and he was beginning to develop skills that no one ever expected him to have. He was ten years old when his counselor, Mr. Cobb, at Reading Special School, saw computer potential in John. Aaron and Susie were delighted to receive such a remarkable progress report and would do all they could to encourage him.

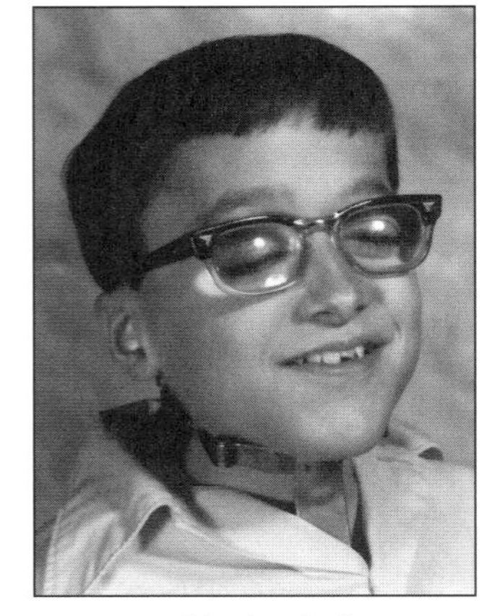

Ten year old whiz kid.

At that same time John had to be fitted for his second prosthesis and God gave him Dr. Jack Smith. It turned out that God gave John to Dr. Jack Smith as well. The doctor was in his early thirties and had recently become a widower. Losing his wife when they were so young had been a great tragedy and was very painful for him; but he and John found something in each other that helped both of them. It did not take long for Jack Smith to see some promise in John's ability to memorize, so he began to challenge John to memorize Scripture. John, in turn, in his good natured way, asked Dr. Jack Smith to learn verses with him. Soon they were memorizing chapters! They became good friends which was pleasant for both of them and most pleasing to God!

A similar situation came about at home on the farm. Aaron had hired a man to paint their large stucco house. He was a kindly Christian man who loved to visit with John. Each day when the painter came to work, John would take notice as to which part of the house the man was setting up his ladders and John would go to the inside window nearest the work site. With his prosthesis removed (he was more agile without it) John climbed up on the sill of the open window. He could then stick his head out of the window and have wonderful conversations with his new friend. They began saying Bible verses and then challenging each other to memorize more. Every morning they found new joy in what they had learned and in making decisions about what more they wanted to memorize. It was a rewarding time for both. The painter developed a great affection for his new little friend. Susie remarked again, as she has many times throughout his life, "John wiggled his way right into his heart."

During the same year, 1970, Lewis Overholt had tent meetings that the family faithfully attended. The meetings were held in a big tent that was pitched on the Pequea Mennonite Church lawn and everyone in the community was welcomed.

All five of the Stoltzfus children looked forward to going and they especially enjoyed the children's meeting. It was during these meetings that it seemed as if John was waking up. In spite of what all his therapists had said through the years about his being a repeater – he was not just repeating words. He was thinking for himself. Lewis asked the children questions about the story he had told them the previous night and John would pop up with the answer!! And not just a one-word answer – he would give every detail. His family was amazed and tearfully thankful!

John was also becoming more aware of his need for a personal relationship with the Lord. One evening after bedtime prayers in his room, he invited Jesus into his heart. About two weeks later, during the night, John called Susie. She went to his bedside to see what he needed, carrying a slight apprehension in her heart that he might be having a problem. She was relieved to see that he was radiant. Sitting up in bed he exclaimed, "An angel is here in my room." He described it in great detail and wanted Susie to see it, but she could not see his Angel. She was certain, however, that it was very real to John.

The next wonderful event of that year was the birth of Louise on October 6, 1970. What a treasure she was and how the family welcomed her into their fold. Now they had three girls and three boys and their family was complete. It was Susie's fifth Caesarian birth and Dr. Rifford had delivered them all. She was thankful for Dr. Munteanu's and Dr. Rifford's care throughout the years and even more thankful for Aaron, Naomi, John, Kathy, Sam, Mahlon and Louise. Susie was *most* thankful for God! Without Him her life would be empty, but with Him she had *everything!*

CHAPTER 7

Lean Times

After Louise was born, for just a fleeting moment, Susie wondered again what had happened to cause John to be born with deformities when their other five children were so normal and there was no history of any abnormality on either side of their families. Just before Mahlon was born, Susie was admitted to Johns Hopkins Research Center in Baltimore, Maryland because Aaron and Susie wanted to know why. Hundreds of doctors and members of medical research teams tested her and checked her over but they had no answers – no answers.

Isaiah 26:3 says, God **"wilt keep him in perfect peace, whose mind is stayed on Thee: because he trusteth in Thee."** Aaron and Susie truly trusted and put themselves under His guidance… they depended on Him which was greatly to their advantage. Those who trust in God must have their minds stayed upon Him – must trust in Him at all times – under all events - must firmly and faithfully adhere to Him with a complete satisfaction in Him. God will keep those who do so in perpetual peace – perfect peace! When unusual things happen, those who trust Him will calmly accept the event and not be disturbed by frightful apprehensions arising from them.

When trials come, and they will, we have two choices: We can run from God thinking that He has abandoned us – or we can run to Him for strength and protection. God had Aaron's and Susie's love, faith and trust – it would not have entered their minds to do anything except run to Him! He kept touching their lives in such meaningful ways that they were left with no doubt of His presence, His love and His caring!

Times were lean for Aaron and Susie. All of the medical care for John, his many operations, long stays in the hospital and the knowledge that more surgery would be required in the future kept them diligent. They spent very little on themselves and were thankful to be farmers – at least they would always have food on the table. They literally lived off the land and had their own milk and meat. The milk check supported them and they were able to sell garden produce.

Susie wanted to do her part and was able to get a job cleaning house for a wealthy woman in the neighborhood. She was a fine lady and Susie felt it was a privilege to be able to work for her. No doubt the woman was pleased to have someone as meticulous and trustworthy as Susie to take care of her valuable belongings. Susie also cleaned a beautiful nearby Episcopal Church. Wherever Susie went John was with her. He loved going to that church because he was allowed to play the magnificent pipe organ. Both the organ and the organ bench seemed oversized when that little boy was sitting at the grand console. He could not reach the foot pedals or the higher manuals but the keys within his reach made a deep and reverberating sound when he touched them. How it thrilled him to play the hymns he knew so well and hear the music swell as it came from the pipes above his head. He sang and played while his Mom dusted and polished the rich woodwork to bring out a soft sheen on the old walnut patina. Even when she did the scrubbing, her heart was made light by the joy that poured out of John's music. He liked to reach a climax with a big chord and stop abruptly. Instead of the sudden silence he expected there was always a lingering tremor that seemed to melt into the cascading sun rays that refracted the vivid colors from the stained glass windows. He listened quietly – hardly wanting to breathe – until the last tone was completely blended and absorbed. It was then that the silence came and a peaceful hush fell over the sanctuary.

Everyone in the family worked to make their produce stand successful. They were all familiar with the long process from seed to harvest and they were diligent to do their part. It took patience to watch for the first crops to mature enough to be ready for selling, but suddenly the vegetables were ripe, and from then on they grew non-stop until frost. Isn't God wonderful! Only the nicest specimens went to the vegetable stand and the family ate or canned the rest. Early morning picking provided a fresh display in their shaded stand and they were careful to have the produce attractively arranged. Freshness, cleanliness and neatness were their standards, and the friendly contact with customers just came naturally.

Susie enjoyed getting acquainted with the people that stopped to purchase vegetables. One woman, Grace Sand, lived nearby and came often to buy corn during the season. She seemed especially nice and soon Grace and her husband, George, were friends of the Stoltzfus family. They took a special interest in John. They were very good people and George belonged to the Masons. One Sunday morning the Sands drove up the lane to Aaron and Susie's, just as they were getting all of the children in the car to go to church George got out of his car, went to Aaron and gave him a slip of paper confirming that the Masonic Lodge had sent $75,000 to the hospital to pay John's bills.

Praise God from Whom All blessings flow!

I Chronicles 29: 11-14 – **Thine, O LORD is the greatness, and the power, and the glory, and the victory, and the majesty: for all that is in the heaven and in the earth is Thine; Thine is the kingdom, O LORD, and Thou art exalted as head above all. Both riches and honour come of Thee, and Thou reignest over all; and in Thine hand is power and might; and in Thine hand it is to make great, and to give strength unto all. Now therefore, our God, we thank Thee, and praise Thy glorious name.**

But who am I, and what is my people, that we should be able to offer so willingly after this sort? For all things come of Thee, and of Thine own have we given Thee.

Matthew 6:33 – **But seek ye first the kingdom of God, and His righteousness; and all these things shall be added unto you.**

Thank You, Lord Jesus, for being our Great Provider. How can we serve You better?

CHAPTER 8

Happy Days in Honey Brook

Every year that John attended Reading Special School made him feel more comfortable there and he always looked forward to September when school began again. His brothers and sisters went to Honey Brook Christian School and Louise was still a toddler so she stayed home with Mom. Louise was happy being the big helper with housework, quilting and cooking, but she was happiest when John and Mahlon came home from school to play with her. Their favorite game was crawl tag. John removed his leg and the three of them would fly around the house gleefully laughing! Around and around the table they would go. Mahlon and Louise crawling on their hands and knees while John did his roll-crawl. Then through the house they scampered again until they were weak from exhaustion. Their lingering spurts of laughter dissolved into happy gasps and sighs. John always out-crawled his brother and sister.

One of Kathy's memories is the fun that the family had

when they attended John's Christmas programs at Reading Special School. The students sang funny, silly songs and as Kathy puts it, "Gave it all they had." One year there was a beautiful Christmas tree with presents underneath it. She was allowed to choose one and she selected a package with play dough in it. Kathy was really pleased!

John was in his glory when he was able to perform with his classmates and having his family in the audience was the whipped cream on the cake! He loved singing the songs and his teachers were very thankful he was there because his voice led the group. Many handicapped children do not have the ability to match a tone so a loud, clear, sweet voice that was on perfect pitch was a blessing to the group, a gift to the teachers and a pleasure to the audience. But the happiest one in the auditorium was John – he glowed!

Thank You, Lord, for the voice You gave to John – please let him always use it to bring glory to You!

This was one of John's favorite songs:

"Love Is"

Love is
A very special thing
A smile, a tear
A soft summer rain
It has no beginning

It has no end
But I like it best when it's shared with a friend.

Love is
Never stuffed up, never puffed up,
never gives up when the going's rough
It's the biggest little word you can say by the way
It's sympathy
Sincerity
It's charity, the main variety
Of everything happiness is made of.

Love is
Never stuffed up, never puffed up,
never gives up when the going's rough
It's the biggest little word you can say by the way
It's sympathy
Sincerity
It's charity, the main variety
Of everything happiness is made of
And I like it best when it's shared with a friend. [10]

(See the Endnotes on page 194 for stories that John learned while they lived in Honey Brook.)

Outdoor fun!

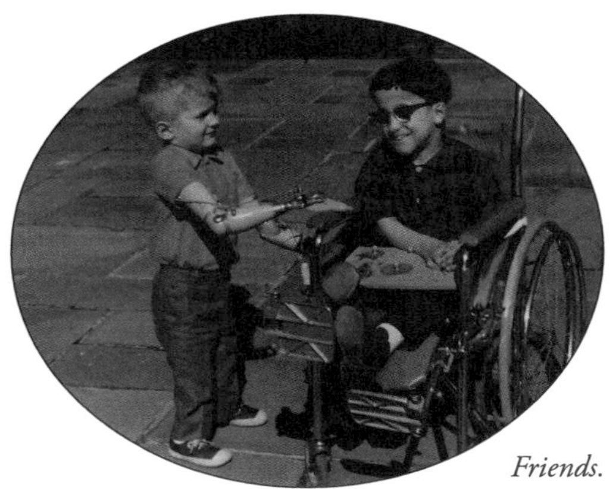

Friends.

John at age nine enjoying the fresh air and sunshine.

John 10 years old, Mahlon 3 years, and Louise 8 months old.

John with Nanny – his pet goat.

Sam, Mahlon (with Toots), Louise and John

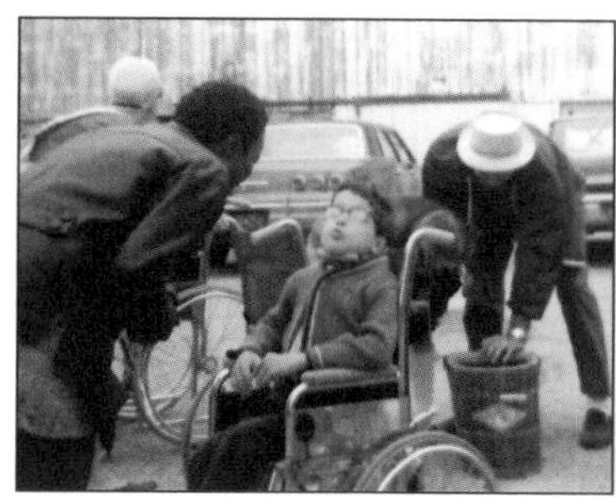

Reading Special School picnic and hayride at Honey Brook Farm, with hand-churned ice cream for all.

HAPPY DAYS IN HONEY BROOK

John on his three wheeler.

Hard to catch.

CHAPTER 9

"Johnisms"

Have you ever thought much about "isms"? There are many! Patriotism, heroism, favoritism, nationalism and realism are only a few; but the Aaron Stoltzfus family has one of their very own. They affectionately refer to some of the characteristic things that John does as "John-isms." When they are together you can hear them roar with laughter as they recall his "isms."

Many toddler age children find comfort in twisting their hair with their finger. They find a way to do it unobtrusively and people don't take much notice of it. John, however, went at it in such a vigorous way that it was hard to keep it from becoming the center of attention – the main attraction. On Sundays when the family went to church, Aaron pulled John in his wheelchair backward up the steps and then they sat in the back pew with John sitting in his wheelchair in the aisle beside Susie who sat in the first space in the pew. When the service began and everyone settled in to worship, pray, sing and hear the Word of God – John's hand would fly to the top of his head. Using his thumb to curl the hair – his palm and fingers would wave in the air in a rhythmic circular motion – non-stop through the entire service. He sometimes became so animated with the flailing motion you would think he was directing the whole congregation. Susie feared it would be a distraction to the other worshippers but John was content and God must have been smiling (just as Aaron and Susie do now when they reflect upon that precious memory).

When John was a little older, he spent hours lying in front of the washing machine. For some reason he found it very entertaining. (Some children had a TV and John had a washer.) The motion was fascinating and the sounds were intriguing, the rush of the water while it was filling, the splash-chug sound as it agitated and the whirring that went on while it was in the spin cycle. He liked it when the washer moved forward a little – he would brace his foot against it to hold it back. Occasionally it would get out of balance and really move forward. John did his best to keep it in its place.

One day the washer had become particularly rowdy with him and that night he had a nightmare. That monster washer was coming after him and chasing him. It was a very heart-thumping, scary dream, but not frightening enough to keep John out of the laundry room. He was back there the next day listening to the treasure of noises it made and cautiously hoping the washer would start rocking again so he could hold it back with his foot.

Thank You, Jesus, for John's brave heart.

John developed a passion for weather forecasts. Since there

was no radio or TV in the house and Aaron needed to keep one step ahead of the weather for the various plantings and harvestings that a farmer has to get done – he would quite often call for the weather report on the telephone. John memorized the phone number by listening and counting the clicks as his Dad dialed the rotary phone. One month the phone bill was over $40.00 – someone had dialed the weather report number six to eight times each day. John was in big trouble, but his love for weather forecasts helped him become an almanac. To this day he can recall major storms or distinct weather patterns for the 1970's – he recalls the day, month and year of each event. The family learned something else from the weather report experience. They never needed a phone book in their home. John could memorize phone numbers after hearing them only once. Whenever anyone wanted to make a phone call, they just asked John. He was overjoyed to come to their assistance.

Soon after that Aaron bought a fire, police and weather scanner. What a happy day that was for John. He became enthralled by the reports and through the reality of the scanners local emergency information he could climb mountains and fight fires with the best of them. He also built up a curiosity about the monitor and started squelching it and then he sat quietly beside it for a long period of time. Suddenly the family would hear a "ch ch ch ch" and then John turned the static button until it made its annoying, hair raising, squealing sound that drove the family into a near frenzy – especially Susie.

The family began to realize that they had no secrets. Whatever was discussed at the dinner table or within the family circle became public knowledge because John felt it was his duty to become the town crier. Susie tried to explain to him that families have secrets. After a long teaching session with him, as a test, she told him "Ivan and Anna are coming tonight and it is a secret." John went directly to his siblings and told them, "It's a secret that Ivan and Anna are coming." They all shook their heads, but Anna thought it was funny. She is Susie's sister who loves John very much. Anna baby sat for Aaron and Susie and was always very helpful.

John developed another habit that his family identifies as a "Johnism." He picked at the cuff of his sock until he loosened a thread and then he pulled it until the sock unraveled. He ruined many pairs of socks. Susie reinforced the cuff by stitching over the existing threads but he picked his way through the toughest reinforcement until he found the thread that unraveled the sock. That "ism" tested Susie's patience almost to the limit. Thankfully it was a short-lived habit; it only lasted about a year.

Because of John's interest in the weather, it seems quite natural that he would find thunderstorms exciting. When he heard that one was predicted for their area, he would hurry outdoors and lie on the ground to wait for the storm. When it arrived, his family would try to encourage him to come in the house, but he loved to stay on the lawn and be a part of the storm. If he was inside he bumped around in cadence with the thunder. If the storm came up during the night he would take the screen out of the bedroom window, climb up on the sill (it was an old stone house with very wide sills) and there he stayed with his head hanging out of the second story window to hear the thunder, see flashes of lightning and feel the rain on his face until the storm faded off in the distance. One year on his birthday his friendly neighbors came with a lovely, decorated cake that she had made for him. Just as they arrived there was a distant rumble of thunder, so off he went, to go up on the hill to be closer to the storm. Susie recalls, "He would not cooperate at that birthday party. He would rather go up the hill and listen to a thunderstorm! Here they came with a cake to have a party for him and he was not at the party."

John has a unique method of brushing his teeth. We should probably all take lessons from him (except for the "jerk" step) because not many of us have adhered to the proper way that we were taught. We hurry and take shortcuts by quickly running the toothbrush over our teeth, rinsing out the toothpaste and then off we go. Not John! He does it exactly as he was taught. Twenty-five strokes up and down on the upper left side (next is the unique part) and then "Jerrk!" – he pulls the brush out of his mouth with forceful fervor – splashing the mirror, wall and sink with a spray of foam. Then – twenty-five strokes up and down on the upper front and, you guessed it! "Jerrk" the brush is out again with a fresh coat of spray on anything in front of him… and we still have the upper right, lower left, lower front and bottom right to go. That makes six hearty jerks – oh, well, every bathroom should be cleaned after each brushing.

John had a tape recorder and enjoyed using it when the family was not aware of it. He recorded the little fights his siblings had and then played it back for them all to hear. Their reactions struck him so funny that he just howled with laughter. It became his hobby and gave him endless delight. He kept the recorder on the floor near his desk and when the family bantering became interesting he could secretly touch it and set the tape in motion. He even recorded conversations with visitors. The family was relieved when he outgrew that "ism."

"*The Budget*" is a collection of hundreds of letters written by Amish and Mennonite people about happenings in their communities. It is published weekly in newspaper form. John read it faithfully from cover to cover and almost came to know the people in many communities personally. Anywhere the family traveled John knew and recognized names of people he read about. His memory is amazing. He was so determined to read everything in "*The Budget*" that he never read the new issue until the previous ones were finished. Sometimes he would be weeks behind and was concerned that Susie might discard some of his old issues. John should be commended for his patience. His tunnel vision allows him with a telescope lens in his glasses, to only see one or two letters at a time (not the whole word). He realizes it is such a blessing that he can read. He has never seen the faces of:

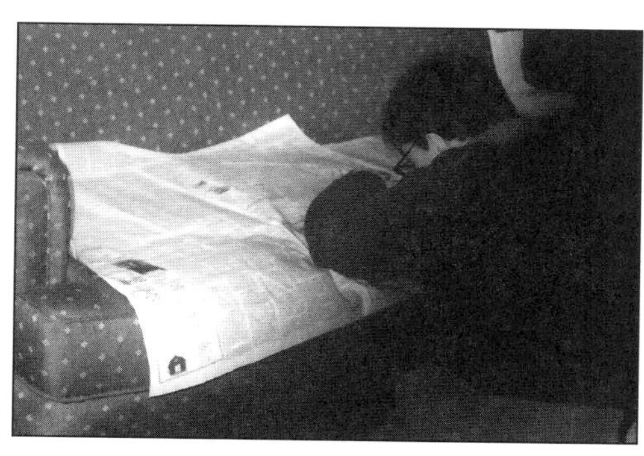

Reading "The Budget".

Aaron, Susie, Naomi, Kathy, Sam, Mahlon, Louise

or anyone else that he loves

– but still, he is thankful for what he has.

CHAPTER 10

CHANGES

John was fifteen and had been wearing the Milwaukee brace for six years when the doctors at Elizabethtown Crippled Children's Hospital said he was ready for back fusion. He was admitted to Hershey Medical Center on August 1, 1975. It took the surgeons five hours to remove one of his ribs and use it to fuse his back. Aaron went in the room to be with John as soon as he was allowed after surgery. He was not prepared for what he saw – all kinds of tubes and monitors were attached to John and he looked so pale and fragile that Aaron nearly fainted and a nurse took him out of the room. Recovery was long and very painful. It bothered Aaron and Susie to see John suffer with the pain. After a few days he was still very pale and had frequent cold sweats but he was cheery and started making new friends. Finally the healing began and they were able to fit him into his full body cast and release him three months later, on November 1, 1975. He had to be in the cast for one year.

When Aaron and Susie took him home they had a hospital bed in the living room. John had many visitors stopping in to see him and they were a wonderful help because he needed lots of entertainment. Friends and family members sat on his bed and played games with him by the hour. Fortunately he loved people and games so he never tired of their attention. It took a great deal of energy to keep him happy especially when there were no visitors and the other children were in school.

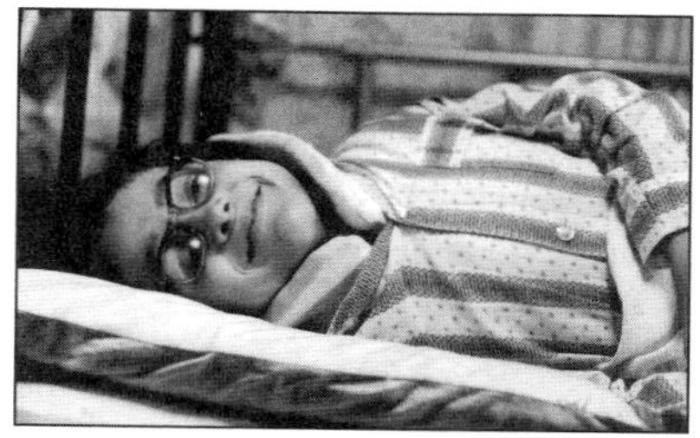

Happy to be home after back surgery.

Folding laundry – his scanner close by.

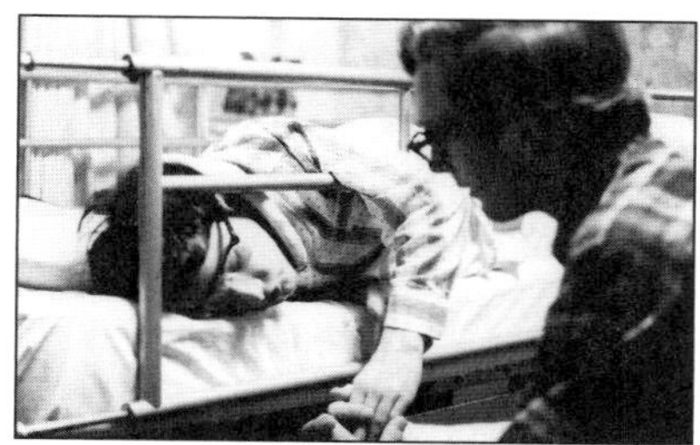

A minister friend comforts John.

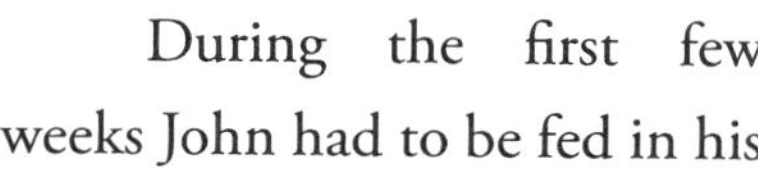

During the first few weeks John had to be fed in his bed but someone brought them a low cart with wheels called a creeper (mechanics use them to lie on and scoot under cars.) The creeper turned out to be a most useful gift. Aaron and Susie could put him on it for a change in position and it also served another purpose. By lying on it on his stomach he started eating by himself with his plate on the floor.

Of all times, John came down with chicken pox while he was in the full body cast and that was not a good experience! The insatiable desire to scratch the incessant itching sensation that was hard to cope with made keeping him occupied even more important. After he recovered from chicken pox, he frightened Susie one day by falling out of bed. In an instant everyone in the house was hovering over him. It was a great relief when they checked him over and found that he had not hurt himself. From then on they kept the sides up on his bed. He was clumsy and yet was always on the move. John was in the full body cast and needed almost constant care for one year.

Adolescence was not an easy time of life but most generally John made the best of it. After eight years at Reading Special School he was ready to go to work at Thorndale ARC. It was a well managed, sheltered workshop and they even had a van that picked John up in the morning and brought him home later in the afternoon. He adapted quickly and was happy to be working.

Things were changing at home. Naomi was driving, Kathy had her learner's permit and Sam was following close behind. All three of them were involved in activities with the youth from their church and that was hard for John, especially when Mahlon and Louise began to go. His little flock was leaving him alone in the nest where he had always been comfortable because they were snuggled against him. Change is not easy for someone who is patterned to routine.

At least the activities around home were staying pretty much the same: chores, church, time for reading, playing games, night-time prayers with his brothers in the room they shared, visits from family and friends and quite often they had dinner guests. The family had become acquainted with a couple that were as opposite as day and night. She was as sweet and caring as anyone could be and they were all very fond of her, but he was abrasive. He always expected perfection, never gave a compliment and consequently the older children felt intimidated by him. They were so accustomed to Aaron's gentleness that they were a little fearful and uncomfortable with this man (we will call him Mr. Stern). For the woman's sake Aaron and Susie wanted to befriend them. Mr. Stern had been the topic of conversation among the family members – you know, some of those "families have secrets" type conversations. Before dinner everyone was seated comfortably in the living room and John was introduced to the couple. When he heard Mr. Stern's name he bellowed, "Ah, Mr. Stern – I have heard much about you." The members of the family, knowing his penchant for truthfulness, were suddenly drawn to attention – their relaxed demeanor changed from a comfortable slouch to an erect stiffness. Sam tells us that the girls "evaporated." Kathy excused herself and ran to hide in the pantry, Naomi flew to the kitchen as if something was on fire while Sam had no excuse to leave so he sat there in agony. Aaron and Susie could hardly breathe. Mahlon and Louise were too young to comprehend the family dilemma and John just smiled – he was waiting for a reply. Mr. Stern said, "What did you hear – was it good or bad?" After a long hesitation John said, "Mostly good – I think." Everyone breathed a sigh of relief (John's response could have been so much worse!). The girls came out of hiding and the dinner went on as if nothing unusual had happened.

John had uncommon eating habits and the family became

more aware of them when they had dinner guests or when they were invited to someone else's home. He just had certain ways of doing things at the table and try as they might, the family was not able to change his routine. John ate so many bites of food and then drank so many swallows of milk. Over the years that habit changed to eating all of the food and then drinking all of his beverage at once. Many times when the family went to someone else's house they would be embarrassed because of the way John ate and then, too, he only wanted certain foods. He loved applesauce and asked the hostess, "Do you have applesauce?" Or in a very loud whisper, "Mom, is there applesauce on the table?" Or he would ask, "What's for dessert?" With most people his behavior was overlooked because it was just John, but the family was very much aware!

They would coach John on the way to the home where they were invited to have dinner. One day Kathy instructed him and said, "Now, today don't ask for applesauce!" At the table he shocked her by saying, "Kathy told me not to ask for applesauce." Was that his sly way of asking for applesauce?

Part of his manner of eating came from the routine he was taught when he was learning to eat and part came from his need to be cautious. Soft foods are still best for him and he hardly ever chews. Some of the habits he developed became irritations to the family and it was such a battle to try to correct him. If someone coughed – he laughed, if someone choked – he laughed. Oh – what could they do with this boy?... Take him home and love him!

John was sixteen when he expressed a desire for baptism. He had been listening to a great number of Christian tapes during this stage of his life and his faith was of utmost importance to him. Their ministers talked with John and agreed that he was ready. He even surprised Aaron and Susie with the insight he had in the Word. After the ministers took him through a time of instruction they gave him a questionnaire that he filled out in great detail. John was baptized by Bishop Elan Kauffman.

> Acts 2:38 – **Then Peter said unto them, Repent, and be baptized every one of you in the name of Jesus Christ for the remission of sins, and ye shall receive the gift of the Holy Ghost.**

In 1977, the whole family went to Spruce Lake. It was a retreat center in the Poconos for families with handicapped children. The children loved going because of all the recreational facilities. John enjoyed being with other handicapped children in such a positive environment and Aaron and Susie found support from the other parents. It would turn out to be an annual event for them until 1989. During their first weekend stay in 1977 the speakers were a great encouragement. Aaron and Susie discovered some of their feelings that were hidden deep inside that they never told anyone – it was so healing for them. When John was born Susie wished that God had given them a girl – if their baby was going to be handicapped Susie would have wanted a girl because it would have been so much easier for her to care for a girl. She wished with all her heart that John could see. There were a lot of things that she just thought God should have done differently but today she very readily says, "God, You did everything right and I just know that with all my heart. I'm glad he's a boy – I'm glad he can't see, if this is how You want it; if he could see he would have a lot more temptations. God, You just did everything right!"

That winter after they first went to Spruce Lake, John's kidney was not functioning properly. He developed numerous bladder and urinary tract infections which caused incontinence, discomfort and a general feeling of illness. Doctors had suggested for several years that he should have an ileoconduit done. This is an ureostomy operation to divert urine from the bladder to an opening in the abdomen. Aaron and Susie hesitated because they were not familiar with the procedure and up to this point they had been able to handle the situation. But now John was on strong medication and as the drugs took a toll on his body he became anemic and very run down. As Aaron and Susie watched his condition worsen they consented to have the surgery done at Hershey Medical Center.

The surgery went smoothly but it took five hours and during the night John started having severe pain. Two doctors came into his room and stayed during the night – they were puzzled. John hurt so much that he held on to the sides of the bed with such a strong grip that his knuckles turned white. The pain was so intense he was grinding his teeth. The doctors worked through the night and by morning they said they might have to open the incision again. They had to go through scar tissue and were afraid something was not in place. Aaron's sister, Lydia, from Morgantown, called the hospital early that morning – she said she felt restless and had to call. Aaron and Susie were so glad to hear someone's voice of concern! They told her what was taking place and Lydia said she would put a prayer request on the Pequea Church relay. She also said she would come to be with them as soon as she could get there.

There was immediate relief from John's pain! God had kept Aaron and Susie very strong through the surgery and all through the long night but they were tense. When the prayers were answered – they broke – they were filled with emotions when their relief came. And then they were thankful and extremely tired.

Dear Jesus, thank You for assisting the doctors and thank You for watching over John. We know that his pain hurt You because he is Your child and You love him. Thank You for the strength You gave to Aaron and Susie. Thank You for nudging Lydia and thank You for the prayer warriors on the relay that called upon You. In Your Word, Galatians 6:2, we are told to bear one another's burdens and by doing that we will be fulfilling the law of Christ – thank You that so many people were fulfilling Your law that day. Thank You for Your perfect timing in answering the prayers to heal John's pain. We praise You, Lord, and all the glory is Yours!

In June 1978, John moved to Plain City, Ohio to help with laundry duties at a retarded children's home called Sunny Haven. John was eighteen and this was his first real job away from home. Sunny Haven was renowned for its dedicated staff and the loving care that each child received. Some other youth from John's church were going for volunteer service – they would work for an allowance and the remainder of their pay would be given to support missions.

Aaron and Susie had come to know the administrator quite well and it was he who suggested that John go there to live and work. In October John went home for Glenn and Naomi's wedding with plans to go back. During the week he was home two of the Sunny Haven staff members were in a bad accident and they were the ones in charge of John. At this same time the administrator told Aaron and Susie that John was more handicapped than he realized and he knew it would not work out for John to go back there.

It happened more than once – people thought they could do more for him. They would judge him by his intellect and say that he was not living up to his potential but then they would try him out at the job site and realize the extent of his physical disabilities.

John went back to work at Thorndale ARC but his heart was not in it. Sunny Haven was such a disappointment to him. One night when Kathy and Sam were at a youth meeting, he was getting ready for bed and had already removed his leg. With a heavy heart he crawled out the back door and down the gravel lane. Would running away relieve the sadness?

John was too hurt in spirit to realize how he was harming his body as he struggled to crawl in the gravel on that quarter-mile long lane. Aaron heard him leave and followed at a distance feeling that it was best to let him work through his frustration. John stopped at the end of the lane and Aaron, filled with compassion, picked him up in his arms and carried his weary son back to the comfort of their home. He was badly bruised; the worst wound was on the top of his foot – all of the skin was gone.

Susie could not hold the tears back when she saw his injury, so Aaron faithfully nursed it for the next three weeks by dressing it with ointment and fresh bandages every day. Aaron and Susie both worked at mending his broken heart. John missed thirty days of work but he was completely healed by then. John was especially happy when Glenn and Naomi came to visit or when the family went to see them. They lived only fifteen miles away in Christianna. Glenn's family owned the Lapp Fruit Farm and they were known for their beautiful peaches, apples and cherries. The activities of family, home and church brought normalcy back to his life. Susie wanted to keep him at home forever so he would never have to suffer through a disappointment like Sunny Haven again.

Job 23:10 – **But He knoweth the way that I take: when He hath tried me, I shall come forth as gold.**

I Peter 1:3 – **Blessed be the God and Father of our Lord Jesus Christ, which according to His abundant mercy hath begotten us again unto a lively hope by the resurrection of Jesus Christ from the dead.**

"God can turn our
Fear into fortitude.
Courage is not absence of fear
But the mastery of it." [14]

Philippians 4:19 – **But my God shall supply all your need according to His riches in glory by Christ Jesus.**

Psalm 31:7 – **I will be glad and rejoice in Thy mercy: for Thou hast considered my trouble; Thou hast known my soul in adversities.**

I Peter 5:7 – **Casting all your care upon Him; for He careth for you.**

"Does Jesus Care?"

Does Jesus care when my heart is pained
Too deeply for mirth and song;
As the burdens press, and the cares distress,
And the way grows weary and long?

O yes, He cares – I know He cares!
His heart is touched with my grief;
When the days are weary, the long nights dreary,
I know my Savior cares. [15]

CHAPTER 11

Hidden In His Heart

Psalm 119:105 – **Thy word is a lamp unto my feet, and a light unto my path.**

Psalm 119:11 – **Thy word have I hid in mine heart, that I might not sin against Thee.**

John was thankful for all the Scripture he had memorized through the years. It strengthened him and kept him joyful. When he was fifteen he found a creed that he felt was worthy of memorization – he liked to memorize because he could always carry what he had learned in his mind and be able to reflect on it. It is good to hide uplifting things in our hearts.

The Bible Contains:

The Bible contains: the mind of God, the state of man, the way of salvation, the doom of sinners, and the happiness of believers. Its doctrines are holy, its precepts are binding, its histories are true, and its decisions are unchangeable.

> *Read it to be wise, believe it to be safe and practice it to be holy. It contains light to direct you, food to support you and comfort to cheer you. It is the traveler's map, the pilgrim's staff, the pilot's compass, the soldier's sword and the Christian's character. Here Paradise is restored, Heaven opened, and the gates of Hell disclosed. CHRIST is its Grand Subject, our good its design, and the glory of God its end. It should fill the memory, rule the heart and guide the feet. Read it slowly, frequently and prayerfully. It is a mine of wealth, a paradise of glory and a river of pleasure. It is given you in life, will be opened in the Judgment and will be remembered forever. It involves the highest responsibility, rewards the greatest labor and condemns all who trifle with its holy contents.*

> *2 Timothy 3:16* – ***All scripture is given by inspiration of God, and is profitable for doctrine, for reproof, for correction, for instruction in righteousness.*** [16]

John was also thankful for music. As his love for the Lord soared, his voice followed suit. Each week in church his heartfelt singing became louder and louder until the rafters nearly shook. At least he was singing on tune but the family began to shrink in their places as if becoming smaller would make them less noticeable. Much as they would try to teach him to soften his voice and hard as he would try – when the Spirit moved him he would "belt it out." After a few months it seemed that he was beginning to comprehend and his voice began to mellow but then someone said, "I like your singing," and he gave it all he had again… God just loved his singing!

> Psalm 100 – **Make a joyful noise unto the LORD, all ye lands. Serve the LORD with gladness: come before His presence with singing.**
>
> **Know ye that the LORD He is God: it is He that hath made us, and not we ourselves; we are His people, and the sheep of His pasture.**
>
> **Enter into His gates with thanksgiving, and into His courts with praise: be thankful unto Him, and bless His name.**
>
> **For the LORD is good; His mercy is everlasting; and His truth *endureth* to all generations.**

Much as God loved John's singing, Aaron and Susie felt that he would fit in much better here on earth if he learned more about using his voice properly – he needed to learn about blending with other voices. They found a voice teacher in New Holland. Her name was Mrs. Mumaw and Naomi usually took John to her home once a week for an hour lesson. The youth group paid for his lessons. He was a very good student and soon learned the proper techniques of breathing, singing from the diaphragm, tone quality and diction. Not long after he began taking lessons he was singing with the youth group and then he was asked to join the men's chorus. He found much pleasure in being a part of that group.

Also hidden in John's heart were the thankfulness, great love and appreciation he had for his family. He felt truly blessed that God placed him there with them. His Mom and Dad were the best in the world as far as he was concerned and his siblings seemed just made for him by God. John had special names for each of them: Naomi was "Yolm," he called Kathy "Kiffry," Sam was "Little Brother," his nickname for Mahlon was "May," and Louise was "Wezie." He also loved his Grandma Stoltzfus, Grandma and Daudy Beiler, his many aunts, uncles, cousins and especially Naomi's husband, Glenn Lapp. How happy his family made his life – how full they filled his heart!

To tell them how he felt would have been difficult but they knew by his actions how much he loved them and depended on them. John longed to tell Jesus how thankful he was for His great love but it worked out best to show his gratitude through song:

"I Love to Steal Awhile Away"

I love to steal awhile away from ev'ry cumb'ring care,
And spend the hours of setting day In humble, grateful prayer.

I love in solitude to shed The penitential tear,
And all His promises to plead, Where none but God can hear.

I love to think on mercies past, And future good implore,

And all my cares and sorrows cast On Him whom I adore.

I love by faith to take a view Of brighter scenes in heav'n,
The prospect doth my strength renew,
While here by tempests driv'n.

Thus, when life's toilsome day is o'er, May its departing ray
Be calm as this impressive hour, And lead to endless day. [17]

CHAPTER 12

Picture Postcard Days

Some events of our lives are stored away in our minds like colorful postcards. Each time one is recalled it comes to the forefront as a picture perfect memory... Every time the family went to Hawk Mountain they were blessed with that kind of day. Susie's dear sister, Anna, and her husband, Ivan, had three birth children and two adopted children. They also had a fifteen passenger van which was big enough to take both families on their short fifteen mile journey to Hawk Mountain which is located near Reading.

How they anticipated this mini-vacation each summer! To begin with – they all loved being with each other so the special events of the day were an added bonus. On the day before the outing Susie and Anna were busy in their own kitchens preparing their favorite picnic foods. The long awaited day finally came and each family eagerly hurried through chores so they could get an early start. When Ivan and Anna's van came up the lane with seven happy, smiling faces shining through the windows, the Stolzfus clan was ready and waiting. Everyone talked at once as they loaded the van with their share of the food and then they all climbed in for the joyous trip to the mountain.

After parking the van they were ready to start their annual hike to the top. All of the children loved this day and couldn't wait to begin the climb. John had the place of honor – he rode on his Dad's back and what a good time he had up there! When they reached the crest the panorama was breathtaking – the vast beautiful valley below supported another mountain and when they lifted their eyes to look across the precipice the other mountain seemed to be resting against the backdrop of blue sky beyond. From their vantage point they could watch the hawks on that other mountaintop. Some perched in treetops with their head nestled into their neck feathers as if they were napping. Some were alert and watching for prey from their roost in the top of a tree; while others were diving into the valley to pounce on a small rodent whose movement caught their eye from their watchtower above. Some were nesting and others were gathering food to fill the wide-open mouths of their young. The hawks kept the watchers almost spellbound as they flew through the air swooping and soaring. When they were gliding you could see their bodies lift in the air currents. It was as if they were weightless and as the two families watched the hawks, their hearts filled with awe and wonder at what God had created.

Aaron carrying John.

The whole effect of perfect day, worn pathways, children's laughter, rugged mountain tops, rocky ledges, magnificent trees, lush green valleys, vivid hues of green and blue with splashes of white, brown and gray, birds in flight and at rest – all these things made them grateful. And then they looked at each other – two families made by God, blessed by God and gladly living for God – sometimes the hearts just overflow!

Time evaporated on that mountaintop but after awhile their stomachs let them know it was time to climb down the hillside. Everyone helped unpack the van, set the tables, empty the coolers, set out the mouth-watering array of food, the jugs of sweetened mint tea and the homemade pies. They had much to be thankful for as they prayed before eating. Mmmm – how good everything tasted – the exercise, the fresh air and wonderful company made it extra special! They spent the afternoon playing, resting, hiking and visiting before returning home to do their evening chores.

Summer all by itself is a beautiful time in southern Pennsylvania but when you focus in on a Mennonite farm near Honey Brook in Chester County, you will frequently see a scene that warms the heart. The Stoltzfus family did not buy ice cream at the grocery store – they enjoyed making their own. They gathered together near the back porch and everyone helped with the procedure. Using the cream that had risen to the top of the milk jug, Susie and the older girls combined it with junket and other ingredients, put the mixture in the metal tube-like cylinder that housed the wooden dasher and then firmly screwed the lid on. The container was placed in the wooden ice cream bucket and they filled the space between the cylinder and bucket with chopped ice and rock salt. After the top with the gears and crank handle were attached and securely latched into place, the churning could begin. Everyone liked to take turns, but most of the churning was done by Sam and Mahlon. When the ice cream began to get firm, the churning became more difficult so Aaron took over to finish the process – it needed his strong arm to blend it to a nice firm consistency.

John observed from his favorite location on summer days. They had a lounge chair which could be flattened out to make a cot – right there in the yard near the back door. From his cot, John took part in the ice cream making with his usual gusto – calling to see if it was done and loudly laughing at the antics of his siblings. His presence always added zest to any family event because of his spontaneity and good nature.

It was hard to define which was the best part of ice cream making – the procedure or the eating. Perhaps the accompanying sounds helped give an indication of preference. The voices seemed quite normal during the preparation but the volume began to get louder when the family (and sometimes their friends) joined together to watch Aaron make those last turns on the churn. It was then the noise level reached its peak, as everyone anticipated the time of completion. Gradually the voices softened as the crank handle and top were removed, the container was lifted from the ice and the lid was unscrewed. Aaron slowly lifted the dasher out while Susie used a spatula to scrape the ice cream from the paddles back into the container. The chatter increased while bowls were being filled, spoons were set in them and they were passed out to everyone. Suddenly all was quiet – the smooth and creamy confection was being savored. Satisfied murmurs rippled from the group when they took their first tastes. Quiet took over again until spoons started scraping the bottoms of the bowls to retrieve every last delicious drop. After a few lip smacks of approval the conversation and activity resumed to normal. Is there anything better than ending a hot summer day with a soothing bowl of hand-churned ice cream and a little time to relax with family and friends?

Another memory maker – a nostalgic picture comes to mind. During harvest time Aaron was so busy that he had little time to be with the family. His days were long and every hour was filled with hard work. Susie liked to think of creative and enjoyable things to do with the children while their Dad was so occupied with the farm. They loved it when she piled them all in the car and drove to the next ridge beyond Honey Brook where nature went wild with all sorts of treasures. Susie parked the car off the road and found a place where John could safely stay on the hill side of the car. Then she and the other children walked up the hill gathering baskets of small wonders that grew close to the ground. With each find they would call to John to keep him informed. They collected tea berries, moss, mushrooms, crowsfoot, ferns and many other small clumps of vegetation.

This time *they* were the picture – a beautiful Mennonite mother and her children dressed in their proper attire – some bent low investigating what lay beneath the tall grass, one sitting and searching, another dancing on to a better spot and all of them thoroughly enjoying their great adventure. John on his crutches and the rest a short distance from him dotting the green hillside were all within the framework of that perfect picture. God was with them – God made the picture!

Susie and the children could not wait to take their treasures home and show Aaron. Every little sprig would be used to make winter gardens. They all enjoyed making the lovely green arrangements in a variety of glass jars and little fish bowls that Susie had found at garage sales. Each jar was topped with plastic wrap to hold the moisture in and keep the gardens alive all through the winter. Susie was able to sell twenty-five to thirty of them each year. She also made pine cone wreaths to sell before the holidays and her little troop of helpers loved to search for them. Wherever they saw a group of evergreen trees they wanted to stop and hunt for pine cones. It can become a fever – the more you find – the more you want to seek. It's the same way with Jesus – when we seek Him, we will find Him, but once we find Him – the more we want to seek Him.

Deuteronomy 4:29 – **But if from thence thou shalt seek the LORD thy God, thou shalt find Him, if**

thou seek Him with all thy heart and with all thy soul.

Jeremiah 29:13 – **And ye shall seek Me, and find Me, when ye shall search for Me with all your heart.**

Matthew 7:7, 8 – *(These are the words of Jesus)* **Ask, and it shall be given you; seek, and ye shall find; knock, and it shall be opened unto you: for every one that asketh receiveth; <u>and he that seeketh findeth</u>; and to him that knocketh it shall be opened.**

CHAPTER 13

JOURNEY TO A NEW LAND

In 1980 John had grown to his full size. He was 4'2" tall and weighed 76 pounds. He was twenty years old and had to be fitted for his third prosthesis. He was excited because he would be spending time with his friend, Dr. Jack Smith, again. Their reunion was grand! When old friends meet – even after a ten year separation – it seems as if they were together yesterday.

In John's mind no one could make a new leg for him as well as Dr. Jack Smith. The doctor first put plaster-of-paris on the stump in order for him to have a perfect mold when he made the leg. John's former leg was made of solid wood with metal rods inside which made it very heavy. His new leg would be much lighter because more refined materials would be combined with the wooden exterior. It took skill and diligence to make it, shape it and fit it into place. The fine-tuning had to be accurate so there would be no rubbing or discomfort in the hip socket, and then the leg had to be made smooth and polished to a soft finish.

These processes took three days and John hardly realized how meticulously the doctor was working because it seemed that all of his attention was given to his conversation with John. They challenged each other with Scripture and learned more verses. John left Dr. Jack Smith's office after the three days had passed with a sturdy new leg and a strong awareness of how lasting and valuable a true friendship is. He hoped he would see Dr. Jack Smith again before they met in heaven.

A few years earlier the Pequea Mennonite Church had reached its membership capacity and they were ready for outreach into other areas. Four families moved to the Finger Lakes Region of New York State. They settled near Dundee, NY and found the area conducive to dairy farming, fruit or vegetable production and small business. They met in each others homes for their church services and by 1980 they were ready for a church building. From the beginning, Pequea joined them in their prayerful efforts to plant this new church and now they felt the Lord's leading for the final steps in the process. More families from Pequea would be needed. Aaron and Susie's minister discussed the needs with his congregation one Sunday but he did not make a request for any families to move north. The following Sunday Aaron and Susie were away, but Kathy and Sam went to church and their minister talked about it in greater detail. He explained that in order to establish a church in the Dundee area more families would have to move up and an ordained minister would be needed. He was not trying to persuade people – he just laid it on their hearts for prayer.

Kathy and Sam were very moved by his words during the church service. When their parents came home that afternoon, Sam met them first and told them that he felt the Lord wanted them to move. Kathy was in her bedroom when they arrived but as soon as she saw them she said the same thing. This was difficult for her because her boyfriend was there in Lancaster County, but she still thought the Lord wanted them to move to New York State and they must do what the Lord wanted. Aaron and Susie had never seen them so strongly convicted – they began to pray about it and soon they felt it was time to make a trip north to see the land they were being drawn to.

They looked at a few farms but only one seemed just right. It was located closer to Penn Yan, NY than Dundee, but those two towns are only eleven miles apart. The children were impressed by its seclusion and they laughingly said the area was uncivilized. It was quite a contrast to the hustle and bustle of the Lancaster County area. They had watched as progress filled in the places surrounding the Amish and Mennonite farms that had been there for so many decades. Fertile farm land was being swallowed up by suburban sprawl and large attractions had been built to satisfy the ever-growing tourist industry.

In 1981 Aaron and Susie sold their farm in Honey Brook – a place with many memories but they were not attached to material things. They were ready to follow the Lord's leading to a new venture in their lives. The only twinge of remorse in their hearts was leaving their six-month-old granddaughter, Crystal, Naomi and Glenn's first baby.

After much preparation and hard work, the caravan was on its way. Aaron drove the pickup truck and Sam and Mahlon rode with him. Susie had John, Kathy and Louise with her in the car and following them were the truck with the household furnishings and the cattle trucks with the whole herd of cows. Last, but certainly not least, were carloads of friends from the Pequea Church who were helping them move. Timing was important because they could not load the cows until the morning milking was completed and after a six hour trip they had to be in place in their new barn before evening milking.

Everyone had a job to do and they were pleased to see that some of the families who had already moved north were there at the new farm to help them move in when they arrived. While the men cleaned the barn, prepared it for the cows and unloaded them from the trucks – the women cleaned the house. Beds were set up and kitchen equipment was put in place or unpacked to be ready for breakfast preparation the following morning. Some of the former Pequea ladies had prepared dinner for the moving crew that first night. Many hands made the work lighter and by bedtime the friends were gone but the furniture was in place, rugs were unrolled, beds were made, boxes had been unpacked and the kitchen was ready for action. The barn chores were done and the cows were bedded down on clean straw – none the worse for wear. The family was tired and weary as they had evening prayers and bid each other good night but they were content to be in their new surroundings. Rest was sweet that night – the Lord covered the Aaron Stoltzfus family with His peace.

Philippians 4:7 – **And the peace of God, which passeth all understanding, shall keep your hearts and minds through Christ Jesus.**

Morning comes early for a farmer and his family but that first morning was special. The spring nights were cooler and the morning dew seemed heavier than in Honey Brook. Consequently sleep had been more restful and the morning air was more refreshing. It was cleansing just taking a deep breath and filling the lungs with the crisp, clean air. The moon was still bright in a sky that seemed larger to them and it softly lit the back step and walkway to the driveway that led to the barn. Inside, the barn was warm from the body heat of the cows who were happy to see Aaron, Sam and Mahlon come to milk, feed and clean them.

The large frame house was coming alive also. Susie, John, Kathy and Louise were up and ready for a busy yet exciting day. It was fun to explore their new home and try to get some semblance of order established. Their first thoughts were concentrated on the kitchen in order to serve breakfast to the hungry family when chores were done. Midway through the preparation, Susie glanced out the window that had been cloaked with darkness only a few minutes before and saw the dawn breaking. She and the children went outside to capture the moment. The birds were chirping their early morning calls to one another – announcing the birth of a new day and in the freshness and chill of that new day Susie took time to feast her eyes on the world around her. Across the road from the house and barn were the flat fields – ready to be plowed, dragged and planted. Their farm was on one of the rolling hills between Seneca Lake and Keuka Lake, but the hill their farm was on was broad and flat for miles across its top. This plateau was ideal for a productive farm and the view was spectacular. In the distance you could see the tops of other hills and as the sun broke over the horizon the sky above them was blue as could be. Looking east toward Seneca Lake, which was a mile and a half away, a long ridge of white puffy fog was still resting in the valley over the lake. The people in their lake-side cottages probably did not even realize it was a glorious day! (But then most likely the majority of them were still sleeping and only a few dedicated fishermen were in their boats on the fog-laden lake.) Susie and the children scurried back to the kitchen to put the meal on the table – they would have a lifetime to "oo and ah" over the beauty of their hilltop farm.

Aaron, Sam and Mahlon were full of smiles when they came in to wash up for breakfast. The food smelled good, the kitchen was inviting and the barn was going to work out just fine. When they sat down at the table they all held hands while Aaron prayed. The Stoltzfus family was thankful that the Lord had brought them to this place. They would do their best to serve Him as they began this new phase of the journey through their lives.

Penn Yan, New York farm.

CHAPTER 14

A New Way of Life

Kathy need not have been concerned about leaving her boyfriend when they left Honey Brook – absence just made the hearts grow fonder! Kathy and John Beiler kept their friendship going through letters and because Glenn, Naomi and Crystal were still in Christianna, the family had to make frequent trips to Lancaster and Chester Counties. John Beiler made sure he saw Kathy when she went south to visit her sister!

John Beiler lived twenty miles from Honey Brook. He and Kathy had met at the Weavertown Mennonite Church where John and his family were members. In 1982 they were married at the newly formed Crystal Valley Mennonite Church in Dundee, NY. It was a joyous day for everyone. John and Kathy Beiler began their married life together in Lancaster County and are still living there with their two sons. The roads are well-traveled between Lancaster County, PA and Yates County, NY.

Next to leave the flock was Sam. Through a Mennonite

Church outreach program he went to South Carolina to serve with another twenty-year-old at a facility for delinquent boys. Sam and the other young man held the title of "Chief" – (Does that mean the boys were called "wild Indians?" …Of course not!) It was difficult work but very rewarding when they saw improvement in one of their boys. Over the two-year period that Sam was there he learned a great deal. His compassionate heart and patience helped him have understanding and the boys responded to him. Sam grew ever more thankful for his own family and the upbringing he had.

One of the prerequisites of moving to Penn Yan had been to find a good work place for John. He had been very happy at Thorndale and they felt assured that an ARC in Penn Yan would just be a continuation of the type work John was used to. But soon after they arrived at the farm they learned that the establishment was new and consequently was not yet in full operation. Penn Yan ARC was not ready for John to work there.

The adjustments of no work plus Kathy and Sam leaving home were difficult. John grew bored. He needed to work. He began to think about independent living – if he lived in his own place he could go home to eat. These were natural thoughts for a young man his age, but he needed help with his physical needs – he could not manage alone.

Aaron and Susie were concerned and began checking on places for handicapped people to work. The most highly recommended was Pioneer Center in Syracuse, NY. They went there to talk with the owner, Mrs. Pike, and were very pleased. She was a fine Christian woman and they were impressed with the facility. Arrangements were made for John to live in a group home and work at Pioneer Center. The workplace was perfect for his needs but he was not happy in the group home so Aaron and Susie moved him to an apartment with one other handicapped young man and a caregiver.

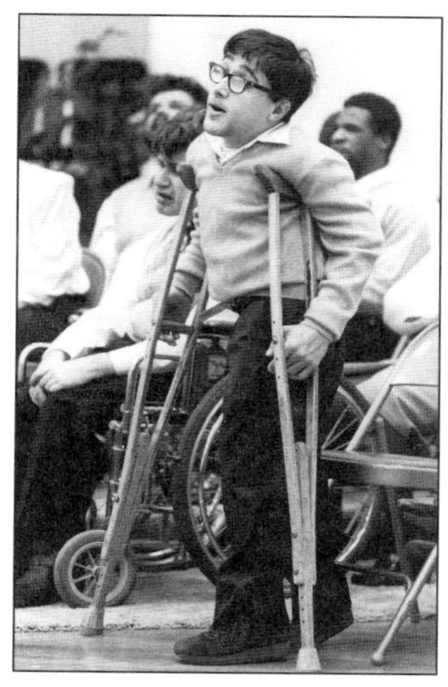

John with fellow workers in Syracuse. He was always ready with the correct answer.

John was pleased to have his first taste of independent living! He would be able to work Monday through Friday and then on Friday afternoon, go by Greyhound bus to Geneva, NY where his Mom or Dad would pick him up and take him home for the weekend. During the week his caregiver taught him how to make out grocery lists, exchange money and do his own shopping. He learned how to use public transportation services and became familiar with the routes he had to take.

Most generally John did very well – he enjoyed learning to be more independent but he did have a few memorable experiences. When John was born his left side was badly damaged and that meant that the left side of his brain was affected as well. The left side of the brain controls our ability to reason – it gives us analytical strengths – whereas the right side of the brain is the more creative side. Artists and musicians generally are more strongly led by the right side of their brain. This was John's case – bright as he was, he did not have very good reasoning sense. Any of us can have a more dominant side – you can check yourself by clasping your hands together by alternating the fingers – if your left thumb is on top you are analytical and if your right thumb is on top – creativity gives you pleasure.

Making out his own grocery list sounded like fun to John. One of his favorite snack foods was prunes so he went to the grocery store and bought a box of prunes. He took the box home and in one savory sitting ate the whole boxful! A few hours later he learned why his Mom had always limited the amount of prunes that he ate. He had counted every delicious, moist, succulent prune in that box as he ate them – there were fifty-three… fifty more than he needed to eat.

John loved to listen to a local radio station. One afternoon they had a contest that required the listener to come into the station if he could identify a song. John heard the clue and knew the melody at once so he hired a taxi to take him to the station where he went in and proudly gave the answer. The disc jockey praised him and gave him the prize, but the taxi driver stood nearby and asked John for the cab fare before the driver would take him home. In his excitement to respond to the contest John had forgotten he would need money to pay the taxi driver. Consequently the riled driver refused to take him home – but a kindly worker at the radio station gave him a ride back home. John carried on an exuberant conversation and was gracious as he expressed his appreciation when they reached his apartment. The kind man sat there in his car and watched his new small, blind friend as he deftly used his crutches to swing his body up the sidewalk.

"Where does his joy come from?
Must be that young man is a Christian!"

Friday afternoons were exhilarating for John. His work-week was over and he was on his way home to be with the family he loved. One Friday he arrived at the Syracuse bus station early and sat down to wait for his departure bus to Geneva to be announced. Before he realized what was happening he was being mugged. A man grabbed him and removed his wristwatch. This is one time John's strong lungs came to the rescue. Immediately he screamed, "Security Guard!" and one ran forward, apprehended the would-be robber and returned John's watch to him. It was over very quickly – thanks to John's quick thinking, his God-given loud voice and the attentive security guard who was standing close by. This is a memory that John would like to forget but it does let us see his ability to respond instantaneously to danger. Sometimes we are the victims of the bad choices other humans make but God was with John to protect him, strengthen him and give him wisdom. We are thankful the Lord kept John safe and uninjured – the experience could have been much worse. John was happy to get home that weekend.

CHAPTER 15

QUILT ROOM

Soon after John moved to Syracuse and Susie was left with only Mahlon and Louise at home, she found herself with more time to pursue one of the great creative loves of her life. She learned to quilt when she was nine years old and always found comfort while sitting at the quilt frame. Some women love to quilt but their stitches are big and uneven. Susie had a natural talent – once the needle was threaded and that thimble was on her finger the needle would fly. Pricking through the three layers and touching her left finger underneath she then picked up a few small stitches on her needle and pulled the thread through – then her needle went back on the quilt top just a stitch width from her last to weave her needle up and down to gather another needle load and pull it through. It seemed so effortless. If she had any frustrations they melted as the stitches flowed to fashion the beautiful quilting design. Some of her most sincere prayers came while she sat there – the calming effect that quilting gave her made her more open to His presence.

Before they left Honey Brook, Susie started quilting for other people. During that time she heard about Arlene Lee – a quilter and quilt shop owner from Rushville, NY and Susie called her. They became very close friends – in fact Susie refers to Arlene as her sister. Within a year after Susie moved to Penn Yan, Arlene wanted her to open a shop but Susie was not interested. She took eight quilts to Arlene's shop to let her sell them.. People soon started going to Susie's home to order quilts. It was then that Susie decided to open a room upstairs in the farmhouse.

John with one of Susie's quilts.

She named her shop "The Quilt Room" and had no regular hours. It did not matter if she and Louise were baking cookies or canning peaches – they just went on doing the things they were used to doing. When customers arrived Susie left her kitchen work and took them up the open staircase, through the hall and into the large front bedroom that she had transformed into "The Quilt Room." The main focal point was the bed – spread high with layer upon layer of lovely quilts. To show them, Susie and

Louise or the customer would stand on either side at the head of the bed. Together they folded the top quilt down to the foot of the bed – uncovering yet another beauty. Her variety of patterns and colors was exciting – the customer could choose between exquisite appliquéd or charming patchwork quilts. The room also had a table of patchwork gift items, pot-holders and pillows. A chair in the corner was stacked with wall-hangings.

Shortly after The Quilt Room opened, a woman from Long Island called Susie. She owned a shop and wanted to come look at Susie's quilts. She flew from Long Island to Elmira, NY (the Chemung County Airport) where Susie met her and took her back to the farm near Penn Yan. Susie was just a little distraught when the woman started removing quilts from the bed one by one. It was not unusual for anyone to buy one or two but this woman bought twelve quilts. "Too many!" thought Susie. Instead of being excited about the sale – Susie was concerned because her supply had been so drastically depleted.

Susie's business grew by leaps and bounds. She had thirty women who quilted for her in their own homes and kept two quilt frames up in the very large living room at the farm. Women loved to go there to have tea or coffee, which Susie served at her dining room table – if it was baking day they received an added treat. Refreshed, they could make the climb up the stairs to go into the cozy Quilt Room.

Susie is such a gentle, humble woman and would not want it to be said, but she became very famous – not only throughout the

Finger Lakes Region but also women started arriving from Canada, New England and many other places. She was frequently asked to demonstrate or teach quilting. Her stitches were small and uniform – she definitely had a gift for perfection. But she would scoff at those praises because she knew that if she had a gift – it came from the Lord!

CHAPTER 16

A Mystery Solved

<u>*The Plan of the Master Weaver*</u>

Our lives are but fine weavings, that God and we prepare
Each life becomes a fabric planned
And fashioned in His care.
We may not always see just how
The weavings intertwine,
But we must trust the Master's hand
And follow His design
For He can view the pattern
Upon the upper side
While we must look from underneath
And trust in Him to guide.
Sometimes a strand of sorrow
Is added to His plan
And though it's difficult for us
We still must understand
That it's He who fills the shuttle

It's He who knows what's best
So we must weave in patience
And leave to Him the rest.
Not till the loom is silent
And the shuttles cease to fly
Shall God unroll the canvas
And explain the reason why
The dark threads are as needed
In the Weaver's skillful hand
As the threads of gold and silver
In the pattern He has planned. [18]

John had been in Syracuse for two years when he had to be admitted to Upstate University Hospital for surgery to have a hernia repaired. Out of the blue the answer to the questions Susie held in her heart for twenty-four years came. Since Upstate is a teaching hospital, many interns walk around with the resident doctors discussing the case of each patient. They dig deeply into past history as well as symptoms, diagnoses and proper treatment.

When one of the resident doctors examined John he knew at once what had happened. He met with Aaron and Susie and told them it was his belief that John had been exposed to radiation. It was as if John's left side had melted together and the doctor felt that his conclusion was the only explanation. Other doctors concurred and began to ask questions about where they had lived in Morgantown and then they investigated what was going on in that area in 1960. They discovered that the government had briefly done some secret experimental testing with radiation in a stone quarry on property that was adjacent to the Stoltzfus farm in Morgantown.

The Stoltzfus farm with the stone quarry in the distance.

What a relief for Aaron and Susie to <u>know</u> – even John had questioned his Mom throughout the years. At one time he read that drinking coffee while pregnant, in rare cases, could cause deformity in the baby. He had asked Susie, "Did you drink coffee before I was born?" She was glad to tell him that she had not. Other members of the family had been perplexed but now it was gratifying to have an answer. A legal group wanted Aaron and Susie to sue but even their questions opened wounds in Susie's heart. Aaron and Susie could have easily followed through, but they did not want to sue – they were satisfied just knowing the mystery had been solved at last. Joseph of Bible times forgave his brothers for betraying him and said, "God intended it for good." Aaron and Susie strongly believed that God intended John's life for good.

CHAPTER 17

God's Plan

Crop rotation and gardening have always been second nature to Aaron and Susie – their livelihood depended on their ability to be good stewards of the land. But when we compare the small cycle of fields of grain, vegetable gardens and flowerbeds with the magnificent cycle of a human life we begin to feel humbled. We cannot help but think about the lives of our children and God's plan for them.

So many of the processes a gardener goes through from planning, preparation, planting, cultivating, weeding, mulching, nurturing, guarding against predators, to harvesting remind us of the processes a parent goes through. Both a plant and a child can survive with little care, but weeds and disease will choke it and cause the harvest to be meager or non-existent. Constant love, care, feeding and pruning will reward the gardener and the parent with a beautiful, healthy, strong and flourishing specimen that produces a gratifying harvest!

And then we start thinking about the Master Gardener and our hearts begin to overflow with thankfulness.

Psalm 33:11 – **The counsel of the LORD standeth for ever, the thoughts of His heart to all generations.**

Isaiah 40: 8 – **The grass withereth, the flower fadeth: but the word of our God shall stand forever.**

Isaiah 64:8 – **But now, O LORD, Thou art our Father; we are the clay, and Thou our Potter; and we all are the work of Thy hand.**

Romans 1:20 – **For since the creation of the world His invisible attributes, His eternal power and divine nature, have been clearly seen, being understood through what has been made, so that they are without excuse.** (NASB)

Hebrews 11: 3 – **Through faith we understand that the worlds were framed by the word of God.**

Matthew 25:34 – (These are the words of Jesus) **Come, ye blessed of my Father, inherit the kingdom prepared for you from the foundation of the world.**

God is so wonderful! He created heaven and earth – all things! He put every star in place and knows them all by name (Isa. 40:26). He made man in His image. He knew us before we were born. He has counted every hair on our head. He made the perfect plan for each of our lives. He calls us and loves us so much that His greatest pleasure comes when we decide to put our hand in His and follow His leading by asking His Son, Jesus, to come into our heart.

He wants us to read His Book of instruction so we can learn exactly how He wants us to live. Oh yes – we can survive and still be assured that He will keep us and love us – but life can be so much richer if we allow Him to prepare, plant, cultivate, weed, mulch, nurture and protect us through the instruction in His Pattern Book – the Bible!

Let us think about creation for a minute. God the Father is the Maker! He used authority as He commanded each event to take place. "Let there be light! – Let there be a firmament! – Let the waters under heaven be gathered together and let dry land appear! – Let the earth bring forth grass and herbs and fruit trees and the seeds thereof!" And He kept saying "Let there be" until everything was completely ready and made perfect. – Then He was ready to make and to place man in the rich, lush garden that He had prepared for him.

As we read these verses in Genesis we can sense a change – the business-like voice of authority softens. He did not say, "Let there be man!" – it is as if He counseled and concurred with Jesus and the Holy Spirit (after all – They are the Three in One) and then with great affection said: "Let Us make man in Our image. After Our likeness" and He did!

He made us able to give and receive love in relationships with each other and with Him. He created us in His perfect love and thus it was --- until Adam and Eve disobeyed God. Because of their disobedience, sin came into the world and the image of God was all but destroyed in mankind.

But God is love. He sent His Son! Our model and our pattern. In Christ, love is restored. Though we are unworthy, Christ's sacrifice lights the tiny flame of love in our hearts and makes it burn strongly. As the flame of Christ's love ignites each of us – those around us will catch the fire. We must let God fill our heart with His love and as He does – let it flow through us to those around us.

It was good of God to come up with the plan of four seasons. We grow tired of winter and hunger for warmer weather and He provides us with spring – a beautiful time for new beginnings. Everything seems fresher and lighter and brighter. We love to hear the birds singing and smell the flowers as they push their way out of the ground and reach for the sunlight. The spring rain washes everything clean – just as Jesus has washed us clean. God's plan is so perfect! He has provided us with a Savior. If we know Him and confess our sins to Him we can let go of the past and look forward to the future with excitement and joy because Jesus provides forgiveness and hope!

> 2 Corinthians 5:17 – **Therefore if any man be in Christ, he is a new creature: old things are passed away; behold, all things are become new.**

Philippians 3:13 – F**orgetting what lies behind and reaching forward to what lies ahead.** (NASB)

Because of God's faithfulness and His perfect provision for our forgiveness, we can step into the new season leaving our dark and gloomy shortcomings behind and start with a bright and shiny new beginning.

Ephesians 4:29-30 speaks to us about a dark and gloomy thing we should get rid of:

Let no unwholesome word proceed from your mouth, but only such a word as is good for edification according to the need of the moment, so that it will give grace to those who hear. Do not grieve the Holy Spirit of God, by whom you were sealed for the day of redemption. (NASB)

It hurts to think that our unkind words would cause the Holy Spirit to grieve! When we realize that – we know we need a shiny new beginning.

New beginnings can happen in all aspects of our lives. First and of utmost importance is a new and personal relationship with the One who made us. He loves us and looks on us as His precious children, He finds great pleasure when we lift our faces toward Him and in turn He blesses us.

2 Corinthians 2:14, 15 – **But thanks be to God, who**

always leads us in triumph in Christ, and manifests through us the sweet aroma of the knowledge of Him in every place. For we are a fragrance of Christ to God among those who are being saved and among those who are perishing. (NASB)

God always leads us in triumph in Christ! Life has its adversities – we all have them – but when we remember that "when we are weak – He is strong" and "His power is perfected in our weakness," and when we come to the full realization that unless He takes over – we will never make it (we must empty ourselves to be filled with Him) – then He will lead us in triumph! Our joyful uplifted hearts will give off a sweet aroma of the knowledge of Him in every place!

Can you think of a grander privilege than to be a flower in the Master Gardener's garden and to bring a smile to His face by being a fragrance of Christ? Whenever you see a flower let it be a reminder for you to lift up the fragrance of Christ in you for Him to enjoy. What a sweet way to give thanks!

If we follow God's plan for our life and allow Him to love, care, feed, prune and protect us – we will be a part of His bountiful harvest. By living for Christ we can be good gardeners for God as we serve and help others to grow and blossom. Our purpose for living is to know Jesus and make Him known.

When we stay within the framework of the plan that God made for our lives and have a humble openness to Jesus, then He has the freedom to work through our lives. We have a high calling – to live to glorify Christ. We can open the hearts of others by glorifying Him in everything we do.

CHAPTER 18

Back Home to Stay

Early Sunday morning while John was in Upstate University Hospital for his hernia surgery, he talked with Aaron and Susie on the telephone. They had visited him on Saturday and planned to make the trip from Penn Yan back to Syracuse again after they attended church that morning. When they heard the discouragement in his voice they immediately left to be with him. John told them that he felt as if there was a great gulf between God and him. Aaron and Susie were subdued and prayerful on their trip – when your child hurts – you hurt.

John felt comforted to have them arrive in his hospital room, but it tugged on his Dad's and Mom's hearts to see him there in his hospital bed looking so distressed. The lifestyle change was wearing him down. Very few of the people in his life were Christians. His whole existence seemed to have a very cold setting both at his apartment with an uncaring caregiver and at the work place. Mrs. Pike was the only ray of sunshine but he did not see her very often. Some of the people he worked with were loud and belligerent.

Their negative comments and crude behavior were very upsetting to John. Because he had time to think about these things while he was alone in the hospital, his heart seemed heavier than when he was actually dealing with the situation. The best way he could describe his feelings was to make the word picture of a great gulf between God and him.

Aaron had a long talk with John – explaining that God was always near – He would never leave him or forsake him! Aaron's wise and loving words encouraged John and made him realize how much Jesus wanted John to seek Him. It was good that John could pray with his Mom and Dad. Their loving presence brought him back to the loving arms of God where he felt safe and secure. John rededicated his life to Christ and the heavy cloud that hung over him was blown away!

> 1 Peter 1:3-8 – **Blessed be the God and Father of our Lord Jesus Christ, which according to His abundant mercy hath begotten us <u>again</u> unto a lively hope by the resurrection of Jesus Christ from the dead, to an inheritance incorruptible, and undefiled, and that fadeth not away, reserved in heaven for you, who are kept by the power of God through faith unto salvation ready to be revealed in the last time. Wherein ye greatly rejoice, though now for a season, if need be, ye are in heaviness through manifold temptations: that the trial of your faith, being much more precious than of gold that perisheth, though it be tried with fire, might be found unto praise and**

honour and glory at the appearing of Jesus Christ: Whom having not seen, ye love; in Whom, though now ye see Him not, yet believing, ye rejoice with joy unspeakable and full of glory.

In 1985 Mahlon was eighteen. After graduating from Faith Mennonite School in Lancaster he attended Calvary Bible School in Arkansas for a three-week course. While he was there he met a sweet girl and her name was Anna Stoltzfus. (She was born in Lancaster County but when she was three years old her parents had moved to Blackville, South Carolina.) A year later Mahlon went south again to be a "chief" at the same home for delinquent boys where Sam had worked.

Speaking of Sam – he had found a special young woman right there in his home church in Dundee. Her name was Ruth Stoltzfus and when they decided to get married everyone was happy. John and she were already friends so he gave Little Brother Sam his voice of approval. Their wedding was a blessed occasion at the Crystal Valley Mennonite Church. They lived in a home up the road and around the corner from the farm and Sam worked on the farm for Aaron.

Progress had been made in the development of the Penn Yan ARC called Keuka Lake Enterprises and by 1987 they were in full operation and ready to have John work there. We can imagine how elated John was! In no time he was bidding goodbye to the friends he had made in Syracuse and saying hello to his family and friends back at the farm and in his church. That five year stay in Syracuse had been a great learning experience for John but he was very thankful to be home. He decided then that it was best for him to live with his family. He would not be interested in a group home or independent living again even though many people would suggest it from time to time throughout his life. The best caregiver was his Mom – she was not glum and disagreeable – she embodied the word caregiver by caring gladly for him and giving of her heart – besides, she was an excellent cook!

Working in Penn Yan was an easy transition. A bus picked him up at the end of the driveway and brought him home. He had another opportunity to get acquainted with the bus drivers. The workplace was clean and comfortable and he liked his coworkers. John spent his day folding newsletters, labeling, counting or doing any other job they needed done.

Louise was seventeen when John came home from Syracuse and they were both happy to be together again. They had their own special way of communicating – they call it "whistle talk." It is not a very easy thing to do – they form the word through the whistle sound. They could get lost in their own little world while they practiced and accomplished this mode of conversing. Amazingly they understood each other. They still "whistle talk" when they are together.

John had a parakeet named Polly and that little bird just loved him. Polly was especially excited when John was lying on the living room floor because then she could fly to him and walk all over him. If John was lying on his chest with his face close to the floor he would say, "Look into my mirror, mirror, mirror," and the little bird would go to John's glasses and peck on the lens. Then John turned over on his back and said, "Whisper in my ear, whisper, whisper, whisper." Polly went to his ear and made a soft whisper-like sound. After they tired of the play John lay there quietly and Polly flew up on his chest or snuggled in his neck and fell asleep.

Over the years John has had two little Chihuahuas and he grew very attached to both of them. Toots was wonderful company for John and his brothers and sisters while they lived in Honey Brook. More recently Aaron and Susie bought another puppy for John. He named it Snooky. The two became so inseparable and were such good companions that the little dog was pouty and dejected while John was at work. He came to life when he heard the bus bring John home. Snooky wanted to make sure John did not leave at night so he slept with John – right on his chest as if to keep him held down.

Toots.

Aaron and Susie's family was growing smaller while Sam and Ruth's was promising to grow larger, so in 1988 they traded homes. Aaron and Susie had bought the home on Himrod Road for Sam and Ruth to live in when they were married – thinking ahead to the day when Sam would take over the farm and Aaron would work for him. The Quilt Room was moved to the finished basement of Aaron and Susie's new home. For the first time in her life Susie had a more modern bright and cheery home to live in and take care of. They would not have to remove five layers of old linoleum from the kitchen floor as they had done to improve their Honey Brook farmhouse. This cozy yet functional kitchen was a delight to work in and the separate dining room had sliding glass doors that went out to a spacious shaded deck. Beyond the dining room was the large living room that took up one end of the house. The front foyer had a half-open staircase that went to the bedrooms upstairs. It was a convenient home for them to live in because at the opposite end of the kitchen from the entry to the dining room was a hallway with John's room on the right, Aaron and Susie's large master bedroom on the left and the bathroom was at the end of the hall. John's room was required to have an outside exit and it went out to the deck. That was pleasant for him because he enjoys being outside in the summertime.

Aaron and Susie finished off and carpeted the double garage that was attached to the house and it made a perfect large area for the whole family to congregate when they came home. Now they have extended and added another double garage. They have also expanded flowerbeds, added a lovely gazebo on the knoll with a water garden and little waterfall in front of the gazebo. The lawn is large and beautifully manicured with quaint planters tucked here and there. The bird houses and feeders keep the shade trees lively with bird families.

Mahlon finished his two-year stint at the home for delinquent boys and then began working in South Carolina. Could it be he had an interest there? Anna lived three hours from Mahlon but they wrote to each other and began to realize that it was God's plan for them to be married and so they were on September 30, 1989. Both families were happy about the union and God has blessed them with six wonderful children.

All through the years Daudy Beiler kept close track of his family that had moved to New York State. He and Grandma Beiler remained members of the Old Order Amish and of course they were growing older but they still hired a driver to bring them to visit Aaron and Susie twice each year. The visits were very special – especially for John – he and Daudy could spend hours talking to each other and catching up on the months they were apart. Daudy and Grandma always looked so tidy in their handsome black clothing – he with his starched white shirt under his black suit coat and she in her fine black dress and white head covering. Grandma still helped her daughter, Susie, in the kitchen. The best time of day was when chores were done, dinner and cleanup were over and everyone could gather together to share and sing. John played his keyboard and led the singing while the family joined in with strong voices and joyful hearts. Did any of them think back to that night nearly thirty years earlier when the doctor told them John would not live through the night?

Thank You, Lord, for giving John life! Thank You for the way his life has blessed us! We love You and give You all the glory!

John's scanner has served him well. He has had countless hours of intense enjoyment from it. Weather forecasts always interest him and he keeps up with other reports as well. Every Christmas Eve the meteorologist follows the travels of Santa (of course, John does not believe in Santa Claus – but he gets a chuckle out of the reports!) The eight tiny reindeer with its sleigh full of toys are followed all over the world and sometimes Santa disappears in the clouds leaving the listener wondering if he will ever be found again. John laughs with glee at the weatherman who keeps the audience informed.

One late evening Susie heard a baby crying and went to the open door of John's room. The crying was coming from his scanner and John was listening intently. John started talking to the baby and Susie heard him say, "Aw – it's alright – don't cry – it's alright." She stood watching him as he tried to comfort and console the baby. They found out later that he had figured out the frequency of Sam and Ruth's baby monitor and it was their baby he was listening to. John was told not to do that again – he had to learn about Sam and Ruth's privacy but in her heart Susie was moved to hear how loving and attentive he was to the sound of that baby crying. It was good to have him home where he belonged.

Singing to his nephew.

John is always ready for a game of Sorry!

John and Michael his nephew.

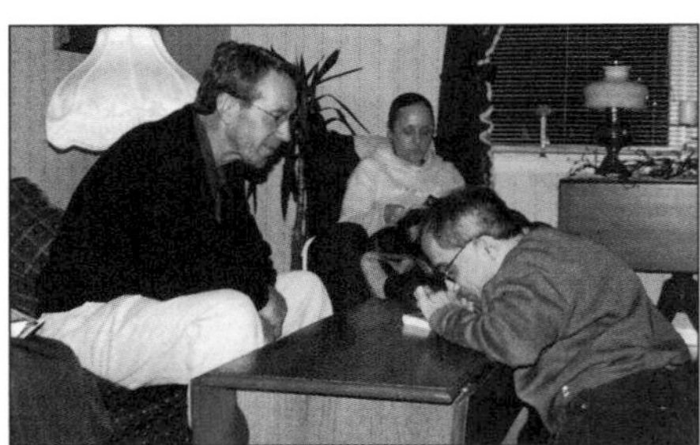

Playing electronic basketball with Glenn Lapp.

John enjoying casual conversation with his family.

Sam and John – not only brothers but good friends as well.

This is how John participates in the "Walk for Habitat for Humanity" each year. Sam is at the wheel.

CHAPTER 19

Last to Leave the Nest

After Aaron and Susie stopped taking John to the handicapped summer retreat at Spruce Lake in 1989, he began to miss it. They found one that was a little closer to them near Buffalo Valley, PA, called Penn Valley and started going there in 1991. All three of them were pleased to see old friends and meet new ones. It was good to meet some of the younger couples that had handicapped youngsters and be able to be supportive to them. John was a great help to the younger ones and always enjoyed being with those he had known for years.

John with his friend Donnie.

Aaron and Susie had many friends with handicapped children but among the dearest to them was a couple from the Pequea Mennonite Church. Emmanuel and Rachel Smucker lived in Lancaster County and had two handicapped sons. The families became very close because Emmanuel and Rachel also had six other children who loved to play with all of the Stoltzfus children. They were what Susie refers to as "picker-uppers." God had given them joyful spirits that just lifted others out of the doldrums. They knew the hearts of Aaron and Susie and always did thoughtful and helpful things to bring sunshine to their lives.

Dear friends – the Smucker family.

Both of their boys were in wheelchairs – they could neither walk nor talk. J. Wendell was quiet and withdrawn but a treasure of a boy – he died at a very early age. John Mark had a great deal of determination and lived to be twenty-one. He was very outgoing and friendly and communicated with his kindly expressive eyes. He was very bright and his cheerful disposition drew people to him. At church people went to him with their secret prayer requests. John Mark loved to pray for them. Young couples told him their secrets about wanting to get married – they knew he would never tell. Everyone loved him.

When Aaron, Susie and John go to Lancaster now to visit Kathy, John and the boys – Rachel plans special days with John. He loves it when Rachel takes him to sing for widows or handicapped children and then she always takes him out for lunch.

Grandma Stoltzfus always remained an important part of their lives and her love for John never wavered. John had stayed close to her and loved to visit her when he and his family went back to Lancaster County. As Grandma grew older she lived one month at a time with all of her children. Aaron and Susie took good care of her when she spent her month with them. During the last two years of her life she had Alzheimer's disease which made her require more special care but they were happy to give it and John was happy to be with her.

Grandma Stoltzfus and John. Mutual admiration

Louise was thinking of marriage – she would be the last to leave the nest – and the fortunate young man was from Ohio. James Bontrager had visited the Stoltzfus home in Honey Brook many years earlier. His father was a Mennonite minister who had been invited to preach in the Pequea Mennonite Church and they were guests in Aaron and Susie's home. Louise was very young and she remembered James but he did not remember her – he only remembered John. It is strange how he noticed and remembered her when she grew up to be a fair-haired, polite young lady with a sweet smile (he didn't know she whistle-talked with her brother). While they were courting, James came to Penn Yan to visit and Susie invited him to dinner. During the meal John choked on his food and soon after that Grandma Stoltzfus started choking on her food (she was having esophagus problems). Aaron and Susie got them back in control and the meal went on but Louise wondered if James would ever come again. He did and they were married on June 10, 1995.

The Aaron Stoltzfus family.

Naomi, Kathy, Sam, Mahlon and Louise made sure, before they were married, that the person they had chosen felt comfortable with John. As far as each of his siblings was concerned, it was a prerequisite that their future spouse enjoyed being with him. They could not have been more pleased – Glenn, John, Ruth, Anna and James not only felt at ease around John – they loved him and oh how John loves each of them! John has a very special affection for all of the nieces and nephews they have given him.

Lord, thank You for the love that abounds in the family. Thank You for being in the midst of them.

Even the parents of John's sisters and brothers-in-law have great respect for him. Following is a letter from Sam's wife – Ruth's father:

Memories of my dear friend and Brother John:

John I want to thank you for the inspiration you have been to me both in my physical and Spiritual walk. Although I have 2 legs to walk, sometimes I might be hesitant to go or walk where God would want me to. Although I have good eyesight sometimes I might be slow to see what God would want me to see.

You never failed to request prayer for the Sunday morning service. Your love for singing has inspired me and been a Blessing to many. Keep on singing till the day when we all gather there and there'll not be one cripple on Hallelujah Square! And don't forget to make preparation to Send your crutches over so they are there when you get there. Crutches in Heaven. Of course not. They would mar the streets of gold. It will be like Paul wrote in Phil. 3:21: Who shall change our vile body, that it may be fashioned like unto His glorious body, according to the working wherewith He is able to subdue all things unto Himself.

And the memories of the Sorry games and being a good sport even if sometimes you lost. How about going to Mac's (oops) I mean Seneca Farms for coffee ice cream. And your love for burnt hot dogs.

Precious memories, how they linger
How they ever flood my soul,
In the stillness of the midnight
Precious sacred scenes unfold

And when all is said and done, Johnny "Die shick dich:"
(You behave yourself.)

Elmer Stoltzfus [19]

CHAPTER 20

HEAVEN

John likes his present bus driver. When you spend five days every week going to and from work together, life is far more enjoyable if you find pleasure in talking to each other. The driver works nights at the county jail and told John that he has named one of the jail gates after him. The driver is not allowed to talk to John on the telephone from the jail but he knows John's scanner frequency and tunes into it when some one has to pass through that gate. John is always pleased when he hears a familiar voice say, "Open the Johnny Gate," on his scanner.

One Sunday recently John's minister gave a sermon on heaven and John was thrilled by it. He grows excited when he hears or thinks about Heaven. His enthusiasm was still at an elevated level when the bus driver picked him up on Monday morning and naturally John expressed his desire to go to heaven to the driver. Not understanding the joy that John felt about someday being in his Heavenly Home, the driver turned with alarm and said, "Are you suicidal?" John assured him that he was not!

If you love Jesus with all your heart – the thought of seeing Him face to face is exhilarating – especially if you have never ever seen a face in your lifetime. But when we stop to think about it – what an honor and privilege to have His face be the very first one you ever see! How can we not look at this through John's mind and be awestruck by the glory that is to come??

Everything in his life has reinforced the happy anticipation that he carries in his heart. John cannot remember when he did not want to go to Heaven – some children get excited about Christmas and receiving new gifts – John grew excited about his gift of a new life in Heaven. In 1992 John acquired a cassette tape of the Antrim Mennonite Choir called "Flight F-I-N-A-L." They persuasively presented hymns to inspire the listener to live in readiness and climb aboard this heaven bound flight as their harmonic voices sang hymns like: *Holy, Holy, Holy*, *Redeemed*, *Face to Face*, *Goin' Home* and many others. John nearly wore the tape out. Now, as a well-adjusted adult who finds joy in living and brings untold blessings to those who know him and love him – he grows even more elated because he knows his life journey is taking him ever closer to that promise of Heaven.

Through his life John has not complained about his struggles and pains. The many operations have been taken in stride and he does not consider any of them as bad memories. His attitude is a reflection of his inner spirit. His love for Jesus and his strong faith have sustained him. One thought has constrained him – he feels like a prisoner in his own body. All the more reason to look forward to the freedom he will experience. He can leave his thick heavy glasses, his bladder flange, his wheelchair, his prosthesis and his crutches behind because he will have no need for them again for all eternity!

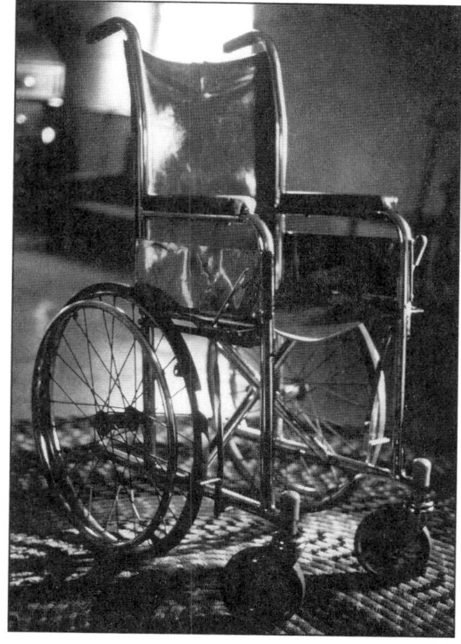

From the time John was a boy he has sung this song for different groups of people:

"HALLELUJAH SQUARE"

I saw a blind man tapping along
Losing his way as he passed through the throng
Tears filled my eyes, I said, "Friend, you can't see"
With a smile on his face he replied to me.

"I'll see all my friends in Hallelujah Square
What a wonderful time we'll all have up there
We'll sing and praise Jesus, His glory to share
And you'll not see one blind man in Hallelujah Square."

I saw a cripple dragging his feet
He couldn't walk like we do down the street
I said, "My friend I feel sorry for you."
But he said, "Up in Heaven I'm gonna walk just like you."

"I'll see all my friends in Hallelujah Square
What a wonderful time we'll all have up there
We'll sing and praise Jesus, His glory to share
And you'll not see one blind man in Hallelujah Square."

I saw an old man gasping for breath
Soon he'd be gone as his eyes closed in death
He looked at me Said, "Don't look so blue,
Cause I'm going to heaven, how about you? [20]

John sings this song with great feeling and his audiences are always moved by his rendition. Who could sing it with more feeling?

We can be assured of our place in heaven because:

John 3:16 – **For God so loved the world, that He gave His only begotten Son, that whosoever believeth in Him should not perish, but have everlasting life.**

In order to experience God's love and His plan for our life we must realize:

Romans 3:23 – **For all have sinned, and come short of the glory of God.**

Romans 6:23 – **For the wages of sin is death; but the gift of God is eternal life through Jesus Christ our Lord.**

Hard as we might try we cannot reach God through our own efforts. Jesus Christ is God's plan for the forgiveness of our sins.

Romans 5:8 – **But God demonstrates His own love toward us, in that while we were yet sinners, Christ died for us.** (NASB)

1 Corinthians 15:3, 4 – **Christ died for our sins according to the scriptures; and that He was buried, and that He rose again the third day according to the scriptures.**

John 14:6 – **Jesus said to him, "I am the way, and the truth, and the life; no one comes to the Father but through Me.** (NASB)

Knowing all of these things is not enough. We must receive him – we must ask Him into our hearts. He stands at the door and knocks (Rev. 3:20) but we must open it.

> John 1:12 – **But as many as received Him, to them He gave the right to become children of God, even to those who believe in His name.** (NASB)

> Ephesians 2:8, 9 – **For by grace you have been saved through faith; and that not of yourselves, it is the gift of God; not as a result of works, so that no one may boast.** (NASB)

John is thankful to be a child of God. He is thankful that God sent his Son to live among men to be our example and John is grateful for the cross – not for the sorrow of Christ's agony but for His great sacrifice in taking on the sin of mankind so that those who believe in Him can have forgiveness. John is thankful for the resurrection and knows that Jesus sits at the right hand of God in Heaven. He is thankful that Jesus left a Comforter – His Holy Spirit – to dwell in the hearts of believers. And most of all John believes and is thankful to know that because the Lord has made these provisions – he will go to Heaven.

After John looks in the face of his Lord and Savior, he wants to see Daudy Beiler, Grandma Beiler and Grandma Stoltzfus. They won't have to look down to see him because John will be standing as tall as they. His grandparents will surely be happy to see him in his new body. They will recognize his handsome face and strong arms and hands but they will rejoice to see how bright his eyes are and how straight his back is. He and Daudy will likely take a little stroll on the golden streets and try some sprinting to a distant hill – just to try out his new limbs. There will be others to see, but best of all will be sitting with them at the feet of Jesus – basking in His loving presence. John will be able to sing with the Heavenly Chorus – he will know all of the words and his voice will blend like warm honey. Oh, what glory that will be! And what satisfaction John receives from knowing that every member of his family believes and will meet him there. Whoever goes first must save a place for those to come.

When John leaves the earthly body that has sometimes felt like a prison to him – his sweet soul will soar toward Heaven and as he draws near he will hear ten thousand voices ring out as all the Saints in Glory shout in one accord – "Open the Johnny Gate!"

CHAPTER 21

Dark Days

Susie's new Quilt Room had its own outside entry with a gift lined stairway that led to a very large downstairs room. She enjoyed having a separate shop from her house and decorating it with all of the handcrafted items that were for sale. The Quilt Room was laden with treasures and on two walls there were large protruding quilt racks – hinged at the top to display the beautifully made quilts. In another well lit basement room there were quilt frames where Mennonite women met to quilt. Their friendly chatter was pleasant to hear.

Another enterprise was growing in the community. A few years earlier, in 1988, Susie began to think about a special outlet for her quilts. She talked with a friend, Pat Gunderman, who made baskets and sold them out of her home. They thought that if they could have a place on the main road with a restaurant or coffee shop in the complex and invite other vendors to participate then people would love to come and buy their wares. Susie and Pat talked and planned for one year and then they began to share the idea with other local crafters who became excited about it. Soon everyone was anxious to set the vision into motion. They needed to buy land and when they could not get financial backing from the local banks they did not let disappointment squelch their desire. By then the group had such a heart to start that they formed a CO-OP. Thus, the Windmill was born from their eager enthusiasm. The CO-OP bought a plot of land on Route 14A between Dundee and Penn Yan and immediately it became a Saturday tourist attraction. They started with one building and now there are three large permanent buildings, which are open year round – housing the market, food services and vendors. Seasonal attractions are: a pavilion for produce, a street of shops with permanent small structures and areas where vendors can set up their own canopies. It has met and exceeded every expectation and dream. Three years after they began, when their success was obvious, the local banks were offering support but it was not needed then. Now there are one hundred sixty six vendors every Saturday during the spring, summer and fall and seven to ten thousand visitors come each week. People enjoy making purchases from the various vendors. The observer can watch them carrying everything from cold meats, cheeses, jams, jellies, woodenwares, birdhouses, quilts and baskets to soaps, candles, porch furniture and rocking horses to their vehicles in the parking lots. Everyone is welcome to come and walk around to chat with the friendly people or just to bask in the ambiance.

With so much on her platter, Susie really did not have time to be ill, but she began to have some health problems. She called her doctor and made an appointment, but just before she was to meet with him his receptionist called and said he was going to be out of town for a few weeks. During that time a nurse customer came to The Quilt Room and noticed how white Susie was. She was so concerned that she made an appointment for Susie with another doctor who ordered blood work. Her platelets were very low so he prescribed medication.

Soon after that – what seemed like a very normal Friday morning turned out to be anything but normal. Susie had gotten John off to work at 7:30 and then prepared the breakfast that Aaron and she would have together when he came in from doing chores at Sam's. While she waited, she started to do their laundry but something was wrong. She went to the bathroom to comb her hair but her hand would not reach up. She felt so strange. Aaron came in and she tried to talk to him but her words came out in a jumble. She could think but she could not talk correctly or tell him what was happening. Aaron told her she had better go lie down awhile and when she did he knew she was sick – she would never lie down during the day unless something was very wrong. By then she could not talk at all. Aaron took her to the hospital where she had to undergo many tests. Not until afternoon did they diagnose it as a stroke – the drug that had been prescribed had caused an irregular heartbeat. A blood clot formed and went to the brain, causing the stroke.

Susie was in the hospital for one week, but it would take many weeks of hard work to recover. She gradually regained her strength but learning to talk again took sheer determination. At times she became very embarrassed to be around people, but her business was a blessing in that it forced her to be with people and try her best to talk to them. Her doctor was a faithful customer and strengthened her a great deal. Her other customers, as well as her family and friends were very helpful and encouraged her to keep trying. After many months she regained her glow and began to feel more comfortable with her words.

It was a blessing that Louise had just returned from doing two years of mission work in El Salvador before Susie was hospitalized. Louise was able to watch the shop and care for John while Susie was ill and until she recovered. One year later Susie had a hysterectomy and they became very concerned for her life. Three days before the operation they had to take her off Coumadin and during surgery she had another stroke. It had been a dark year for Susie and this was the culmination, but her family and many friends were praying and even the doctor felt the power of those prayers while he was operating on her. He was also moved by Susie's tenacious faith and inner strength. She would not give up and God would not let her. God still needed her here to fulfill her job as caregiver to John.

Susie could not have made it without the prayers, without Dr. Lindenmuth and without the constant support of Aaron. He always encouraged her and gave her the will to fight through her disability until she was normal again. Our same sweet, caring and serving Susie emerged in full radiance from the cloak of cloudy darkness that had numbed and engulfed her for so many long months. Her children had all been extremely concerned and were there to help in any way they could. Her recovery brought the light-hearted joy back into their lives again also.

Because of Susie's health, Glenn and Naomi left their home in Arkansas where they had lived for two years and moved to Yates County so Naomi could take over Susie's business. They bought twenty acres just off Route 14A near the Windmill and put a trailer on the land to live in while Glenn built a charming building nestled among the trees for The Quilt Room. After everything was moved from Susie's shop and the new Quilt Room was open for business, Glenn started building a beautiful home for his family.

When the large basement room that had been the Quilt Room was emptied, more quilt frames were set up and the quilters that quilted for Susie continued to come. They were a steady and constant help in Susie's full recovery. They still meet there every Tuesday and Thursday and spend those whole days quilting. John has endeared himself to them and even spent time teaching them how to whistle talk. When he comes in from work a little after 4:00 each Tuesday and Thursday – his first greeting is to go to the top of the stairs and call down to them, "Hello Girlies!" – they respond with happy voices. They love him as we all do.

CHAPTER 22

A Day to Remember

John hardly had the opportunity to enjoy being thirty-nine because he was so excited to be almost forty! Many people look at it as a dismal time of their life and never want to leave thirty-nine for fear of going "over the hill" or coming face to face with the dreaded "black forty." To John it was a day to look forward to – a day of accomplishment and celebration so he began planning the glorious event many months ahead of time. He had long lists of people to invite and things to get done. It is a good thing that Susie was in good health and able to assist him in his great endeavor. Invitations needed to be sent, tents had to be ordered, tables and chairs could be borrowed from the church and a menu had to be planned.

The final few days before his birthday were full of anticipation for John – he was thankful his Mom and Dad would supervise the preparation of the home, food and lawn because he had important things like the weather to think about. For years John has set his alarm every night to go off at eleven o'clock PM and at five o'clock

AM to get a weather report. When the alarm goes off he climbs out of bed and the thump of his foot generally awakens Susie as he takes one hop to the scanner nearby to listen to the update. The weather report for June 26, 2000 was perfect. He went back to bed and slept like a baby. Susie found sleep hard to grasp as her mind began racing through the things that had to be done. But she was thankful for the early morning wake-up call; it allowed her time to pray for the events of the day, the people who were coming and for John – what a day of thanksgiving this was! Her grateful heart filled with joy that sustained her through that busy festive day and never let her realize she had not had enough sleep the night before.

From the moment John woke up his heart was singing "This is the day, this is the day that the Lord has made…!" When he remembered that he was really forty he raised his fist and said "YES!" His great day of celebration had finally arrived, his family members were all there, the sun was shining in a bright blue sky, colorful tents were all over the flower brimmed lawn, tables and chairs would soon be set up and friends would start arriving in a few hours. Even the birds sang more loudly as if to drown out all the ruckus that was going on in their yard. Perhaps they were looking forward to the extra crumbs they would find at the end of

the day. John gave a satisfied sigh – this surely must be as good as life can get!

John's wry sense of humor helped him decide what to wear on his birthday. He looked very dapper when he went out to greet his first guests dressed in black slacks with a defined crease, shiny black shoes and a crisp black shirt. His crutches seemed to have extra "zip" as he lithely moved about to make everyone feel welcome and his whole demeanor defied the belief that this was to be his "black forty" day. His smile was radiant and never faded. How wonderful was the Lord to hold the rain drops back and in their place to reign down sparkling drops of joy that filled John's heart with effervescence and spilled over to saturate everyone around him. Love abounded because the sweet Spirit of God had been invited and because of that the day was perfect indeed!

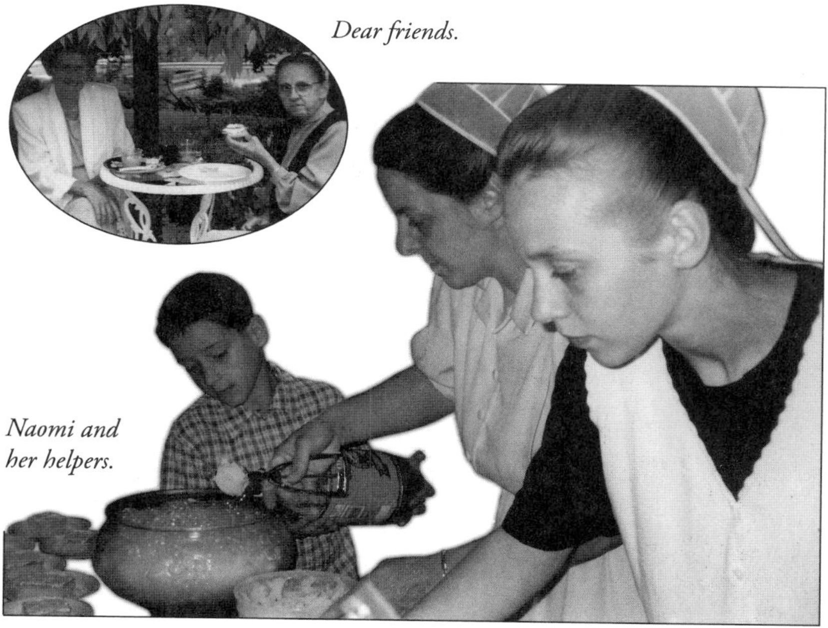

Dear friends.

Naomi and her helpers.

A beautiful day for a party!

Friends from ARC.

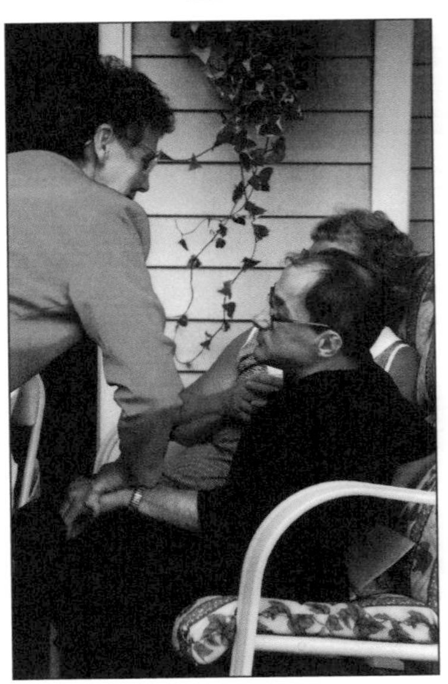

Loving well-wishers.

Opening gifts.

Susie and a friend.

John with nieces and nephews.

Two hundred people came to John's party and he was able to visit with every one. There were friends from far and near; friends from childhood and through all stages of his life: bus drivers (even one who had pleased John by pumping the brakes as she drove in rhythm with the music they were listening to), doctors, teachers, ministers and neighbors. They all enjoyed punch, sandwiches, vegetables, dip, birthday cake and most of all, wonderful fellowship with each other.

John's friend, Jim Youngman, read "Forty Things the Bible Says That You Can Do When You Get Old" (on page 204) and John enjoyed that. John and James (Jim) are such close friends that they are called "Sons of Thunder" (Mark 3:17) by the people in their church.

John was delighted to be able to buy a very nice computer

with the gifts of money that he received for his birthday. The computer has proven to be very practical and helpful to him because he can store all of the songs, poems and stories that he has memorized over a lifetime in it. He is not on the internet but he enjoys his large magnifying video screen and printer. He spends time at his computer every evening and the dexterity he has acquired qualifies him to do specific jobs at ARC.

Enjoying his new computer.

John was exhausted by day's end on June 26, 2000 but he was able to stay alert and attentive to each guest until time for them to depart. It was a glorious day – one he will never forget! His family and friends came to pay tribute, congratulate and express their love and respect to John, but as always, it was John who was the blessing to them – "He wiggled his way right into their hearts!"

Dear Jesus – thank You for overseeing John's party from his first inspirational plans to the end of his big day. Thank You for watching over him for a lifetime and making him such a blessing to others. Thank You mostly for the love that overwhelms us because of Your Presence in his life.

John is unable to read cursive writing – he can only read uniform type written words, but he did learn to write in cursive when he was a boy. After his birthday he wrote this letter to his friends:

Dear Friends,

Thank you for coming to my party my 40th birthday celebration. It was wonderful. Thank you also for the gifts. They are appreciated and I love you all very much.

John

CHAPTER 23

Late Bloomer

Just as John had nicknames for his siblings – they had their own special names for him. They called him "Boy" or "Woy" and as the years went by Mahlon changed that to "Boiler." Aaron and Susie call him "Late Bloomer" and isn't that fitting?

Everything John did took longer and required extra patience but the rewards were blissful: his first smile, the unique method he developed to roll crawl, the sweetness of his singing, the fact that he learned to talk when they said he never would, the struggle of trying to walk and the determination he showed in learning to read in spite of being legally blind. His lack of fear or worry about the many operations he had was commendable – his thoughts seldom seemed to be about pity for himself but rather on the excitement of making new friends during his long hospital stays. As he grew, the accomplishments became more monumental when he began to answer difficult questions, used his mind to develop memorization skills, worked through his teenage frustrations, committed his life to Christ and became a productive adult. All these accomplishments!

– when so little – almost nothing was expected from him. He is a remarkable work of God – and "Late Bloomer" fits him to a "T."

We are reminded of a bouquet of wild flowers. The fields are full in early summer and the stewards of the meadow are enthralled by the colors, variety and fragrance. For many years they had been gathering seeds from the flowerbeds around their home and had cast them on this plot because they wanted to please God – the rightful owner. It was their hope that passersby would be warmed by their beauty and they knew God's birds would be nourished by the seeds.

The lady steward did most of the gathering. She enjoyed having freshly cut flowers in their home. On this balmy summer day, the tall graceful stems with perfect, perky blossoms are swaying and dancing above the stockier flowers and they are the ones that catch her eye. She reaches down to cut long stems to fit the elegant vase she has chosen to put them in. Sometimes there are two or three flowers in bloom at the top of the stem and further down are buds that look as if they will never bloom. She expects little – almost nothing from them but they add interest to the bouquet. One by one the flowers are selected and cut; Daisies, Lupines, Coreopsis, Gaillardia, Black-Eyed Susans, Echinacea, Delphinium, Columbine, Bachelor Buttons, Larkspur, Foxglove, Sweet William, Canterbury Bells, Queen Anne's Lace and other nameless beauties until the arrangement satisfies her.

Carefully and happily she carries them back to the kitchen (bending her head from time to time to catch the wonderful fragrance and thank her Lord again for the awesome treasures He has created). She puts them on the counter while she gets the intended vase and fills it with water. Arranging the lovely jewels is such a pleasure and when the last stem is slipped in place the bouquet looks spectacular – special enough for the dining room table.

A few days pass – the flowers have been appreciated by those that walk by the dining room and happen to glance at them, but the real place of activity is the kitchen – everyone congregates there. The blossoms have begun to fade and droop, some petals and pollen have dirtied the table and the once clear water has turned murky and smelly in the vase. Most bouquets are thrown in the garbage at this point but our gatherer sees potential in the still tight little buds on the lower part of each stem. The wilted blossoms are cut off and discarded, stalks and stems are shortened and trimmed, stems of parsley are gathered from the herb garden, an old blue pint Ball canning jar is filled with fresh water and a new arrangement is made. The little buds are happy to be nestled amongst the greenery of parsley in a jar that is just perfectly suited for the kitchen table. They drink their water and snap to attention to give pleasure to the family and friends that sit there to eat or chat or study. The little bouquet is noticed and enjoyed by everyone. They see that the buds are beginning to come to life. The small flowers are so delighted with all of the care and attention they are receiving that they respond by opening up and amazing the family with a dazzling display of color and fragrance. Neglect would have left these little late bloomers stunted forever but love, encouragement and confidence in what was hidden inside brought them to life – life that gave pleasure to all.

In John's case, nothing was expected but all was hoped for and prayed for and because God loved his family – abundance was given – John is a Bloom beyond belief!

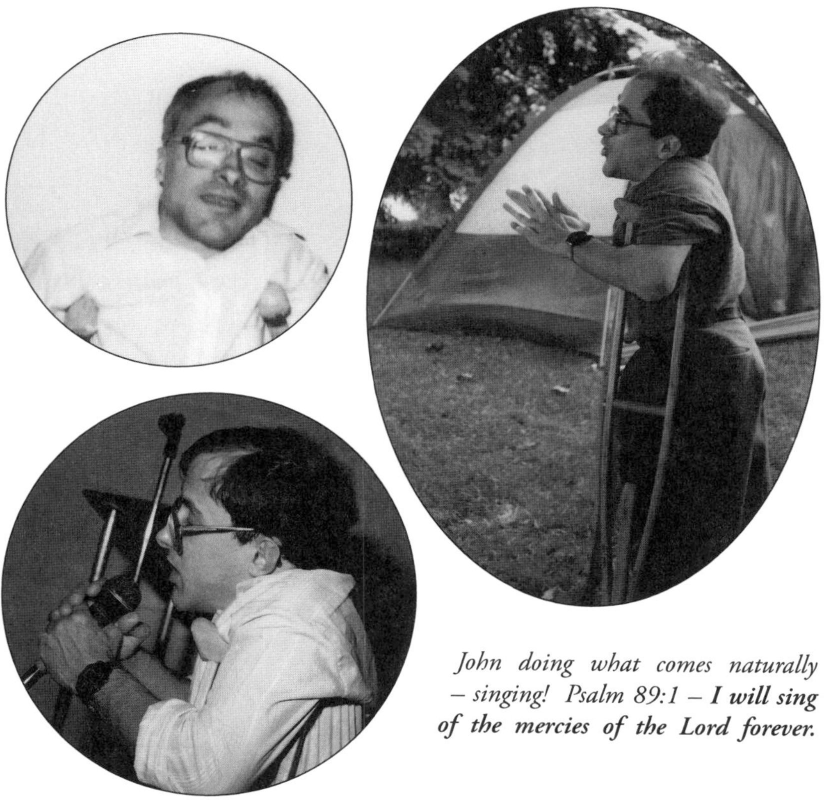

John doing what comes naturally – singing! Psalm 89:1 – ***I will sing of the mercies of the Lord forever.***

Blindness is a disadvantage but God blesses those without sight with keener senses of hearing and smelling. John's friend, Ken Riehl, came to the house to visit one evening. After they shook hands John observed, "You must be doing chores for Alan Faust," to which Ken replied. "How did you know that?" John smiled and said, "You smell like his barn." How many of us would know or recognize one barn smell from another? At another time John was visiting with a woman at church and some people walked in. He turned and said, "Hi, Mom," the woman he was talking to laughed and said, "John, you can't see. How did you know that was your mother?" With all sincerity he answered, "I can tell by the way she breathes." One Sunday someone found a sweater after the church service and wondered who had left it. John asked the person that found it to bring it to him. He smelled it and named the woman it belonged to. His keen senses, alert mind and sharp memory make him a valuable commodity to have around! Susie relies on him for many things – if she cannot remember something she quickly says, "I'll ask John when he gets home." She knows he will have the answer.

The name Late Bloomer seems even more appropriate with each passing year because he has mellowed, can sense his problem areas and has become more patient and content with his life. Even the way he has learned to cope with frustrations has shown remarkable maturity. John's greatest cause for disturbance to the point of depression has been caused by friction and the bad behavior of others. From the naughty boy who rode the school bus to the antics of fellow workers in Syracuse to his present workplace – if people are loud, unruly and disrespectful, John is deeply affected. When he was little he could ask his bus driver to sing and now he raises his hand at work to let a supervisor know that the irritation is beginning to bother him. At home John is very content because the routine is pretty much the same but when the large family is all together for special weekends or holidays – occasionally John has to retreat to the security of his room for solitude. Much as he loves his nieces and nephews it is hard when he has to shuffle over toys that he cannot see and his crutches do not help him feel. Rather than fear stumbling he finds his room to be a safe haven. Most generally the children seek him out to play Sorry or Probe and then he is very happy again. After dinner John goes to his keyboard to play and when he starts to sing the whole family is drawn to listen and then sing along. It adds a festive touch to their time together. The family tells John that he is singing for his supper and he is delighted.

Smaller groups are more to his liking and quite often on Friday nights there will be a Boys Sleep Over at the Stoltzfus home. Boys, ages ten to fourteen, arrive with their sleeping bags. Some are nephews of John (Sam's boys) and others are sons of his friends (Jim Youngman and others in the church.) Susie plans a favorite meal and she and Aaron enjoy the boys as much as John does. John and his young friends "have a ball" playing Sorry and then they play electronic basketball. They take turns pushing the buttons and get a little loud as they shout out the play-by-play description of what is taking place. John loves it and they do have a good time with each other! At bedtime the boys spread out their sleeping bags on the living room floor and John goes to his room where he can sleep comfortably and tune into his scanner at eleven and five to check the weather. Susie enjoys making breakfast for the mop-headed crew on Saturday morning.

Wednesday is John's favorite day and purple is his favorite

color – if you know John you must know that! He always wears a purple shirt on Wednesday (sometimes it is hard to find new ones to buy in the stores so Susie looks for them in out-of-the-way places like the Salvation Army, consignment shops or yard sales). Several of his supervisors wear purple on Wednesdays and one supervisor always takes time to have a Wednesday morning coffee break with John. Talk about wiggling his way into hearts!!

Off to work.

In the workplace at ARC.

Singing with the Men's Chorus is one of John's greatest pleasures. He and eleven other men from Crystal Valley Mennonite Church have joined together to use their voices to bring glory to God. Their a cappella voices blend in four-part close harmony. The moving baritone part adds a special quality that is pleasing to the ear. The inspirational message is clear and sung with humble sincerity.

The men all dress alike with black slacks and white shirts and hold black folders for their music. John stands in center front next to his brother-in-law, Glenn Lapp – they sing lead or melody while the rest sing the harmonies. John is the only one without music but he knows every word. He takes cues from Ken Riehl (his friend and director of the group) who stands directly behind John and Glenn touches John when he needs to sing softer. John is so comfortable in front of an audience that he keeps his right crutch under his arm pit but moves the left crutch forward and with raised bent arm he can rest his upper arm and forearm in the curve at the top of the crutch. In that position he looks relaxed and can sing to his heart's content.

In the middle of the program all of the men except Ken Riehl and John go to the back of the church. Then John sings *Hallelujah Square* and Ken harmonizes with him. It is very moving. After they finish, the children are invited to the front for children's ministry. They sit in a semi-circle around John and he tells them two of his stories with clever sound effects. He changes his voice for the various characters and emotes in the climatic parts of the story. The children are enthralled and quiet as church mice as they sit wide-eyed not missing a word of what the storyteller is saying (the adults are just as attentive!) After the children are dismissed to return to their parents the chorus members go to the front again to do the last half of their program.

Some churches where they are invited to sing are large – especially in Lancaster County, PA with congregations of three or four hundred and some are small as in Kossuth, NY with about sixty people (members and visitors) in attendance and that was a capacity crowd. Large or small the Lord fills each church with His presence and as the Men's Chorus sing His praises the congregations are blessed and filled with God's love.

The men travel in a fifteen passenger van and John loves their camaraderie. They joke, laugh and sing together and what holds them close is that they pray together. Their mission is to serve God by using their voices to draw the listener closer to Him. John is safe with his friends in the Men's Chorus because they all watch over him, lift him over the high places and take good care of him.

John is thankful to be a Late Bloomer because his life just keeps getting richer and richer.

CHAPTER 24

Crystal Valley Mennonite Church

Traveling from Watkins Glen, NY to Dundee, NY on an early Sunday morning is a pleasant experience – particularly on a chilly November morning. Watkins Glen seems quite deserted when we compare this morning with its usual summertime hustle and bustle. Only one native resident is braving the early hour dressed in windbreaker and knitted cap. We can tell he is headed for the local coffee shop – he has his Sunday paper tucked under his arm. Seneca Lake looms ahead and as the highway follows the hillside and rises on the west side of the lake we can look down and see its cold bleakness. Just a few weeks ago it was alive with the activities of sailing, fishing, water skiing, swimming or riding on the scenic cruise boat.

We continue on our way. The tourist season has long been over – the lake dwellers have packed up and returned to their winter homes, the strawberry, cherry, raspberry, blueberry, peach, plum, pear, grape and apple seasons have passed. Even the colorful leaves that bring foliage-gazers out by the carload have dropped from the trees and only the oaks are left with their nut brown stick-tight leaves still intact. The evergreens stand stately showing off their green furry coats. Their half-brothers, the larch trees, will lose their needles and look like skeletons during the winter months but for now they have turned yellow and are making a final splash that casts a golden glow to add dazzle to the hillsides.

Very little traffic is on Rte. 14A but as we near Dundee, a horse and buggy pulls out of a farm road and soon we see another. Three more are trotting through Dundee and as we pass them we see more on the road ahead. Outside of town we begin to see boys on their bicycles leading the way for their parents and siblings in the buggies. They look cold with their black rimmed hats almost hiding their red ears and noses but when we get close enough we cannot help but notice how bright with excitement their eyes are – Sunday is a good day!

The now almost steady stream of horse and buggies is joined by more children on bicycles as they turn off Rte. 14A onto Rte. 230. Our destination is Crystal Valley Mennonite Church which is five and a half miles out on Rte. 230, but curiosity gets the best of us and we make a left turn to follow all these eager children and Sunday morning worshippers. A short distance ahead is a large white boxy building – plain and unmarked, but the long lines of horse and buggy sheds on either side of the extra wide driveway that encircles the building confirm to us that this is their church – especially after we see the children parking their bicycles and running to greet each other. Then the horses begin to lead their buggy loads into the stalls they seem accustomed to filling.

As we leave this pleasant scene we return to Rte. 230 and turn left again to make our way to our destination. The church we just left was an Old Order Mennonite but Crystal Valley is a Conservative Mennonite Church so its members arrive in modern vehicles. The same glow is on the faces of these children and young people. They express pure joy in joining together with the families they know so well. How good it is to see young people who greet you with gentle smiles and shy innocence – there is no sign of pride and no one seems to have an attitude problem here. The girls wear dresses and head coverings like their mothers and the boys wear dark slacks and white shirts. The men look tidy in their black suits and white shirts. Everyone has a sincere greeting for one another and all are quick to make the visitors feel welcome and comfortable.

Upon entering the building the large greeting area is beginning to fill. Not one is so caught up in his or her own concerns that they do not notice who is arriving. Pleasant greetings are given to everyone. Some of the women are carrying covered dishes downstairs and the tantalizing aromas of baked ham, red cabbage and apple dumplings that are being cooked in the church kitchen are wafting up the stairs to tease what should be a dormant appetite into activity. There is a loving softness in all of the conversation and activity.

You realize Sunday School will soon begin as the members start to move from the foyer into the sanctuary. A hushed quiet falls over the group as everyone takes their place – men on one side and women and small children on the other. As you sit in the comfortable pew covered with immaculate soft blue upholstery fabric, you sense the real meaning of church. We have joined together to come into His presence. He is here, filling the sanctuary. In the quiet you read the sign on the wall behind the pulpit, "I will put My Spirit within you to walk in My ways." ***Thank You, Lord.***

The devotions are led by Pastor Mel Lapp. After uplifting hymn singing the men remain in the sanctuary and everyone else disperses to the various Sunday School rooms. Naomi Lapp teaches one of the women's classes and what a gifted teacher she is. Her deep and prayerful study to prepare for the lesson has given her an enlightening insight that she is eager to convey to her students. If her students knew how much she pretended and yearned to be a good Sunday School teacher when she was a little girl, perhaps they would love her more. When Naomi became an adult and was first asked to teach a real Sunday School class she found that it was not at all like pretend teaching when she had John and her wooden children in front of her. She felt inadequate and nervous so she took her problems to the Lord – she wanted to serve Him but she did not see how she could get past her fear. She asked for His help and He so lovingly gave it to her. Now she can teach with joy because He is her strength. Today as we look around the classroom at the gentle, wise and radiant faces of these women, we realize how fortunate she is to have them for students instead of her line-up of slab wood students.

Sunday School is dismissed and everyone moves back to the

sanctuary. This is a day of celebration! It is the thirtieth anniversary of the Crystal Valley Mennonite Church. Their minister, Josh Beiler, acknowledges the first family, James and Rachel Smoker who moved from Lancaster to Dundee in 1972. They had looked for two years before they bought a farm in 1974 and after that, four ministers came up from Lancaster to check out the area. They gave their approval in November 1974. John and Mary Stoltzfus moved up in 1974 and Josh Beiler moved his family here in 1975. It gives us a feeling of nostalgia to hear about the first church services in their homes and the way they meshed their lives together to be united in their service to God, His church and His people. Much was said about their desire to build this church on a sound foundation and when the church was built they hoped that people would not just see the steeple – they should see a congregation who believed in Christ.

> I Peter 2: 1-5, 9 – **Wherefore laying aside all malice, and all guile, and hypocrisies, and envies, all evil speakings, as newborn babes, desire the sincere milk of the word, that ye may grow thereby: if so be ye have tasted that the Lord is gracious.**
>
> **To whom coming, as unto a living stone, disallowed indeed of men, but chosen of God, and precious, ye also, as lively stones, are built up a spiritual house, an holy priesthood, to offer up spiritual sacrifices, acceptable to God by Jesus Christ.**
>
> **But ye are a chosen generation, a royal priesthood,**

an holy nation, a peculiar people; that ye should shew forth the praises of Him who hath called you out of darkness into His marvellous light.

After the Aaron Stoltzfus family and a few other members from Pequea moved up, the church was built in 1981. Wonderful helpers came up from Lancaster County to help build the church – many of them young men. They lived with the church families and put in long hard days of labor but the work was made light because they carried a deep love for God and a strong desire to serve Him in their hearts. It was an exciting and uplifting time for everyone.

The church was built on the hill side of the road at the edge of a cleared plot of land. The double front doors lead into a foyer with a stairway to the basement on the right and a wide windowed hallway to the left where there are rest rooms and a classroom at the end. The large foyer, the open greeting area, at the doorway extends to the back with a wide entry into the sanctuary on the right and a wall with doors to classrooms on the left. Back outside – if you follow the driveway around to the left of the building, you will find another double door entry and that is the entrance to the school. Across the drive to the left is a playground shaded by the woods that skirt the cleared land the church is built on. The woods are deep and extend for many acres along the roadway and up over the hillside. It is a beautiful setting and from the front steps of the peaceful white church you can look down across the road to the valley that looks like a patchwork of farm land – not all smooth and flat, but rolling and hilly with higher hills in the distance.

This mind picture brings us back to Pastor Josh Beiler's message. He is talking about the teamwork that it takes to not only build a building but also to build up the people that make the church – the body of Christ. His example is **T**ogether **E**veryone **A**chieves **M**ore. He explains that, "We need to hold the ladder instead of shaking it." "The highest reward is not what we get for it but what we learn by it." The Crystal Valley Mennonite Church gives evidence that Christ is its cornerstone and the congregation reflects His Spirit!

The present membership consists of fifteen Mennonite families – many of them are four generations now – from babies to great grandparents. With their lives so intertwined is it any wonder they care for each other the way they do? A few members have joined them from other denominations and they all bless each other because their bond is Christ.

Only Mennonite women could prepare and serve a fellowship dinner like this! After being lured by the enticing aromas from the basement kitchen for nearly two hours, we are more than ready to eat. And yet we savor the fellowship on the way. How gently the group moves from sanctuary to foyer and then down the stairs. The large dining area is set up with white covered round tables and chairs. The food is so attractively displayed that you want to sample everything. It is a planned menu consisting of homemade bread, apple butter, baked ham, sweet and sour red cabbage, scalloped potatoes, squash, mixed vegetables, Waldorf salad, applesauce, apple dumplings, mulled cider or coffee. It is satisfying to enjoy the tasty food with such good company and refreshing to watch them interact with each other.

Aaron helps John get down the stairs and has him sit at one of the tables. Susie prepares his plate and takes it to him but from then on he is on his own. He is never alone – people of all ages spend time with him and it is humorous to see him bantering with some of his friends – my, how they pick on each other! But it is all done in good fun. Through their joking you are warmed by their unspoken affection and respect for each other. John's nieces (Naomi and Glenn's girls) spend much time with him in a happy and comfortable manner. If people are not sitting at his table with him, he is roaming about chatting with someone else. Susie once said he was the Dandy at church and now we can see how true that is – people are drawn to him like bees to honey and he purrs like a kitten when he is with his church family.

After the last delicious morsel is eaten and our plates are carried away, we still linger. Our hunger has been satisfied but better than that our hearts have been filled. We keep wanting to savor what we have found here and never let it go.

Dear Lord, please continue to pour Your blessings over this precious church.

Following is a letter from John's minister:

> ***I will instruct thee and teach thee in the way which thou shalt go: I will guide thee with mine eye.***
> *– Psalm 32:8.*

God had created us and designed our lives in many different ways. And with that our awesome God said He will instruct and teach us in the way that he wants us to go, and also guide us in the right path with His eye.

I have been blessed and privileged to know the Aaron Stoltzfus family and especially Johnny. As a young boy and teenager I remember seeing him in his wheel chair as his parents would bring him to the Pequea Amish Mennonite Church on Sunday morning.

Many years later we again lived in the same area at Dundee, NY. As many people know, Johnny loves to play Sorry, and on occasions our family would spend an evening visiting, and of course, playing Sorry.

One big event that was special to John and many others was his 40th birthday party when his parents invited church families, friends, and teachers for a Sunday afternoon get-together. About one year later I asked John what he plans to do for his 41st birthday. He thought a bit then said he would like a ride in the big truck which I drive. My thoughts went to the ***Make A Wish Foundation*** *which does very special things with handicapped and*

Josh Beiler and John – trucking buddies.

underprivileged people. I told John it's a deal and that we would plan a short ride together. It was a great time with him. It also meant blowing the horn at times and stopping to visit a friend. About a year later I again asked John what special thing he would like to do on his birthday. Since John knew that I also do some flying, the request was, let's go for a plane ride somewhere for lunch. We waited for a beautiful day then flew to the Perry Warsaw airport and a friend picked us up and we had lunch at Lantz's store and restaurant.

These very special times together have allowed John and I to share in different ways and to get to know each other just a bit better. Once a person gets to know John he will never forget you and may also attach a different name to you. Somewhere in our life John and I have gotten attached to the name "Boova" which means boys in PA Dutch. Where it all started and where it might end I don't really know, but we have had a lot of fun with it. Since I was ordained into the ministry at the Crystal Valley Mennonite Church John has added more to the special name, and I'll let you guess just what that might be.

Our family also had two mentally and physically handicapped girls which have gone on to be with the Lord. These experiences in life have also allowed us to reach out and minister to the needs of others.

I also wish to thank and praise God for a church family

and friends who have in the past reached out and helped us when we had children with special needs.

John, you will always be a special friend, and may you serve God, with singing, and your life each day.

I'd like to share a thought that goes like this "What you are is God's gift to you. What you make of yourself is your gift to God.

God's richest blessing to you.

Josh Beiler

CHAPTER 25

Sweeter Gets the Journey

John's life has been a journey – sometimes barely clinging, sometimes difficult, sometimes slow and plodding and sometimes free and easy. At all times his journey has been enlightening because he has Christ in his heart and wonderful lessons have been learned along the way.

Someone gave Susie this clipping from a newspaper a few years ago:

"Welcome to Holland"

by Emily Perl Kingsley

I am often asked to describe the experience of raising a child with a disability – to try to help people who have not shared the unique experience to understand it, to imagine how it would feel. It's like this:

When you're going to have a baby, it's like planning a fabulous vacation trip – to Italy. You buy a bunch of guidebooks and make your wonderful plans. The Coliseum. Michelangelo's "David." The gondolas in Venice. You may learn some handy phrases in Italian. It's all very exciting.

After months of eager anticipation, the day finally arrives. You pack your bags and off you go. Several hours later, the plane lands. The flight attendant comes and says, "Welcome to Holland."

"Holland?" you say. "What do you mean, Holland? I signed up for Italy! I'm supposed to be in Italy. All my life I've dreamed of going to Italy."

But there's been a change in the flight plans. They've landed in Holland and there you must stay.

The important thing is that they haven't taken you to a horrible, disgusting, filthy place full of pestilence, famine and disease. It's just a different place.

So you must go out and buy new guidebooks. You must learn a whole new language. And you will meet a whole new group of people you would never have met.

It's just a different place. It's slower-paced than Italy, less flashy than Italy. But after you've been there for a while and you catch your breath, you look around and you begin to notice that Holland has windmills. Holland has tulips. Holland even has Rembrandts.

But everyone you know is busy coming and going from Italy, and they're all bragging about what a wonderful time they had there. And for the rest of your life, you will say, "Yes, that's where I was supposed to go. That's what I had planned."

And the pain of that will never, ever, ever go away, because the loss of that dream is a very significant loss.

But if you spend your life mourning the fact that you didn't get to Italy, you may never be free to enjoy the very lovely things about Holland. [22]

The story was meaningful to Susie because she had also made a similar comparison – not with the same destinations, but the idea of an unusual journey as she and Aaron traveled through their life with John.

Sometimes the road was obscure while driving at night through fog and rain so torrential the wipers could barely keep the windshield clear. But there was always a Light to give them a glimpse of the center-line. As they slowly continued on with caution – the storm subsided and the way ahead could be seen more clearly.

The storms were more frequent at first but the glimmer of

Light was always leading them forward. They clung to the hope that the Light gave them and then the storms that once surrounded them and tried to smother them rumbled off in the distance. They were left with only a sprinkle now and then but most often with refreshing sunshine overhead. The rough terrain was wearing smooth. The winding, narrow, bumpy, unpaved roads were the most difficult at night but as daylight appeared the darkness melted away and those same roads seemed picturesque and beautiful. Sometimes the highway stretched straight ahead for miles and there were no obstacles in sight. How free they felt – the exhilaration was refreshing. Strengthened, they were better able to handle the smaller potholes in the road when they came upon them.

During the early part of their journey they could have driven off the road and fallen into a bottomless precipice if it had not been for the Light that was guiding them. They realized that and never let It get out of their sight. They did not want to be lost forever. The Light led them ever upward to a higher plain where the air was purer, the way seemed clearer and the view was grander. They took time to stop and appreciate this resting place in their journey. They gave thanks to the Light and as they breathed in the freshness of the air they realized how very sweet it was. So incredibly sweet in fact, that tears of joy filled their eyes as they humbly expressed the great depth of their gratitude. They could continue on now with confidence – the Light would never leave them. The Light would always draw them ever closer to the Source at the end of their journey.

Family time means everything to John. Soon after James and Louise were married in 1995, someone suggested that the whole family start meeting each summer for a vacation together. Of course, everyone agreed that it was a great idea so they made reservations and the following summer met at Timberwind Lodge in the mountains near Lewisburg, PA. It is the perfect getaway for them; each family has their own rooms for sleeping, there is a large kitchen for food preparation and a central common area for eating, game playing and lounging. A wonderful deck overlooks the spacious grounds where the children (and adults) can participate in all kinds of outdoor activities.

John and his nephews playing electronic basketball.

Father and son – Aaron playing his thousandth game of Sorry with John.

One family game they enjoy teaches them teamwork and how to trust each other. One person stands lengthwise on a log, six people (three on each side) stand on either side of

Susie singing with John at the keyboard.

the log behind him with palms up and arms outstretched and interwoven over the log, but not touching each other. The one standing on the log must close his eyes and fall stiffly backwards into the waiting arms. It takes courage to release yourself and trust that the outstretched arms will not only be there, but will also be able to hold you. It is scary but it always works. When the breathless part is over everyone roars with laughter and someone else steps on the log to prove his or her trust in the family.

John loves the deck where he can play electronic basketball, enjoy the fresh air and always have someone available to play Sorry with him. The deck has no steps to the ground so it is a safe place for John to sleep at night. What a wonderful place to camp out! He can listen to the katydids each night until they lull him to sleep.

One night he really frightened his brothers. At three o'clock AM, John had a nightmare and kept crying out for help. Sam and Mahlon woke up with a start. Leaping out of their beds in a state of alarm and confusion they both grabbed their car keys and ran out to the parking lot (remembering they had left money in their cars) to lock them up for safe keeping. They felt a little sheepish when they looked at each other and realized that they had not run to help whoever it was that was in distress. Was someone being attacked by a wild animal? Was there an intruder on the grounds? With hearts still pounding, they followed the cries that led them back to their own complex and out to the deck where their brother was restlessly sleeping. Their wide eyes relaxed when they grinned at each other – but in the morning, how were they going to explain their reactions to a family that was sure to tease them and never let them hear the end of it?

Last winter, Glenn had to make a business trip to Ohio and he took John along to spend two weeks with Louise and James. John was thrilled! His time with Glenn was enjoyable (as it always is). John has always been **so** comfortable with his little sister. Having the opportunity to spend that much time with Louise, James and their four wholesome boys was a wonderful treat for him. He is planning to do that again this winter and now everyone is excited because Louise is expecting their fifth child.

John has become quite the coffee connoisseur and his favorite is Starbucks. He gets to satisfy his taste buds every Saturday morning in his older sister's home. Naomi and John look forward to this special time together when they can just drink their Starbucks coffee together, tell each other about their week and talk about everything under the sun. Sometimes they visit for four hours and who knows how much coffee they consume! Being with Naomi is a highlight in John's week. He loves her very much and Naomi is just as happy to spend her Saturday mornings with John – it is a time that she gladly sets aside for him.

Lately John has been desirous of spending some one-on-one time with Sam. They see each other often and are always together at family gatherings but it is not the same as being alone together. Sam is a busy man. He had to give up farming a few years ago because it was affecting his lungs. He went to work at a local mill as a feed consultant, then as a salesman, and now he owns the mill. He is also busy at home being a good husband and father to their seven children. John understands but he still mentioned his longing to Sam a few weeks ago.

John's favorite singers are Michael Card and Michael W. Smith and Sam knows that. To John's surprise, Sam bought two tickets for a Michael Card concert and they went to hear him in Canandaigua, NY – just the two of them. What a wonderful concert it was and what a great time those brothers had together. John still calls Sam, Little Brother. It kind of makes you smile to hear it because John is so short and Sam is so tall.

That night John had a peaceful sleep but he was so happy that Susie heard him call out four times during the night, "Sam – oh Sam, my brother!" He woke up in the morning with a big smile on his face – Sam had made him ever so happy!

These are just examples of the love that John has for all of his brothers and sisters, Naomi and Sam have the advantage of living close by, but he cares just as deeply for Kathy, Mahlon and Louise. They are all attentive to his needs and stay in close touch with him.

Ready to travel.

Much as John appreciated his night out with Sam, Aaron and Susie are realizing that John is becoming more and more of a homebody. He still looks forward to the trips to visit his siblings. Everyone in the family merged to South Carolina for Christmas and spent the holiday with Mahlon and Anna. It was a rich and blessed time for all and John thoroughly enjoyed it. But here at home Aaron and Susie can hardly get him to go for a drive whereas *he* used to be the one who begged to go somewhere. He seems tired and sleeps more. It is not unusual for him to take an hour nap when he gets home from work and then be ready for bed between seven thirty and nine in the evening. His doctor says not to be worried, he is just slowing down. He has the mind of a forty four year old but the body of a seventy five year old.

Resting after a tiring game of electronic basketball.

Though John may have fewer waking moments, his spontaneity and exuberance for life are as alive as ever. He is such a joy to be around – such a lifter-upper – such an example of what God can do in a life that wants to bring honor and glory to Him. John is a satisfied, happy, contented and thankful man and we are grateful and enriched to know him.

Recently we were in Lancaster thinking about John's journey through life. We went back to the farm in Honey Brook. We remembered that in 1970, when John was ten,

A typical Lancaster County scene.

the county bought land from Aaron and some of the neighboring farmers. The local government was in need of a reservoir. They brought in earthmovers and bulldozers. The Stoltzfus family had watched a lake come to life in the meadows below the farmhouse. Today the lake looks like it has always been there. They named it Lake Struble and it must take up nearly one hundred fifty acres.

Honey Brook farmhouse overlooking Lake Struble.

This was the children's favorite tree on the Honey Brook farm. Aaron climbed it and made a wonderful swing for them.

From the road we are on, we can look across the lake and see a charming stone farmhouse – Susie said it was stucco but the stucco has been removed and the wonderful old stones are a pleasant sight. How this place has changed! It is not a farm anymore. The quarter mile lane is gone and the stone free fields no longer reap grain. They are cut up into individual lots (at least they are large) and beautiful homes have been built. The lawns are well kept, shrubs are established and people have been living here for years.

The only landmark (besides the house) that we can define is the old tree on the hillside not too far from the stone house. It is the tree Aaron had climbed to hang a swing from and the children played there for years.

From the Honeybrook farm we drive on to see the Pequea Mennonite Church. What a beautiful setting! The red brick church sits on a little knoll and there is a perfect view of the Pequea Valley in every direction. The church has an added wing now and across the blacktop drive is a new church school. The blacktop area

Pequea Mennonite Church. New wing at the back and new church school far right.

extends from the road and goes completely around the church. It is wide enough for ample parking. There are many memories here – a wonderful hair twisting little boy, a ten year old who seemed to "wake up" during the tent meeting, a youth who sang (a little too loudly) and a young man who was baptized here. This place is an important part of John's journey through life.

We drive from the church to the Old Beiler homestead where Susie grew up and where Daudy and Mummy Beiler welcomed John so many times when he came to visit them. It looks the same but with larger giant shade trees. The farm gives a general appearance of tidiness. The large barns are clean and well kept, the

Beiler homestead, view from the East.

Beiler home from the West.

fields are prepared for winter and the home is magnificent – it seems to go forever. Of course, it was built to hold two families. When Susie was young she lived there with her parents and twelve brothers and sisters. Her grandparents lived in the Daudy part of the home. It is interesting that the wall that separates the two homes is made to fold up for Sunday morning church service. That gave them a large open area for all the worshipers to gather. Susie's brother owns the farm now. He and his family are still Amish.

Just around the corner from the farm the one room schoolhouse where Susie attended is still very much alive. Young Amish boys are playing touch football in the front yard and the Amish girls are jumping rope in another section

One room school house where Susie attended.

of the play area. Recess will soon be over and they will return to their classroom.

In back of the school is a fenced-in mowed lawn. When we look more closely, we see a horizontal iron bar attached on the inside length of the fence. It is the hitching post for the horses when the cemetery in the next plot is visited.

The cemetery makes you feel as if you are stepping back in time. The thin upright markers are nearly all alike – plain and unobtrusive. Daudy and Mummy Beiler are buried here along with many other dear relatives and friends.

We travel on – leaving "Beiler Country" behind us. We can call it that because so many of the original Beilers still own the farms in that area. Next we are going to "Stoltzfus Country" and see once again where Aaron grew up. The farm is beautiful!

The Stoltzfus homestead – where the journey began.

The stone homestead with the frame attached Daudy house seems unchanged. The barns and outbuildings are in wonderful condition. Aaron's warm and friendly brother, David, comes out to greet us. What a fine Amish man he is!

Beyond the fields is a small hill with a wall of stone on one side. My heart sinks to my stomach and I know without being told that this is the stone quarry. Was Susie carrying mint tea to the field to refresh Aaron while he was working the land when they were experimenting with radiation? I picture her as a young expectant mother. The field is so close to the quarry. I can see her waving at her young husband – the love of her life. I can sense their joy when he caught her eye and waved back at her. How gladly he stopped for that thirst-quenching drink and a pleasant chance to be with his Susie. And then I think of that innocent baby. God had made him perfect and in an instant, a cutting instant, man had damaged and injured that perfection.

That is where the journey started so many years ago. That is where God knew what had happened to that little boy they would name John. That is where God knew Aaron and Susie would need extra strength and courage and that is when God breathed His love and His power into them. He knew their hearts and knew they would always be true to Him.

Without Jesus the burden would have been so heavy that their backs would have broken under the stone-like weight of despair and grief, but He said His yoke is easy and His burden is light. His gentle comforting arm around their shoulders was all the weight He wanted them to feel.

God watched over John in the field that day and prepared the way for his journey through life. He made John a blessing to his family and everyone who would ever know him. God made him unique, spontaneous, unforgettable and marvelous. God gave him a quality that penetrates our hearts with a desire to be as trusting a follower of Christ as he is. God made John extra special because He knew that when his journey was done God would "take him home and love him."

Thank you Jesus, for John!

God gave man the ability to make choices. We can choose good or we can choose evil. Either choice affects those around us. God would like us to always choose good and in a perfect world we would – but we are human and humans are not perfect. That is why Jesus had to take on our sin and die on the cross.

The men in that quarry or those who directed them made a choice which deeply affected an innocent family. But Romans 12:21 tells us, **"Be not overcome of evil, but overcome evil with good."** Without Christ in their lives, Aaron and Susie would have been overcome by that evil, but with Him they conquered it. All things do turn out for good to those who love God and keep His commandments! (Romans 8:28)

Jesus must have wept when Aaron and Susie were in the field that day. Our Savior is like that – tender hearted toward the ones whom He loves. He would have all the more reason now, to hold this family in the palm of His hand.

Sweeter gets the journey as we go through life with Jesus in our heart. We can not help but wonder what our lives would have been without Him – dear me! We shudder at the thought! But we can rejoice! He is ours! He is in our heart to stay! Life may have its pitfalls but He will never let us go to the bottom and get blackened in the tar pit. He will swoop us up to safety and not only place us on solid ground, but He will gently dust us off and smooth our ruffled hair. He will take time to tenderly dry our tears and relax our racing, fluttering heart and fill us with strength to go on. But that Sweet Savior does not stop at that. He takes extra time to fill us with joy and put a smile on our face, a twinkle in our eye and a lilt in our step. He lifts us up to realms on high as His love spills over on us. Oh – how wonderful He is! He is the best of the best! Our Friend forever! How sweet life is when we belong to Him.

The End

To God Be the Glory!

ENDNOTE A.

SONGS JOHN HAS LEARNED BY HEART

"STOP, AND LET ME TELL YOU"

Stop, and let me tell you
What the Lord has done for me
Stop, and let me tell you
What the Lord has done for me
For He forgave my sins and He saved my soul
He cleansed my heart and He made me whole
Stop, and let me tell you
What the Lord has done for me.

Go, and tell the story
Of the Christ of Calvary
Go, and tell the story
Of the Christ of Calvary
For He'll forgive your sins and He'll save your soul
He'll cleanse your heart and He'll make you whole
Go, and tell the story

Of the Christ of Calvary. [4]

"Why Should I Care if the Sun Doesn't Shine"

Why should I care if the sun doesn't shine
Jesus is mine
All of the time
Why should I care if the storm clouds hang low
Jesus is with me
I know He will never forsake me
I'm under His wings
Tho' trials o'ertake me
I will praise Him and sing
For I'm ever so happy
So why should I care if the sun doesn't shine
Jesus is mine all the time. [5]

"Whispering Hope"

Soft as the voice of an angel, breathing a lesson unheard
Hope with a gentle persuasion, whispers a comforting word
Wait till the darkness is over, wait till the tempest is done
Hope for the sunshine tomorrow after the shower is gone.

Chorus:
Whispering hope! O how welcome Thy voice
Making my heart in its sorrow rejoice.

If in the dusk of the twilight, dim be the region afar
Will not the deepening darkness brighten the glimmering star
Then when the night is upon us, why should the heart sink away
When the dark midnight is over watch for the breaking of day.

Hope, as an anchor so steadfast rends the dark veil for the soul
Whither the Master has entered robbing the grave of its goal
Come then, O come, glad fruition, Come to my sad, weary heart
Come, O Thou blest hope of glory, Never, O never depart.[7]

ENDNOTE B.

STORIES JOHN HAS LEARNED BY HEART

SHERRY WAS A FRAIDYCAT

Sherry was a fraidy-cat. She was afraid of little wriggly worms, loud noises, and the dark. Sherry was afraid of animals, too. Imagine living on a farm and being afraid of animals!! Her brothers and sisters weren't a bit afraid. They played with the goats and ran in and out among the cows. They played circus and rodeo with the ponies and horses. Sherry heard Bible stories about people who were afraid and how God helped them. She heard about missionaries who were afraid and how God helped them, too. But all the Bible stories, and missionary stories, and Bible verses didn't seem to do any good. Sherry was still afraid. Sherry knew Jesus didn't want her to be afraid. He wanted her to be a happy child, and she couldn't be a real happy girl with all that fear in her heart. Everyone thought Sherry would get over being afraid, but the day she was eight years old, she was still a fraidy-cat. Just before she blew out the candles on her pretty cake, Sherry closed her eyes to think what she should wish for. All of a sudden, she knew just what she wanted most. So, she made her wish, gave a big blow, and out went every candle. As part of Sherry's birthday treat, the family had planned to drive to town to see a missionary film. But the baby had a temperature and Mother couldn't go. Sherry said she'd stay with Mother. She was glad to because one of her big brothers had told her the film was a scary one. About an hour after Daddy and the other children left, the baby became very sick. Mother did everything she could for her but nothing helped. Finally Mother said, "I'll have to call the doctor." But when she tried to call, the phone was out of order. Mother was worried. "Our baby's so sick. The car isn't here or I'd drive her to town to the doctor. I don't know what to do." "Oh," thought Sherry, "If I weren't afraid, I'd go and ask Morgan's to call the doctor." (The Morgan's lived three miles down the road.) Sherry went to the window and looked out. It was dark, but the moon was shining, and the stars were big and bright. "God, I know You're up there behind those stars."

Then she looked down the path to the big, dark barn. "You're everywhere, aren't You, God? You're in those dark bushes; and You're in the barn, aren't You?" Mother saw Sherry go to the desk, open a drawer and take out a flashlight. "What are you going to do?" asked Mother. "I'm going to ride Peanuts over to Morgan's house. I'm going to ask them to call the doctor. Mother almost said, "It's dark and you're afraid." But she didn't. She just said, "God bless you, dear. I know you can do it. God will help you." As Sherry walked up the path, the bushes looked dark and scary. But Sherry kept saying, "God's in the bushes." The barn was big and spooky. But Sherry kept saying, "God's in the barn." As she climbed on the pony, she said, "God's on the pony with me." The moon seemed to grin at her a happy grin. The stars twinkled merrily. Peanuts was glad to be out of that stuffy old barn. Sherry thought of a Bible verse she had learned. "What time I am afraid, I will trust in thee." And all of a sudden, Sherry realized something; she wasn't afraid. She was having fun. She liked God's beautiful, soft night. She liked the shining moonbeams on the road and the twinkling stars. She liked the cool breeze blowing through her hair as she galloped down the road. After the doctor had come and taken care of the baby, Mother hugged Sherry and said, "You've had a nice birthday, haven't you?" "The best part of my birthday was I got my wish. I wished I could be brave, and I was, wasn't I?" "You were very brave. Not many children your age would go to a dark barn and saddle up a pony and ride out into the night." Sherry looked kind of puzzled. "Mother, I wonder why I wasn't afraid." "You were trusting God and thinking of others," said Mother. "When we trust God to take care of us and think of others, we forget all about ourselves." Sherry thought for a moment, and then she said, "I don't think I'll ever be real afraid again. Not even of squirmy, wiggly worms." The next day Sherry wrote a little rhyme. Wanna hear it?

God was in the bushes
God was in the barn
God was on my pony,
Keeping me from harm. [11]

It's Mine

Cal grabbed his bike and glared at Leon, the boy from next door. "No, you can't ride my bike, it's mine." When Cal came into the house, his brother, Tim, was reading a book. "Hey, gimme that book, it's mine."

Myron, Cal's little brother, was playing traffic cop. He had a string of cars lined up in the hall. Cal saw that three of the cars were his. "Say, small stuff, what are you doing with my cars?"

"Mommy said I could play with them," said Myron.

"They're not Mom's, they're mine." He grabbed the cars and took them to his room. Mother heard Cal and shook her head. She was tired of hearing, "It's Mine!"

But she heard it again that evening. Cal's sister, Millie, wanted one of his African stamps. "You keep your hands off my stamps, they're mine."

"But you have three of one kind," insisted Millie.

"I don't care if I have ten. You leave my stamps alone."

Later Dad and the other children were in the den. Mother came in with a paper bag. "Grandma made you some of those chocolate mints you like so much." Mother took a mint out of the bag and started to put it into her mouth.

"Hey, Mom, Grandma made those for me, they're mine." Cal saw the hurt look on Mother's face and hurried to say, "But you can have one." Mother put the mint back in the bag.

Cal saw the look on his Dad's face. "Calvin, tell your mother you're sorry."

"But the candy's mine."

"Calvin, I'm ashamed of you. You forget that God gave us everything we have. You talk as though everything's yours. How it must hurt the Lord Jesus to hear you say that. Now listen, son. Jim Garland was going to give you a collie puppy. I was going to bring it home tonight and surprise you, but all we'd hear would be, "Don't touch that dog, he's mine." Well, you're not going to have a chance to say that. You get no dog until you try to break that "It's Mine," habit. I suggest you go to your room and ask the Lord Jesus to help you. And don't forget to tell your mother you're sorry."

"I'm sorry."

But he wasn't really sorry. He was saying to himself, "I don't care. Those things are all mine." But when he thought, the dog isn't mine, he was very unhappy. He knew he'd rather have a dog than a bike, or stamps, or cars, or anything. Cal dropped off to sleep and when he opened his eyes, he saw Grandma. She was glaring at him and saying, "Get off my bed."

"But, Grandma, you said I could use it."

"I know I did, but it's mine and I want it back." And with that Grandma shoved Cal right out of bed.

"Grandma's sure acting funny,"** thought Cal as he walked downstairs. **"The bed is hers, not mine."

When Cal came downstairs, the family was sitting around the table eating breakfast. "Leave that cereal alone," said Mother. "It's mine."

*"**She's** right," thought Cal. "The cereal is hers." Then he asked his Dad, "Hey, Dad, when are we going to school this morning?" Dad always drove the children to school.*

"I think you'd better walk, you know, the car's mine." As Cal was on his way to school, he saw a beautiful collie dog in Leon's yard. Cal ran over to pet the dog, but Leon yelled at him, "Don't touch that dog, he's mine."

*As Cal walked away he thought, **he's right, the dog is his.** Then he remembered a chorus he'd learned in Sunday School.*

Mine, Mine, Mine, Mine
Jesus is mine.

But if Jesus is really mine, *thought Cal, I oughta act like Jesus would act.*

Just then Cal heard his brother, Tim, say, "Cal, wake up, Mom's called you three times."

"Boy, did I have a dream!" When Cal came downstairs, Mother called out in a cheery voice, "Good Morning, would you like to have banana on your cereal?"

Dad ruffled Cal's hair when he went by his chair. "Don't dawdle over your breakfast, son. We're going to leave a little early today."

Cal was glad Dad was going to drive the children to school. The family laughed when Cal told them about his dream. "I guess I'd been pretty selfish saying everything was mine; but I'm gonna try not to be so selfish." Mother and Daddy noticed how hard he tried and how much he improved. It wasn't long before he got "you know what" – a darling little puppy dog. When Cal saw the puppy, he knelt down and gathered him up in his arms. Then he looked up at his mother and daddy and his brothers and sister and said, "He's not just mine. He belongs to all of us." [12]

Miss Speedy

Miss Speedy was a pretty little sailboat. She had a tall mast and on the mast was a big white sail that fluttered in the breeze. When the wind blew it filled Miss Speedy's sail. Then the sailboat traveled far, far away. Captain Happy was Miss Speedy's jolly captain. He had a spyglass which he looked through. Then he knew that the way ahead was safe. "Such a lot of fuss to sail a sailboat," Miss Speedy told Pokey the rowboat, who was tied up beside her. "The wind is blowing today. The sky is clear. No storms are in sight. I think I shall go sailing by myself."

"Oh, no, no, don't do it. You can't go sailing alone. You need cap'n."

Miss Speedy looked down at the leaky old rowboat. "Ha! What do you know about sailing? You're only a rowboat! You can't go anywhere unless somebody rows your oars! I'm a sailboat! The wind will take me anywhere I want to go!" Miss Speedy held her sail high. The wind blew hard. On and on sailed the pretty sailboat until a big fish swam up beside her. "Go back little sailboat," the big fish grunted, "You haven't got a captain."

"Haw, haw, who needs a captain? I can sail by myself." The white seagull swooped down out of the sky. He perched on the sailboat's mast and said, "Go back, boat without a captain. The water's shallow here. The

sandbar lies ahead." Miss Speedy shrugged her shoulders. "I'm not worried. I've never struck a sandbar in my life." GGGGGGGWWWWWWWWW! Something scraped against Miss Speedy's keel. She stopped with a jerk. She was stuck on the sandbar. Miss Speedy began to cry. "If only I had listened to Pokey the rowboat, or the big fish, or the seagull." Suddenly Miss Speedy heard something. It was the chug, chug, of a motorboat; and Captain Happy was at the wheel.

"Oh, here you are," Captain Happy shouted.

"Yes, yes; please take me home," cried Miss Speedy. Captain Happy tied a rope to his sailboat. He took her off the sandbar and all the way home. "You were right, Pokey." Miss Speedy told the rowboat. "Boats, like children, need someone to take care of them." [13]

ENDNOTE C.

40 Things the Bible Says You Can Do When You Get "Old"

1. (Gen. 7:6)—You can build a boat, and take your family for an around the world cruise when you turn 600.
2. (Gen. 12:4)—You can organize a camping trip for your extended family when you turn 75.
3. (Gen. 17:1-5)—You can have your name changed from John to John-a-ham when you turn 99.
4. (Gen. 21:5, 31)—You can plant an orange grove when you turn 100.
5. (Gen. 27:1)—You can order your favorite meal to be delivered fresh.
6. (Gen. 43:27)—When you get old, people will wonder if you are alive and ask about your remaining health.
7. (Gen 47:7-9)—You will finally get invited to the white house for a meeting with the president,

only to be asked how old you are!

8. (Ex. 7:7)—When you get to say 40-ish, God may send you and your brother-in-law on a special assignment.
9. (Lev. 19:32, 1 Sam 12:2)—You know you are getting old when people begin to stand in your presence and admire your new silvery hairdo.
10. (Lev. 27:7)—You know you are getting old when even the Lord begins to extend to you tax breaks.
11. (De. 29:5)—You know you are getting old when your clothes stop wearing out.
12. (De. 31:1)—You know you are getting old when you can't go out anymore.
13. (De 32:7)—You know you are getting old when people come to you for lessons in Ancient History.
14. (Josh 13:1)—You know you are getting old when the Lord notices that you can't get all your work done.
15. (Josh. 14:6-15)—You know you are getting old when you can plan and fight a battle on your own.
16. (Josh. 23:1-2)—You know you are getting old when you finally get some well deserved rest.
17. (Josh. 24:26-29)—You know you are getting old when you can carry a great stone and place it under an oak tree.
18. (Jud. 19:16-21)—You know you are getting old

when you work all day out in the field and still have time to entertain some strangers.

19. (I Sam. 2:22)—You know you are getting old when you can still hear the gossip for the day.
20. (I Sam. 4:18)—You know you are getting old when your weight is getting out of control and you fall off the chair you are sitting on.
21. (I Sam. 8:1)—You know you are getting old when you need to get others to do your job.
22. (I Sam. 28:14)—You know you are getting old when you need your coat on to go outside.
23. (2 Sam. 19:31-33)—You know you are getting old when someone else needs to feed you.
24. (2 Sam. 19:35)—You know you are getting old when all foods taste the same.
25. (2 Sam. 19:35)—You know you are getting old when you can't tell if it is the men or the women who are singing.
26. (I Kings 1:1)—You know you are getting old when you just can't seem to keep warm no matter how many clothes you wear.
27. (I Kings 1:15)—You know you are getting old when others need to minister unto you.
28. (I Kings 12:6-8)—You know you are getting old when people ask for your advice and then choose not to follow it.
29. (I Kings 13:11-13)—You know you are getting old when someone else needs to put a saddle on your ass for you.

30. (I Kings 15:23)—You know you are getting old when your feet get feeble.
31. (I Chron. 29:28)—You know you are getting old when you are wealthy and respected.
32. (2 Chron. 24:15-16)—You know you are getting old when your reputation for doing good in the community is highly spoken of.
33. (Job 30:2)—You know you are getting old when your handshake loses its firmness.
34. (Job 32:6)—You know you are getting old when people are afraid to offer you their opinion.
35. (Ps. 71:9)—You know you are getting old when your strength begins to fade.
36. (Ps 71:18)—You know you are getting old when you talk about teaching the new generation.
37. (Ecc. 4:13)—You know you are getting old when you can no longer be admonished.
38. (Joel 2:28)—You know you are getting old when you begin to dream dreams.
39. (Zech 8:4)—You know you are getting old when you start to carry a staff with you.
40. (Luke 1:13-18)—You know you are getting old when you have the persistence and patience to ask and wait for God's best.

    (John 21:18)—You know you are getting old when others need to guide you around.

    (Rom. 4:19-20)—You know you are getting old when you stop questioning God's ability.

    (Titus 2:2)—You know you are getting old when

your patience is highly spoken of, your love flows to all, the sound of your faith is melodious, you stop getting upset at life's challenges, you are sincere with all your relationships, and your life is under the Lord's control.

P.S. Remember you can stop counting.
You reached ***"40."***

Hope you enjoyed this, "Brother of Thunder."

Happy Birthday!
James Youngman [21]

ENDNOTE D.

"Who Am I"

Who am I, that the Lord of all the earth
Would care to know my name
Would care to feel my hurt
Who am I, that the Bright and Morning Star
Would choose to light the way
For my ever wandering heart.

Not because of who I am, but because of what You've done
Not because of what I've done but because of who You are.

I am a flower quickly fading
Here today and gone tomorrow
A wave tossed in the ocean, a vapor in the wind.
Still You hear me when I'm calling
Lord, You catch me when I'm falling
And You've told me who I am
I am Yours, I am Yours.

Who am I, that the eyes that see my sin
Would look on me with love and watch me rise again
Who am I, that the Voice that calmed the sea
Would call out through the rain
And calm the storm in me.

I am Yours
Whom shall I fear
Whom shall I fear
'Cause I am Yours, I am Yours [23]

FOOTNOTES

1. Notes taken by Susie from a visiting Minister's sermon.

2. Hymn, "*When Peace Like a River*" by Horatio G. Stafford (1828–1888)

3. Hymn, from "*The Christian Hymnal, Christ Receiveth Sinful Men*" by Erdmann Neuminster (1671–1756), translated by Emma F. Bevan (1827–1909).

4. Song John learned during his Easter Seal School days – he still remembers every word.

5. Poem John learned during his Easter Seal School days – he still remembers every word.

6. Letter from his bus driver, Lavern Petersheim

7. Words and music by Septimus Winner, 1868. Hymnals often list author as Alice Hawthorne, one of Winner's several pseudonyms.

8. Letter from Rachel Stoltzfus

9. Notes taken by Susie during a church service.

10. A song John learned at Reading Special School.

11. John listened to "Aunt Teresa" on a phonograph record and memorized this story – he still remembers it.

12. John listened to "Aunt Teresa" on a phonograph record and memorized this story – he still remembers it.

13. John listened to "Aunt Teresa" on a phonograph record and memorized this story – he still remembers it.

14. Notes Susie had taken during a church sermon.

15. Hymn, by Frank E. Graeff (1860–1919).

16. John memorized "The Bible Contains" when he was fifteen and he still recites it.

17. Hymn, from *The Christian Hymnal, "I Love to Steal Awhile Away"* by Phoebe H. Brown (1783–1861).

18. Author Unknown

19. Letter from Elmer Stoltzfus

20. Author unknown – this song is from John's memory bank.

21. Jim found this on the internet.

22. From a "Dear Abby" column

23. From a "*Casting Crowns*" CD, composer Mark Hall

ABOUT THE AUTHOR

JEANNE WILBER

Jeanne Wilber and her husband Gene have been married fifty-two years and live in the hills of northern Pennsylvania. They feel blessed to have their four married children and spouses, twenty grandchildren and three great grandchildren all living nearby. Their story has been recorded in Jeanne's first book, The Patchwork of My Life (box43 books, formerly RCW Publishing).

Jeanne first met Susie Stoltzfus in 1982. At that time Susie, a beautiful quilter, had just opened 'The Quilt Room' and sold quilts from her home. Jeanne was the owner of 'The Strawberry Patch Calico Shop' – specializing in quality fabric, quilting supplies and gift items. Quilting was the common interest that brought them together.

It seemed that with each meeting the love of God was foremost in their endeavors. No matter the length of time or the physical distance between them, their hearts were always in tune. In fact it seems they beat in unison!

Jeanne had an accident in October 2003 which left her with a cervical spine disorder. What distressed her most was that she lost her capability to actively serve the Lord, her family and others. She began praying for a new way to glorify God. Guess what?! Susie called!! Susie said that her family wanted a book written about her son John's life – similar to the one that Jeanne had written about her own experiences.

To make a long story short, the prayers of Jeanne and Susie were answered. Their two hearts started work on this most important story about John. As the Stoltzfus family realted events – Jeanne, with God's help, put them into story form and published them. It is the prayer of Jeanne and Susie that John's precious story, Sweeter Gets the Journey, will open the hearts of the readers and draw them closer to Jesus. They also hope this book will help eveyone look more deeply into the souls of the disabled and see clearly how very much God loves each one of us.

To contact the author, please write to:

Attn: Jeanne Wilber
box43 LLC
RR 3 Box 43 | Old Post Lane
Columbia Cross Roads, PA 16914

FROM THE AUTHOR: **A STORY OF LOVE AND FAITH**

This is the inspiring story of how one woman's abiding love and faith in her childhood sweetheart husband, in her country and in God carried her through difficult experiences and prepared her for a fulfilling life as a wife, homemaker, and businesswoman. You'll be amazed by the grace, energy and faith that flows from these pages as Jeanne Wilber, who founded and ran a successful Pennsylvania quiltshop for many years, recalls the lifetime of experiences and events that make up the stitches and fabric of her "patchwork" life. Available from box43.

YOUR FRIENDS IN PENN YAN

If you have been encouraged by John's story, you may write to him at his home address. He would love to hear from you:

John Stoltzfus
2666 Himrod Road
Penn Yan, NY 14527

Sometime your travels may take you to the New York Finger Lakes Region – if that happens, a stop at The Quilt Room would be an enjoyable treat. It is located on Hoyt Road, just off of Rte. 14A (NY).

Phone: (315) 536-5964
Hours: 9:30 to 5:00, Monday through Saturday
Naomi would love to meet you!

Susie is generally at The Windmill Farm and Craft Market – Penn Yan, NY – each Saturday (10:00 – 2:00) from late-April until mid-December. Look for The Quilt Room booth in Building #1.